Chris Marker

Manchester University Press

FRENCH FILM DIRECTORS

DIANA HOLMES and ROBERT INGRAM *series editors*
DUDLEY ANDREW *series consultant*

Auterism from Assayas to Ozon: five directors KATE INCE
Jean-Jacques Beineix PHIL POWRIE
Luc Besson SUSAN HAYWARD
Bertrand Blier SUE HARRIS
Robert Bresson KEITH READER
Leos Carax GARIN DOWD AND FERGUS DALEY
Claude Chabrol GUY AUSTIN
Henri-Georges Clouzot CHRISTOPHER LLOYD
Jean Cocteau JAMES WILLIAMS
Claire Denis MARTINE BEUGNET
Marguerite Duras RENATE GÜNTHER
Georges Franju KATE INCE
Jean-Luc Godard DOUGLAS MORREY
Mathieu Kassovitz WILL HIGBEE
Diane Kurys CARRIE TARR
Patrice Leconte LISA DOWNING
Louis Malle HUGO FREY
Georges Méliès ELIZABETH EZRA
François Ozon ANDREW ASIBONG
Maurice Pialat MARJA WAREHIME
Jean Renoir MARTIN O'SHAUGHNESSY
Alain Resnais EMMA WILSON
Eric Rohmer DEREK SCHILLING
Coline Serreau BRIGITTE ROLLET
André Téchiné BILL MARSHALL
François Truffaut DIANA HOLMES AND ROBERT INGRAM
Agnès Varda ALISON SMITH
Jean Vigo MICHAEL TEMPLE

FRENCH FILM DIRECTORS

Chris Marker

SARAH COOPER

Manchester University Press
MANCHESTER AND NEW YORK

distributed exclusively in the USA by Palgrave

Copyright © Sarah Cooper 2008

The right of Sarah Cooper to be identified as the editor of this work has been asserted by her in accordance with the Copyright, Designs and Patents Act 1988.

Published by Manchester University Press
Oxford Road, Manchester M13 9NR, UK
and Room 400, 175 Fifth Avenue, New York, NY 10010, USA
www.manchesteruniversitypress.co.uk

Distributed exclusively in the USA by
Palgrave, 175 Fifth Avenue, New York NY 10010, USA

Distributed exclusively in Canada by
UBC Press, University of British Columbia, 2029 West Mall,
Vancouver, BC, Canada V6T 1Z2

British Library Cataloguing-in-Publication Data
A catalogue record for this book is available from the British Library

Library of Congress Cataloging-in-Publication Data
A catalog record for this book is available from the Library of Congress

ISBN: 0 7190 8364 8 paperback

ISBN 13: 978 0 7190 8364 8

First published 2008 by Manchester University Press

First digital, on-demand edition produced by Lightning Source 2010

Contents

LIST OF PLATES	*page* vii
SERIES EDITORS' FOREWORD	ix
ACKNOWLEDGEMENTS	xi
Introduction	1
1 The early years: 1950–1961	11
2 A second beginning: 1962–1966	38
3 Collective endeavour: 1967–1977	73
4 Continuity and change: the 1980s	112
5 To *Level 5* and beyond: 1990 onwards	142
Conclusion	185
FILMOGRAPHY	187
SELECT BIBLIOGRAPHY	196
INDEX	199

List of plates

1 A repeated image: workers levelling a road surface in *Lettre de Sibérie* [© Chris Marker 1958, Argos Films]	page 67
2 Aerial vision and the land of Israel in *Description d'un combat*	67
3 Fidel Castro in *Cuba Si!* [reproduced by kind permission of Laurence Braunberger, Les Films de la Pléiade]	68
4 The enshrined cats of happiness in *Sans Soleil* [© Chris Marker 1982, Argos Films]	68
5 Laura and the O.W.L. in *Level 5* [© Chris Marker 1996, Argos Films]	69
6 Memory's scar in *La Jetée*	69
7 Life and love, death and eternity in *La Jetée*	70
8 Bloody encounters in *La Sixième Face du Pentagone* and *Le Fond de l'air est rouge* [reproduced by kind permission of Chris Marker]	70
9 The montage cat of *Le Tombeau d'Alexandre*	70
10 The way of all flesh in *Les Statues meurent aussi*	71
11 Metaphysical tracking and the circular insert in *Une Journée d'Andrei Arsenevitch*	71
12 The graffiti cats of Paris in *Chats perchés*	72
13 Collective protest in *Chats perchés*	72

Series editors' foreword

To an anglophone audience, the combination of the words 'French' and 'cinema' evokes a particular kind of film: elegant and wordy, sexy but serious – an image as dependent upon national stereotypes as is that of the crudely commercial Hollywood blockbuster, which is not to say that either image is without foundation. Over the past two decades, this generalised sense of a significant relationship between French identity and film has been explored in scholarly books and articles, and has entered the curriculum at university level and, in Britain, at A-level. The study of film as art-form and (to a lesser extent) as industry, has become a popular and widespread element of French Studies, and French cinema has acquired an important place within Film Studies. Meanwhile, the growth in multi-screen and 'art-house' cinemas, together with the development of the video industry, has led to the greater availability of foreign-language films to an English-speaking audience. Responding to these developments, this series is designed for students and teachers seeking information and accessible but rigorous critical study of French cinema, and for the enthusiastic filmgoer who wants to know more.

The adoption of a director-based approach raises questions about auteurism. A series that categorises films not according to period or to genre (for example), but to the person who directed them, runs the risk of espousing a romantic view of film as the product of solitary inspiration. On this model, the critic's role might seem to be that of discovering continuities, revealing a necessarily coherent set of themes and motifs which correspond to the particular genius of the individual. This is not our aim: the auteur perspective on film, itself most clearly articulated in France in the early 1950s, will be interrogated in certain volumes of the series, and, throughout, the director will be treated as one highly significant element in a complex process of film production and reception which includes socio-economic and political determinants, the work of a large and highly skilled team of artists and technicians, the mechanisms of production and distribution, and the complex and multiply determined responses of spectators.

The work of some of the directors in the series is already well known outside France, that of others is less so – the aim is both to provide informative and original English-language studies of established figures, and to extend the range of French directors known to anglophone students of cinema. We intend the series to contribute to the promotion of the formal and informal study of French films, and to the pleasure of those who watch them.

DIANA HOLMES
ROBERT INGRAM

Acknowledgements

This book was completed in Paris in December 2006. I thank King's College London for granting me sabbatical leave in Autumn 2006 to focus on my research. Diana Holmes and Robert Ingram have been the most efficient of editors; Matthew Frost, Stephanie Matthews and the team at Manchester University Press have been been thoroughly professional throughout; and Michael Janes was an excellent copy-editor. I am indebted to the team at ISKRA and at Les Films du Jeudi for providing me with films unavailable elsewhere. I owe a huge debt to the Centre National de Cinématographie, especially Sophie Le Tétour and Caroline Patte, for facilitating access to their precious archives. The advisors at the Inathèque de France were also helpful. Several of the images reproduced in the book appear courtesy of the Bibliothèque du Film. Min Lee supplied me with some invaluable research material for which I was very grateful. I should also like to thank the following people: Mark Betz, Lucy Bolton, Colin Davis, Richard Dyer, Simon Gaunt, Stephanie Green, Markos Hadjioannou, Tijana Mamula, Ruth McPhee, Michele Pierson, Davina Quinlivan, Keith Reader, Mark Shiel, Rosa Torrado and Leila Wimmer. Ginette Vincendeau in particular has been an indispensable source of encouragement to me. Emily Tomlinson first introduced me to Chris Marker's work, and Emma Wilson first suggested I write a monograph on his films: I am extremely grateful to them both. Finally, I thank my family for their inspiration and unstinting support: this book is dedicated to mum, dad, Clare, Bjørn, Ella-Sophia and Otto, with much love.

Introduction

Screening life

> Mourir est tout au plus l'antonyme de naître. L'antonyme de vivre reste encore à trouver.[1] (Chris Marker, *Le Cœur net*)

The subject of this book – the man otherwise known as Chris Marker – has multiple aliases. Chris Marker, Chris. Marker and Jacopo Berenizi are just three of the pseudonyms that distance him from his original name of Christian François Bouche-Villeneuve, who was born in 1921 in Neuilly-sur-Seine. To accompany this slipperiness, many conflicting biographical stories circulate to provide alternative places of birth (sometimes as far afield as Ulan Bator), and to extend his family lineage to Poland and the surname Krasna, which Marker also adopts occasionally as a fictive guise. These names and narratives stand as so many smoke screens around the life of this notoriously elusive man. While they undoubtedly intrigue and cause people to wonder all the more about what lies hidden away, they serve most importantly to deflect attention towards his work.

Marker began his career as a writer. He published his first essays and articles in the journal *Esprit* in 1947, and continued to contribute to this publication in the 1950s. His output of written work was prolific throughout this first decade, in keeping with the tremendous productivity of his subsequent years in varied media. His first two books were published in 1949: one a novel, *Le Cœur net* (translated into English as *The Forthright Spirit*), the other a montage of different texts on

---

1 'Death is no more than the antonym of birth. The antonym of living remains to be discovered' (*The Forthright Spirit*).

theatre, *L'Homme et sa liberté*. In 1952, an extended essay, *Giraudoux par lui-même*, gave early confirmation in print of one of his strongest and longest literary passions, the work of Jean Giraudoux. In addition to his writing in this period, Marker took on editorial work in 1947 for the newly founded journal *DOC*, and in 1954 he was to become editor for the Petite Planète travel guides at the Seuil publishing house, a series that he founded. During this time, he was also an active member of the groups Travail et Culture and Peuple et Culture, both of which promoted the educational dissemination of culture to a broad cross section of the general public. He has continued to publish articles and essays throughout the years, and has brought out further books, most notably *Coréennes* (1959), *Le Dépays* (1982), and *Staring Back* (2007), which combine photography and prose. But in the midst of his early writing and related activities, Marker made a decisive turn to filmmaking.

Since the early 1950s he has made an astonishing variety of films – features, shorts and co-directed works – as well as participating in numerous collaborative projects. He has also made several multimedia installations for gallery exhibition. As many commentators have observed, Marker was a multimedia pioneer a long time prior to the more precise use of this term to designate the most recent new media technologies. The different media in which he works filter in to one another and the distinctions between them become fluid. For example, *La Jetée* (1962), his celebrated brief incursion into the realm of science fiction, is termed a photo-roman (photo-novel), and exists in book form as a ciné-roman (cine-novel): the cinematic, photographic and novelistic weave through one another suggestively here to question the generic boundaries between them. Additionally, some later works move freely between the gallery space, the cinema and the home entertainment screen, and challenge any easy categorisation in terms of where they belong or how they might be labelled. The DVD release of the film *Chats perchés* (2004), for example, is accompanied by an endearing series of short video films on animals, *Petit bestiaire*, which form part of the installation *Zapping Zone: Proposals for an Imaginary Television* (1990 onwards). One element of this installation – *Chat écoutant la musique* – also serves as an interlude in the television documentary, *Le Tombeau d'Alexandre* (1993). Furthermore, a later addition to *Zapping Zone* in 1994, *Bullfight/Okinawa*, then found its way into the film *Level 5* (1996). This boundary crossing, which unsettles stable definitions, also informs his approach to documentary, the form of filmmaking for which he is best known.

Marker's idiosyncratic documentaries reassess what the term 'documentary' means. This is fitting with regard to his critical comments in interview when he says that the term leaves behind it a trail of 'sanctimonious boredom' (Marker 1984: 197) and that he only uses it because nobody has come up with anything better (cited in Walfisch 1996: 38). The elegance and erudition of his commentaries combine creative prose and factual observation to varying degrees, depending on the film. Some bear a more open relation to fiction than others, as each in its own way features valuable testimony of historical events or people, social commentary and critique, along with a focus on different cultures. Marker has travelled the world with his camera: he has taken still and motion pictures, has gone back to his native France occasionally, and has also returned repeatedly to some other destinations (Japan, Russia and Latin America in particular). His ability to marshal vast amounts of material – both his own and other people's footage – makes the label of 'l'as du montage' (the montage ace), which Laura gives him in *Level 5*, appropriate to a range of his films. His documentaries have traversed the gamut of styles with which this mode has been associated. Two key essayist interventions – *Lettre de Sibérie* (1958) and especially *Sans Soleil* (1982) – have earned him a stellar reputation in the manipulation of this personalised form. The advent of direct cinema in the early 1960s influenced the making of *Le Joli Mai* (1962), even though Marker's film is different in style from the work of the American directors to which the label usually applies. His occasional forays into the observational mode are balanced with more participatory works, in which Marker's distinctive voice is heard, but he is never seen. In the early 1960s he and his crew took advantage of the new lightweight camera equipment available and luxuriated in the possibilities it afforded of recording synchronous sound. His early films range from black and white to Eastman colour, and the qualities and material effects of filming in 16mm or 35mm stock are valued through the decades, with a more recent preference for video. His adoption of Super 8mm film, popular in experimental cinema in the 1970s, is used to striking effect in *L'Ambassade* (1973). This was the decade in which he spent as much time enabling other people's work as he did completing his own, most of which was collaborative. From the late 1970s through to the present, his turn to computer technology, followed by the digital, shows how he has kept pace with, and been an innovator in, the use of new technologies. His embrace of the new does not jettison the old, however. His work just bears witness to the accretion of ever more layers through the years: photographic, film and computer technologies build up like experience, and the relevant technological combination of the moment informs each fresh project.

Among his countless collaborations and friendships throughout these years, the connections with Alain Resnais and Agnès Varda are signal and abiding. These were the filmmakers with whom Richard Roud placed Marker in the early 1960s to speak of a 'Left Bank' group as distinct from the *Cahiers du cinéma* group who worked on the other side of the Seine during the Nouvelle Vague (Roud 1962–63: 25). A mutual admiration, along with a shared aesthetic and political sensibility has linked them ever since these early years. Resnais was the first director with whom Marker worked, and Resnais's films are a continual reference point for Marker through to his most recent work to date. Varda worked on Marker's *Dimanche à Pékin* (1956), and Marker's appreciation of her documentary *Les Glaneurs et la glaneuse* (2000) is recorded in the follow-up, *Deux ans après* (2002). Their longevity and mutability runs parallel to Marker's own: each still makes films and, in the case of both Marker and Varda, has also crossed into the terrain of new media. In accordance with this lifelong devotion to film, and bearing in mind its relation to other media throughout, Marker's filmmaking will be the concern of this study. At the time of writing, there are three comprehensive books that variously address the different media within Marker's work (see Alter 2006; Gauthier 2001; Lupton 2005). The aim of this book is to provide detailed readings of his directed and co-directed films made for cinema and television, along with his unsigned works of the late 1960s and 1970s. The particular focal point from which this study approaches his films is through their engagement with time. It is the interruption of movement in the first instance, which forms the basis for understanding the specificity of Marker's filmic treatment of temporality.

A fascination with stillness runs throughout Marker's work, even though it is not central to every film. It manifests itself principally through the existence of photographs, but also in more diverse ways, through the filming of statuary, painting and other static images, including the film still, in addition to a fondness for fixed frame shooting, which can give the effect of immobility, even though the footage we see is 'moving' in its duration. And on the way to stasis, there are also delays, which slow down the temporal progression of the images, or pause them, if only for a moment. Repeatedly the filmmaker responds dynamically to the emergence of stillness, as if it is conjured forth perpetually only in order for it then to be undermined. Camera mobility or the pace of montage reinsert stasis into the film's flow: both create harmonious links or bring out tensions between the mobile and immobile, and leave many works poised between the two. This relation between immobility and mobility leads us to definitions of cinema's temporal progression as a celluloid strip running through a projector at twenty-four frames per second, in which the quick succession of still frames animates them to give the illusory impression of the movement we perceive on screen. In an amplification of Jean-Luc Godard's definition of cinema as 'truth 24 times a second', Laura Mulvey brings out the moving image's connection to immobility and the inanimate more readily, when she refers to it also as 'death 24 times a second' (Mulvey 2006: 15). Marker's openness to the new film technologies of the twentieth and twenty-first centuries has taken him beyond the celluloid strip, through analogue video, computer graphics and into the digital era. But the bond between life and death, stillness and movement that Mulvey pinpoints manifests itself even throughout the periods of the films that are not made on celluloid. To say this is not to make the tautological observation that his films repeatedly illustrate Godard's and Mulvey's definitions. Rather, it is to introduce his frequent returns to stasis and moments of pause as part of a broader rethinking of temporality, beyond a mechanical or technological description of cinema. Equally importantly, his work occasions a broadening out of the relation between stillness and mobility as currently conceived in existing theoretical writings.

The second tome of Gilles Deleuze's seminal work on cinema, *L'Image-Temps*, is an extended reflection on film and time. There have been excellent points of contact made between Marker's work and Deleuze's thought (see, for example, Bellour 1990; Rodowick 1997: 4–5; and Tryon 2004), yet Marker is strikingly absent from Deleuze's study. Not by way of providing a reason for this, but certainly relevant to my argument in this book, Raymond Bellour points out that interrupted movement does not concern Deleuze (Bellour 1990: 99). It is in work on the photographic image that stasis has been explored in the most sustained ways. Marker's own passion for photography manifests itself in multiple forms throughout his career, even though, as Jan-Christopher Horak notes, he is less well-known as a photographer (Horak 1996: 60). Photographs feature notably in his books *Coréennes*, *Le Dépays*, *Staring Back*, and in Marie Susini's *La Renfermée: La Corse* (1981); in the *Photo Browse* section of the installation *Zapping Zone* and in his CD-ROM *Immemory*; and in his films, three of which are formed almost exclusively from photographs, and many of which make use of photographic images. For Susan Sontag, '[a]ll photographs are *memento mori*. To take a photograph is to participate in another person's (or thing's) mortality, vulnerability, mutability' (Sontag 1979: 15). It is through the question of mortality that the photograph will introduce us first to film in general and then to Marker's films in particular.

For André Bazin, writing in 1945, the very being of cinema is rooted famously in photography. The photograph, like the ancient Egyptian process of mummification, which he links to the origins of statuary, is a form of preservation that is directed against death. To photograph someone is not to override their literal death, according to Bazin, but to save them from a second spiritual death. Photography, by virtue of this act, embalms a moment in time. As a logical extension of this, Bazin understands filmic images to capture temporal duration and act as the mummification of change (Bazin 2002: 9–17). The spiritual survival of the photographic subject after their inevitable physical death has a religious association. The one image that accompanies the essay in which these thoughts are outlined – 'Ontologie de l'image photographique' ('Ontology of the Photographic Image') – is of the Turin shroud (*ibid.*: 15). The imprint of Christ on the holy shroud serves to illustrate how a material substance is impressed upon by an indexical trace. New technologies of film and photographic production have necessitated a rethinking of the way that Bazin theorises the transfer of reality from recorded subject to recording image. Suffice it to recognise here, however, Bazin's faith in the mummified endurance of the filmed or photographed subject, since Marker's own interest in stillness and mortality is not limited to a concern with the materiality of the film image. Bazin's theory serves here not only to bring in the contrastive views of a different theorist; it will also provide the subsequent basis on which Marker's difference from both can be felt.

Roland Barthes states an open preference for photography over cinema, without ever being able to separate the two fully and finally. When he does write on a film, he locates the filmic dimension within the film still rather than the moving image. Yet he observes that film and still exist as a palimpsest in which one cannot say which is on top, or which is drawn from which (Barthes 1993: 67). It is his later and most famous text on the photographic image, *La Chambre Claire*, which provides the most explicit counterpoint to Bazin's thoughts outlined above. The writing of this text is intimately bound up with the death of his mother and the search for a photograph – which he finds but he never publishes (the Winter Garden photograph) – that captures her essence and what she meant to him. For Barthes, photography is haunted by death: it is the return of the dead that he describes as 'cette chose un peu terrible qu'il y a dans toute photographie' (that slightly terrifying thing that is there in all photography) (Barthes 1980: 23). Barthes's famous discussion of the future anteriority of photography suggests that this medium captures a past moment, which has foreknowledge of the future, both of which signify death: 'Que le sujet en soit déjà mort ou non, toute photographie est cette catastrophe' (Whether the subject is already dead or not, all photography is this catastrophe) (Barthes 1980: 150). In contrast to Bazin's thought, then, which has the photograph transcend death, Barthes's work on photography invokes a death encounter from which there is no escape. What neither Barthes nor Bazin question in their work, however, is a sole focus on the mortality of the individual photographic subject. This is where Marker differs significantly.

Whether the photograph of a person foretells their death (Barthes), or whether it preserves them from a second spiritual death (Bazin), these theories of loss or embalmment relate uniquely to the subject we see imaged before us. Such theory is particularly relevant to documentary or realist modes, which preserve a link to the lives of those filmed, albeit differently in celluloid or digital forms. For Bazin, the human lifetime that we know will come to an end is suspended forever, and the photograph provides a spectral semblance of life after death, but one that is fixed. In this, and although writing negatively about the artwork in an early essay, philosopher Emmanuel Levinas seemingly concurs when he states that art immobilises being and freezes time eternally. This eternal stasis suggests for him an instant that endures without a future, 'a future forever to come' (Levinas 1998: 138). Even the introduction of time in cinema 'does not shatter the fixity of images' (*ibid*.: 139). Yet what if the link between stasis and film were to give rise to life after death of a different kind, one that is not to be understood in a religious sense, and one that challenges fixity at every turn? Marker's films, in their form and subject matter, conceive of precisely this. Death and stillness are bound up with alternative understandings of time beyond an individualistic focus on the subject(s) whose mortality is captured on, or explored within, his films. Consequently, his films do gesture towards an afterlife through their images, but this refers to the life of others who will live on after the death of the imaged subject(s). François Niney labels the time with which Marker concerns himself 'le temps historique' (historical time) (Niney 1996: 15), and thereby establishes a connection to the past and future. Reintroducing the subject and the image to time that stretches out prior to birth and after death, but without positing a linear progression between the two, my study labels such temporality the time of others. This term aims to register both the ethical and the political disjunctions and solidarities that Marker charts throughout his explorations of mortality. The temporal vertigo to which his films give rise opens out to varied visions of the past and future, some more welcome than others.

Temporality in Marker's work is sometimes closed in on itself, the future pre-known, and time impossible to change – a scrambled logic enables us to look back at a future in some films, as we may look at history in others. Dystopias are frequently apparent. At other times, and always mindful of the past in his ceaseless concern with memory, more utopian possibilities are explored in relation to a future that has yet to be invented. Closer to the later writings of Levinas than to his early work on art, Marker envisages such time as an opening towards what lies forever beyond the subject. In *Dieu, la mort et le temps*, rather than understand time on the basis of death, Levinas thinks death as a function of time, and thus time opens to the Infinite and the Other. The philosopher writes: 'Le temps, plutôt que courant des contenus de la conscience, est la version du Même vers l'Autre' (Levinas 1993: 127).[2] The filmmaker replies in more grounded terms with a socio-

2 'Time, rather than flowing from the contents of consciousness, is the turning outwards of the Same towards the Other.'

historical exploration of self–other relations that suggests a means of survival and a mode of connection to unknowable future generations. This relation to time sometimes takes the form of politicised collective struggle, solidarity and revolution. Fittingly, this is most prominent in the period when Marker's own identity in his filmmaking is veiled through his participation in collective projects, in the late 1960s and 1970s, but it does make a more recent return in *Chats perchés*. Crucially – and this gestures beyond Levinas's principally humanist ethics – Marker also explores relations between the human and the animal world. Ecological issues only feature explicitly in one co-directed work (*Vive la baleine*, 1972), and his infamous love of owls and cats, along with an attachment to other beasts, does not always lead to their being the focus of his filmic reflections. Yet flesh, fur, feathers, scales and blowholes are caught up in a similar struggle, as the continuing existence of the human race relates to that of the planet.

One of Marker's photo-films, *Si j'avais quatre dromadaires* (1966), connects animals and children in its specific vision of a different time. It suggests that we look again at their activities in the photographs we are shown, and also at photography itself, in order to learn something from them that may prompt a change to the status quo. In the published commentary of *Soy Mexico* (1965), a film that was never made, the second half of which is titled 'La Maison des morts' (The House of the Dead), an unborn child is given the final word. The child speaks in the first person and positions himself as the hope of Mexico (Marker 1967: 81). These life-affirming thoughts emerge from contexts intimate with death, which give pause to any uncritical alignment with the discourse of futurity. For Marker, film is not unequivocally on the side of mobility, duration and life, but nor is photography always an avowal of immobility, temporal stasis and death. The pull of stasis, the hesitation between life and death, lives on throughout Marker's filmic oeuvre in manifold ways. His concern with temporality turns on the intertwining of beginnings and endings, as well as memories and future imaginings. But it is at those moments that gesture beyond the limits of a lifetime, and where the ontology of the image is not bound only to ceaseless movement or death and eternal stasis, that this protean director registers an enduring bond between film and survival.

References

Alter, Nora M. (2006), *Chris Marker*, Urbana and Chicago, University of Illinois Press.
Barthes, Roland (1980), *La Chambre Claire: note sur la photographie*, Paris, Seuil.
Barthes, Roland (1993), 'The Third Meaning: Research Notes on Some Eisenstein Stills', in *Image, Music, Text*, London, Fontana, pp. 52–68.
Bazin, André (2002), 'Ontologie de l'image photographique', in *Qu'est-ce que le cinéma?* Paris, Éditions du Cerf; orig. publ. 1945 in *Problèmes de la peinture*, pp. 9–17.
Bellour, Raymond (1990), 'The Film Stilled', in *Camera Obscura*, 24 (September), pp. 99–123.
Deleuze, Gilles (1985), *L'Image-Temps: Cinéma 2*, Paris, Minuit.
Gauthier, Guy (2001), *Chris Marker: écrivain multimédia ou voyage à travers les médias*, Paris, L'Harmattan.
Horak, Jan-Christopher (1996), 'Chris Marker's Reality Bytes', in *Aperture*, 145, pp. 60–65.
Levinas, Emmanuel (1993), *Dieu, la mort et le temps*, Paris, Grasset.
Levinas, Emmanuel (1998), 'Reality and its Shadow', in Seán Hand (ed.), *The Levinas Reader*, Oxford, Blackwell; orig. publ. 1989, pp. 129–43; article orig. publ. in *Les Temps Modernes* (1948), 38, pp. 771–89.
Lupton, Catherine (2005), *Chris Marker: Memories of the Future*, London, Reaktion.
Marker, Chris (1967), *Commentaires 2*, Paris, Seuil.
Marker, Chris (1984), 'Terminal Vertigo' Computer Interview with Chris Marker, in *Monthly Film Bulletin*, 51/605 (July), pp. 196–97.
Mulvey, Laura (2006), *Death 24x a Second: Stillness and the Moving Image*, London, Reaktion.
Niney, François (1996), 'Remarques sur *Sans Soleil* de Chris Marker', in *Documentaires*, 12 (Summer–Autumn), pp. 5–15.
Rodowick, David (1997), *Gilles Deleuze's Time-Machine*, Durham, Duke University Press.
Roud, Richard (1962–1963), 'The Left Bank', in *Sight and Sound*, 32/1 (Winter), pp. 24–27.
Sontag, Susan (1979), *On Photography*, London, Penguin; orig. publ. 1971.
Tryon, Chuck (2004), 'Letters from an Unknown Filmmaker: Chris Marker's *Sans Soleil* and the Politics of Memory', in www.rhizomes.net/issue8/tryon.htm [accessed 30 December 2006].
Walfisch, Dolores (1996), 'Interview with Chris Marker', in *Vertigo*, 7 (Autumn), p. 38.

1

The early years: 1950–1961

The first decade of Chris Marker's filmmaking career encompasses what Chris Darke terms the 'lost period' of his oeuvre (Darke 2003: 48). The years from 1950 to 1961 are the least discussed because the films made in this period are difficult to find. Reassuringly – for the passionate researcher, at least – the films are still held in French archives, and it is the fervent hope of those who see them that availability will widen beyond this one day. In this early period, Marker collaborated on a number of projects (see Alter 2006: 167–78; Dubois 2002: 171–72; and Kämper and Tode 1997: 371–76 for detailed lists of his collaborations). He co-directed one film with Alain Resnais (*Les Statues meurent aussi* (1950–1953)) and directed five of his own (*Olympia 52* (1952); *Dimanche à Pékin* (1956); *Lettre de Sibérie* (1958); *Description d'un combat* (1960); and *Cuba Si!* (1961)): these six works are the focus of this chapter. Marker entered filmmaking in the first instance as a writer. His finely tuned skills in this capacity are evidenced from the outset in the richness and beauty of his poetic commentaries, all of which (with the exception of *Olympia 52*) are published in the first volume of the 1961 Seuil publication, *Commentaires*. This text also features the commentary of an unmade film, *L'Amérique rêve* (1959), about America's dreams of other times and places – a new America to be discovered – whose present is set up prophetically in conclusion as the Europe of the future. Marker establishes himself as a globetrotter: his first film takes him to Helsinki. Thereafter, he is attracted to countries in transition, and he travels from China through Siberia and Israel to Cuba. This period bears witness to fruitful first contacts with two important French producers – Pierre Braunberger and Anatole Dauman – while testifying less happily to draconian censorship of his work in France and beyond. It is to the first of these encounters with the French censors that we turn as we take a chronological journey through the films of the early years.

Les Statues meurent aussi

Begun in 1950 and completed in 1953, *Les Statues meurent aussi* was commissioned by the organisation Présence Africaine. Ghislain Cloquet was the cinematographer, Resnais was responsible for the editing and Marker provided the commentary, which is read by Jean Négroni. It won the Prix Vigo in 1954, but has had an otherwise chequered history. As well as constituting a study of African art, the film is highly critical of colonialism, and links the disappearance of African art to the process of western colonisation. Its incendiary capacity in this regard resulted in it being promptly censored on 31 August 1953. In the letter to the directors from the Film Censorship Commission in Paris (reproduced in the appendix to *Commentaires* (Marker 1961)), there was no indication of what should be cut, even though the committee specified that the second half of the film was particularly problematic. Marker notes that the film came out in a truncated version (minus its second half) in 1963, with the agreement of the directors, on the condition that it be accompanied by a disclaimer: 'Copie tronquée – à ne pas confondre avec l'original' (Truncated copy – not to be confused with the original) (Marker 1961: 185). But the producer who agreed to insert this statement forgot at the last moment. It was not until 1968 that the film was shown in its entirety. On a more positive note, it is now readily available on the 2004 Argos Films/Arte DVD release of Resnais's *Hiroshima mon amour* (1959).

Death is the leveller of manifold differences within this documentary that moves between statues and human beings from the outset. For Marker and Resnais, stone goes the way of all flesh: statuary crumbles, decomposes and reveals its mortality in the process. Yet this mortality is a sign of life that enables the filmmakers to mobilise stasis in the service of a political and ethical filmic critique. For Emmanuel Levinas: 'Within the life, or rather the death, of a statue, an instant endures infinitely [...] An eternally suspended future floats around the congealed position of a statue' (Levinas 1998: 138). This severed link to a future locates the statue, and the artwork, outside of time for Levinas. In contrast, Marker and Resnais imbue their filmed statues with life beyond the eternal suspension of an instant. For both filmmakers, the African artwork is not cut off from time or history, and this is what sets their filming of it apart from its demise under colonialist rule.

At the start of *Les Statues*, culture is described by the commentary as the botany of death, and is introduced through images of sculptures scattered among grass and trees, some roughly hewn, others – stone faces, a headless bust – more finely honed but disintegrating. The documentary immediately encompasses a museum space to designate the place where the western world has hitherto confined African art, disconnected from the culture that produced it. The film will work gradually to reinstate this connection between art, culture and world. The animation of the inanimate is key to the life that this documentary breathes back into its subject, while it also resuscitates links to African culture. Suddenly, the art objects are freed from their captivity behind the glass of the museum cases and are animated through the mobile gaze of the camera. The statues and other objects appear to glide past as if moving of their own accord. Different intensities of light and dark heighten the transition that we witness from stasis to movement, facilitated at times by a smooth series of dissolves from one image to the next, and at others by crisp cutting. As the voice-over returns, we are reminded that all of this belongs to another world: the statues are mute and the eyes that we see do not see us. However, the rendering mobile of stasis here suggests that even the most fixed of positions can be subject to question and change, along with reinsertion into a more dynamic conception of temporality and history. The initial setting in motion of the African artwork is this film's entry point to shaking a static colonialist and racist vision of African culture at its very foundations.

Contrary to an amnesiac colonising vision, *Les Statues* emphasises that African art and civilisation are as old as western and other cultures. The film as a whole strives ultimately to unite Africa, the West and the rest of the world in a fraternal embrace. At one point we are shown images of wood, cloth and earth, before the editing speeds up to such an extent that the surfaces we have been scrutinising become a hypnotic series of fast-moving wavy lines. The images thus question distinctions between different substances and suggest that the entire world is woven from the same material. The impact of the westerner's arrival on African culture is understood to rip this fabric. Registered by the commentary over disparate extracts from archive footage filmed in Africa, the negative effects of colonialism are seen in the commercialisation and subsequent vulgarisation of African art, the importing of illness (although the film concedes that westerners have also been healers) and the introduction of money to this culture of gift and exchange. African culture is described as being torn between Islam and Christianity, and the attempt to create a bond between the two through art is said to have failed. Yet the film finds traces of a link between art and life elsewhere. The motion of athletes is said to be an art form and the struggle against death is discernible everywhere. Footage of African men working on machines tells of how mechanisation has changed things irrevocably, but there is an affirmation of parity between the gestures of the worker and the artist. In its penultimate sequence, the commentary declares that we (Africa and the West) cannot recognise ourselves equal in our inheritance of a past, unless this stretches into the present. The commentary concludes: 'Les visages de l'art nègre sont tombés du même visage humain, comme la peau du serpent. Au-delà de leurs formes mortes, nous reconnaissons cette promesse, commune à toutes les grandes cultures, d'un homme victorieux du monde. Et Blancs ou Noirs, notre avenir est fait de cette promesse.'[1] Continuing the connection between art and culture, life and its double, a slow panning camera movement finally surveys an array of masks reputed to fight against death, and thus epitomises the overriding gesture of this film.

Today the vision of African culture glimpsed in *Les Statues* may seem all too simple, and the presentation of colonialism broad-sweeping rather than specific to individual African countries, even though it is still abundantly clear that it comes from a committed anti-racist and anti-colonialist perspective. Furthermore, the universalism of the film's humanism, while it was essential to a drive towards racial equality at the time, levels out distinctions in favour of commonality, thereby forestalling the recognition of non-hierarchical differences – both within Africa and between Africa and the West – that the post-

[1] 'The faces of African art have fallen from the same human face, like the skin of the serpent. Beyond their dead forms, we recognise this promise, common to all great cultures, of a man who is victor of the world. Whites and Blacks alike, our future is made of this promise.'

colonial era strives towards. Nevertheless, the film's questioning of colonialism abides convincingly and powerfully in the context of its innovative reflections on African art. Through a very precise focus on statuary, Marker and Resnais reanimate the artwork in order to highlight and question manifold colonial injustices. The promise to the future that the commentary refers to in conclusion is thereby opened crucially to everyone and everything.

Olympia 52

While Marker and Resnais were still working on *Les Statues meurent aussi*, Marker completed and released *Olympia 52* in 1952. It focuses on the fifteenth Olympiad, held in Helsinki in that same year. Marker was part of a team from the popular education organisation Peuple et Culture, established in the post-war period, who obtained the funding necessary to make a film on the games. Bénigno Cacérès, a key member of the group, recalls (as does the film commentary) that this was the first year that the USSR had participated in the Olympics, which made them particularly significant (Cacérès 1982: 35). In spite of the apparent contrast in subject matter with Marker's previous co-directed film, the humanism of *Olympia 52* takes up the earlier film's concern with mortality in its different context. A connection between Marker's work and that of Jean Giraudoux makes this thematic interest in mortal fragility even more resounding.

Marker's book *Giraudoux par lui-même* came out in the same year as *Olympia 52*. Giraudoux's second play, *Amphitryon 38*, reverberates like a distant echo in the title of Marker's second film. According to Giraudoux, there had been thirty-seven dramatic adaptations of the legend of Amphitryon prior to his own play. When Marker writes the introduction to his critical study he picks up on this, and titles it 'Giraudoux 52' (this becomes 'Giraudoux 62' in the second edition, published in 1962), while saying that this is not to be understood in the sense that Giraudoux meant when he wrote *Amphitryon 38* (Marker 1952: 5). Likewise, *Olympia 52* is not the fifty-second film of the Olympics, but the implicit link to the focus of Giraudoux's play is important. In the tales of antiquity, Jupiter regularly renounces his privileges of an Olympian God in order to conquer mortal beings. As in the myth of origin, Alcmène is the woman of Jupiter's affections and is married to Amphitryon in Giraudoux's play. Jupiter assumes the form of her husband to be able to have her through deception. His ultimate offer to her is immortality. Alcmène refuses this, however, having been steadfast throughout in confessing herself to be happy with her human status. As she says: 'Devenir immortel, c'est trahir, pour un humain' (To become immortal is a betrayal for a human being) (Giraudoux 1929: 79). Choosing to live with the imperfections of the human condition, Alcmène also speaks for the thrust of *Olympia 52*, which focuses on mortal limitations through the disappointments, as well as some of the undisputed achievements, in the 1952 Olympics.

Marker and crew left Paris for Finland on 10 July 1952. Images from their train journey across Europe at the start of the film lead into Helsinki's preparations for the games. Thanks to an ever more rousing musical soundtrack, along with the anticipation of the commentary (read by Joffre Dumazedier, co-founder of Peuple et Culture), the pace at this stage suggests exhilaration. The stadium is empty and the workers who are finishing the grounds are defined as the true gods in this place. The streets bustle with people and vehicles, as we also see planes and luggage, and glean through the editing that everyone is heading for the same destination. Momentum gathers in a festival-like atmosphere before everything stops, for lunch. There are humorous touches here: we are told that one would expect a group of statues of workers to put down their working implements, but the union will not let them. And the first cut to a lunchtime meal is to a sea lion being fed in a zoo. (A white cat will make a brief appearance later, as Marker finds space for one of his signature animals in this early work.) As the commentary announces a date – 19 July 1952 – and the start of the fifteenth Olympiad, we see people in raincoats. Not without irony, we are told that this opening date was chosen because it had not rained then in Helsinki since 1902.

In his record of the trip, Cacérès remarks that the most useful word that they learnt while in Helsinki was Finnish for 'sit', in order to prevent people in the crowd from jumping up in front of the camera while they were filming (Cacérès 1982: 36). Quite how popular this made the crew with the spectators they sat among is not something he discusses, but the shots of the races from a spectator's vantage point are admirably unobstructed. In some cases, close-ups of individual members of the crowd show them in more detail than the athletes they are watching. Dumazedier's usually well-paced commentary speeds up from time to time, as he gets quite excited during some of the races. We see moments in which athletes bond with one another, in spite of the fact that they are in direct competition, or in which the montage establishes relations between ideologically opposed camps, which is the case of the US and USSR, still in the grips of Cold War hostility. The film lingers on training sessions, particularly those of the Americans and the Soviets (who will share most of the victories). They are filmed working hard, but also in more relaxed circumstances, with their families or signing autographs. Although the length of each event is obviously edited substantially, the pace of *Olympia 52* still drags at times and its structure is loose. Nonetheless, there are moments of beauty and grace scattered throughout. The use of slow motion for selected events (most striking in the filming of the high jumpers and divers), and the rapid cutting between shots of wheels, bodies and heads in the cycling race are cases in point.

In a brief historical survey of the Olympics early on in the film, its darker moments are touched upon, and images from Leni Riefenstahl's *Olympiad* (1938) feature as the Nazi associations of 1936 are broached. Finland is linked with a return to peace, yet this is not accompanied by a rose-tinted vision. The film cuts from a Greek statue to a photographic image of Baron Pierre de Coubertin (responsible for reinventing the games of antiquity at the end of the nineteenth century), followed by still images of winners of past Olympics. The narrative that introduces the former champions is not wholly celebratory. The photographs immortalise their moment of glory, but some of their subsequent lives progress in a starkly contrasting manner, as the commentary explains that a number of them have fallen into poverty and obscurity. *Olympia 52* features the sadness and failures of the losers in the 1952 Olympics alongside the winners. The pole vault and the high jump are two of several events in which successful and unsuccessful attempts to clear the relevant obstacle are juxtaposed; one of the male runners in a sprint race is seen limping off the track, the camera focused on him rather than on the winner; and a female runner in the hurdles race abandons it, as the commentary announces the end of her career. More positively, the games culminate with the triple victory of the Czech athlete Emil Zátopek in the 5,000 metres, 10,000 metres and marathon. This is one of few successes that are mentioned.

As the champions of yesteryear are seen to fall from glory, the suggestion is that this year's may too, even though their current victories place them in a more prestigious position than those competitors who meet with defeat. The athletes remain largely de-idealised and are left to walk among mortals rather than being raised to the status of gods in the Olympian heights. *Olympia 52* chooses to embrace humanity, its sorrows and flaws, rather than an impossible ideal. The immortalisation of moments of victory in this film – incarnated in photographs of past champions – does not deny the onward temporal progression of a lifetime, whatever it brings and wherever it may lead.

Dimanche à Pékin

Marker's voyage to Helsinki inaugurated a decade of travel across several different continents, which began with a visit to China. *Dimanche à Pékin* (1956) was filmed in a fortnight in September 1955 during part of a longer trip facilitated by the 'Amitiés Franco-Chinoises' (Franco-Chinese Friendship Organisation). Marker confesses to having only the most rudimentary knowledge of the rules of photography at the time, but says that his heart was in it and that this, along with level-headedness, is what counted most (Marker 1961: 29). Banned in Germany because it was deemed propagandist, it was granted a visa number in France without fuss, thereby avoiding the censorship issues that still plagued *Les Statues meurent aussi*. Upon its release in 1956, the 22-minute short won the 'Grand Prix du court métrage' at the Festival de Tours. This is Marker's first film not to be made in black and white, and his use of Eastman colour is well suited to the visual richness of Peking. Even the opening credits are lavish. Each is given in French and Chinese and features intricate colour drawings of animals, flowers or more abstract symbols. Marker is listed as being part of the 'Groupe des Trente' (Group of Thirty). The group was originally formed in 1953 to protest against the threat to short film production in France. Marker joined later, as did Agnès Varda, who is credited as being the advisory Sinologist for *Dimanche à Pékin*. With its first-person narrative (read by Gilles Quéant), and a specific concern with memory and images, this short initiates a series of connections between subjectivity, memory, film and time that Marker will re-visit in myriad ways in subsequent works. Marker recounts how he screened the film to friends in Peking in 1958. He notes that their response was to laugh politely and to agree that this was how it *was*, rather than how it still is only a couple of years later (Marker 1961: 29). For them, it represented the preservation of, and reflection on, an instant, which soon became a thing of the past. The film thus reveals its age as quickly as a photograph does in relation to its ever-changing subject, but is, however, more complex in its structuring of temporality than merely showing us a present which is now past.

Dimanche à Pékin begins on the balcony of a Parisian apartment. The camera pans over an array of items, from brightly patterned fabric to miscellaneous colourful objects. It surveys them through a subjective eye, aligned with that of the first-person narrator, before it moves up some railings to the sky, to take in a view of the Eiffel Tower. The male narrator explains that he is in Paris, remembering back to Peking, and counting his treasures. The travellers' souvenirs are connected to a childhood memory of an engraving that he saw in a book thirty years ago and had been dreaming about ever since – a statue-lined road in China, which leads supposedly to the tombs of the Ming Emperors, but who are actually buried elsewhere. We are shown this black and white still image in a book. The narrator adds that one fine day, he found himself there, and the book image is then replaced by a replica film image, which features giant statues of elephants, camels and warriors. He notes that it is rather rare to be able to go for a walk in a childhood image, and this inaugurates the largely present tense narrative that takes us through this day in the life of Peking. Film provides not only the possibility to look at images and, through them, to move back in time but also to stage a future visit to a place whose emotional geography was first set out in an image from childhood. These ideas and temporal leaps will be taken up differently in *La Jetée* of 1962. For the time being, this narrator of 1956 takes us from Paris to Peking, and back in time, through the entry point of a black and white still image.

The journey starts with the day itself, at dawn, as Peking comes slowly to life through a mist that the poetic commentary suggests makes the whole city look as though it has just got out of the bath. Brighter colours emerge with the increasing daylight as more traffic and passers-by become visible. Thoughts of China's recent and more distant past are never far away. In relation to shots of cyclists who go by wearing face masks, we are told that they are not absent-minded surgeons, but just that the anti-capitalist revolution was also fought against dust, microbes and flies. Tomorrow's China is introduced to us too, as some schoolchildren walk past in pairs with their teachers, laughing and pointing at the camera. The city is presented as the locus of nostalgia, yet the price of modernism is palliated by the explicit recognition of few halcyon days in the past, as we see an old woman who can barely walk because of her mutilated feet. Changing areas, the traveller visits a school and shows pupils a picture book from France, which fascinates them: France here becomes the exotic other. The different areas of Peking take the traveller through time. The old Chinese quarter is described as a cinematic vision in an age that is now past (the narrator muses on seeing Humphrey Bogart in a white suit coming out of an opium den); the modern city is that of the future (Peking in 2000); and Beijing's Forbidden City is described as that of Jules Verne and Marco Polo. At one point, the film leaves the city momentarily, and focuses on still painted colour images, which furnish both the stuff of dreams and the occasion for a brief glimpse of Chinese history. A time journey forwards from Genghis Khan and his invading cavalry is accompanied by the filming of painted horses, men and women through rhythmic cuts and zooms set to music, all of which enlivens the original still illustration of the narrative we hear. An animated watercolour episode that features a princess and a tiger (by Antonio Harispe of the Arcady team), accompanies the concluding summary of how this history lives on into the present. As the film returns to the city, and China is said to be opening out to the rest of the world, having been shut away for so long, the commentary registers the need to understand what we have seen here, since we will soon share history with its inhabitants.

At the end of the day – and the film – the pace slows. The shared gaze of the camera and narrator settles on young girls and boys in a rowing boat. The narrator describes himself as breathing in all of the images that he sees and hears, which emphasises how he literally lives these sensate moments. As the film ends, it leaves him in the present of his past, rather than returning him to the future. It remains with the slow-moving images, instead of taking him back to the still image with which the journey started. The commentary of *Dimanche à Pékin* began with the contention that the memory of a place is the only thing more beautiful than the place itself. Through memory, the traveller is able to enter a childhood image and move around in time from there. His return to temporal progression is suspended, but this does not deny the onward march of historical time.

In spite of the indisputable accomplishment of *Dimanche à Pékin*, one significant initial respondent was still left wanting more. André Bazin declared it admirable, but ultimately disappointing because the short film could not do justice to such a vast subject. The images, he writes, 'nous laissaient un peu sur notre faim' (left us a little hungry for more) (Bazin 1998: 258). It is in his subsequent film that Marker was amply to satisfy Bazin's desire for a more extended study.

Lettre de Sibérie

Contracted by Anatole Dauman's production company Argos Films, a team comprising Marker, Armand Gatti, André Pierrard and Sacha Vierny set off for Siberia at the end of August 1957 to make a film that was provisionally titled *Baikal* but that would become *Lettre de Sibérie* (1958). (A copy of the original contract is in Dauman 1989: 154–55.) Pierrard was to be the executive producer, Vierny the camera operator and Gatti was responsible for collecting documentation. The documentary aimed to avoid the infinitely positive Soviet style of representing this land and, consequently, to take a more dialectical approach instead. This approach was aided by the first emergence in Marker's work of an epistolary format and the particular relation thereby created between the images and the letter-based format of the commentary. Formally innovative, the film sets out to show previously unseen images of Siberia, to dispel prejudices and to reveal how it is so much more than the frozen, unforgiving land of myth. It takes us the length and breadth of the country to meet its population, to explore landscape and wildlife, rural and urban life, along with science and industry. The film won the Prix Lumière in 1958. It was the relationship between commentary and image that attracted high praise from André Bazin in a landmark article that would set some of the key terms by which Marker's work would be discussed in subsequent years.

Bazin speaks of *Lettre de Sibérie* as an essay documented by film. From this point onwards, the label of essayist has been applied repeatedly – and used by Marker himself (see Dauman 1989: 157) – to refer to this important strand of his filmmaking, which valorises his skills as a writer. Bazin states that whereas the image is usually the raw material of film, in *Lettre de Sibérie* this alters: 'Je dirai que la matière première c'est l'intelligence, son expression immédiate la parole, et que l'image n'intervient qu'en troisième position en référence à cette intelligence verbale'[2] (Bazin 1998: 259). Bazin orients our attention first to the soundtrack and the intelligence of the commentary, which then leads us to the images. Additionally, in opposition to traditional montage, he coins the term horizontal montage to describe a zigzag motion in which images do not refer to other images but to what is said about them. Marker's editing, in Bazin's view, moves from ear to eye, and the primordial element is the aural beauty through which the mind subsequently gains access to the image. Consideration of an early example will show how the film's view of Siberia fleshes out the connection between commentary and image that Bazin speaks about in terms of imaged intelligence.

'Je vous écris d'un pays lointain' (I am writing to you from a far-off country). With these words, cited from Henri Michaux's *Lointain Intérieur* (1938) and read by Georges Rouquier, the commentary of *Lettre de Sibérie* begins. The subjectivity of the film's narration is established at the outset as the speaking 'I' who is writing to someone back home and the eye of the cameraman are revealed to be one and the same: 'Tout en vous écrivant, je suis des yeux la frange d'un petit bois de bouleaux, et je me souviens que le nom de cet arbre, en russe, est un mot d'amour: *Biriosinka.*'[3] The camera movement enacts the motion of the eye spoken about here, and we too follow the line of birches. Early on, we are told that the Siberians understood death for a long time as the work of the devil who would steal people's souls. We see images of graves among trees, the cold earth and isolation, but the commentary then envisages the possibility of reanimating such lifelessness: 'Dans ce sol gelé où les cadavres ne changent pas, sous ces tombes où la glace apparaît en creusant, la vie et la mort ne diffèrent que d'un rien, d'un souffle ... Qu'on le lui rende, et le corps est prêt à

---

2 'I will say that the raw material is intelligence, its immediate expression speech and that the image only comes in third position with reference to this verbal intelligence.'

3 'As I write to you, my eyes are tracing the edge of a small wood of birches, and I remember that the name of this tree, in Russian, is a word of love: *Biriosinka.*'

revivre, à revenir partager la vie lente et frileuse des villages de bois, à ramener les chevaux errants, à construire les chasse-neige, à conduire les troupeaux dans leurs pélerinages à des terres plus douces.'[4] Here, the film's images conjure what the commentary speaks about: from the graves among trees to a view of a village of wooden huts, to errant horses, and finally to herds of animals, with men shepherding them in the right direction. The commentary breathes into these images, injects life into the frozen tundra and thaws out death. The revivifying force comes thus through words, and this verbal power manifests itself elsewhere in this film. In a particularly well-known section, the commentary is set up as the determining feature in our reception of images.

Midway through *Lettre de Sibérie*, and in order to reflect on the influence that a commentary with a particular slant can have over images, the same sequence is shown three different times, each with an alternative verbal gloss. The apparently unchanging images comprise a shot of a crossroads in the city of Yakutsk where a bus passes a luxury Zim car and a pushbike, before the film cuts to workers levelling a road surface on their hands and knees, and a man who looks into the camera lens as he passes in front of it. The first commentary on this scene is upbeat, Soviet-style and extremely positive about the modernity and comfort of the city. It declares its pride in the transport system and the happiness of its workers; the music matches the mood and the man who passes in front of the camera is labelled picturesque. The second is entirely negative and has sombre music to match: the car that featured in the previous sequence as the triumph of the Soviet automobile industry is now portrayed as expensive and uncomfortable. Public transport is described as crowded, social inequities are blatant and the workers are miserable slaves to the State. This version labels the man who passes in front of the camera a sinister-looking Asiatic. The third commentary attempts a greater degree of objectivity. It compares the bus to its counterparts in Paris, describes the car as excellent, praises the courage and tenacity of the people, and the workers devoted to improving a city still in need

---

4 'In this frozen ground where the corpses do not change, under these tombs where the ice digs through, life and death differ by very little, by a breath ... Let someone restore it, and the body is ready to live again, to come back and take part in the slow, cold life of these wooden villages, to retrieve stray horses, to build snowploughs, to steer flocks in their pilgrimages to gentler lands.'

of embellishment. The final man is described this time as a Yakut suffering from strabismus. Rouquier's voice-over reflects back on this series of commentaries and declares that even the final objective example is not right, since it pauses and judges the reality of Siberia and still deforms it, albeit differently from the other biased views. The earlier revitalising force of the commentary or, as in these three examples, its sway over our perception of the images, are two ways in which the words take priority. As this self-reflexive sequence reveals, however, this verbal power is something that *Lettre de Sibérie* is fully aware of, and, in addition to illustrating the authority of documentary commentary, the film works simultaneously to challenge the primacy of word over image. Indeed, it places emphasis on the materiality of its images in ways that lead us gradually to expand and question Bazin's description of *Lettre de Sibérie* as imaged intelligence.

The use of different types of image is an important facet of this film. The first animated sequence, produced by Paul Grimault and William Guéry of the Arcady team, shows a herd of black mammoths that marches in unison across a pink background to a humorous song written about them. The sequence is light-hearted and is accompanied by several songs, but still conveys information about the genealogical lineage of the mammoth and the explorers who set out on its trail. The animation is repeated later on in an imaginary publicity slot for reindeer, although there are other variants in the image, as *Lettre de Sibérie*'s collage is also indebted to archive footage and photographs. As the film continues to traverse the Siberian terrain later on, an album of old photos serves to introduce the region of Aldan, which then bears comparison to Dawson in the US in terms of it being the gold capital of Siberia. This sequence is pitched as a form of 'sentimental competition' preferable to the Cold War, and comparisons ensue between the two countries. (In a similar vein and in an extended sequence of black and white newsreel footage elsewhere in the film, termed 'actualités imaginaires' (imaginary news), Marker inserts Pathé-Journal newsreel footage of forest fires in Montana. He states in the published commentary that this is probably the only film to date in which Soviet firemen are to be seen extinguishing an American fire (Marker 1961: 65).) We see photographs of the interior of the Trans-Siberian express, the Aldan landscape that it crosses, and the people one could meet along the way. Some of the images are said to introduce us to an Arizona-style landscape, along with Siberian 'cowboys and Indians'. Each photograph is filmed with a mobile camera, and such mobility works in line with the revivification of stasis implied at the outset of the film, as the commentary breathed life into the images. The movement between photographs involves the kind of shifts that Marker will use elsewhere when he films both photographs and stills: a mixture of dissolves, straight cuts, and the equivalent of a slide show effect. Yet what this photographic sequence reveals, in addition to focusing our attention on a different medium, is a particular trait of the verbal structure of the narration of *Lettre de Sibérie* that is worth considering in more detail. For, it suggests a way in which the images – whether originally static or moving – take on a life of their own, never wholly independent from the commentary but importantly distinct.

The verbal narration of the film functions largely on the basis of comparisons made mainly between Siberia and France, but also brings in many other places. Marker's films are deft in their use of a comparative style of thinking, and *Lettre de Sibérie* is certainly not unique in this respect. Its difference inheres, however, in the abundance of references the voice-over makes to places beyond Siberia, and the fact that the image track does not enact the journeys of which the commentary speaks. The first time that the river Lena appears in the film, for example, we see its vast open expanse, and then its banks, sprinkled with small houses and vegetation, reflected in the water. The commentary announces that to picture the Lena, we need to imagine a river five times the length of the Seine and fifty times its breadth. The images never cut to the Seine, however, and we are told to imagine something that we are actually shown without the need of the comparative tool. These verbal comparisons continue: workers on the Irkutsk barrage and fishermen on the Angara river are given counterparts in the Renault factory and on the Seine. The commentary also hops around the globe as it gives time checks, from Baghdad, through Malta, to New Zealand. We see young girls in Irkutsk who guide the movement of giant cranes, and cars that move around their bases are likened by the voice-over to cats following one another in the metro system, as the barrage stages a performance which the film sets to music. In each case, the images remain steadfast in their focus on their Siberian subjects, while the commentary travels around the world.

These voice-over comparisons between Siberia and other places, which run from the beginning to the end of the film, demonstrate that what the spectator's ear hears, the eye does not always see. This visual difference from what the commentary designates encourages us to see more than the imaged intelligence that Bazin pinpoints in this film. To refer back to Bazin's statement cited earlier, the images only come in third position with reference to intelligence and speech if we understand the commentary to recuperate them illustratively throughout. *Lettre de Sibérie* ultimately resists this very move, however, even as it showcases verbal dexterity. The implied recipient of the narrator's letters is not in possession of the visual images we see as spectators of the film, hence the need for comparative descriptions. The commentary introduces the unfamiliar in familiar terms in order to domesticate its strangeness and to make it comprehensible to the addressee who cannot see what the commentator, and we, are seeing. The narrator's correspondent is asked to imagine, to conjure images forth on the basis of what the commentary describes. The film we watch is, in one sense, the very production of those images. But in showing us these alongside a commentary that requires a comparative imagination to visualise them from home, or to imagine something different from what is shown, we are positioned simultaneously in conflicting places and times. This disjunction relates to the kinds of dislocations that Hamid Naficy speaks of in relation to exilic filmmaking (Naficy 2001: 101–51). As spectators we are identified with the imaginary position of an implied addressee who sees no images but who receives the written letter, and we are also seeing through the writer's eye/I. The eye/I that writes is split between image and commentary, as is the viewer, and consequently there is discordance within the sites of enunciation and reception of this film. The image track and the fictional addressee of the traveller's letters thus become the silent partners in a complex dialogue. Caught between home and this far-off land, between aural commentary and mental impression, the film's images are very much at home in their distant country of origin, whereas the intelligence whose expression is the spoken word constantly veers away from the time and place of writing.

As the film closes, it comes full circle and cites once again the Michaux lines with which it opened, while showing us different images of the countryside from those that we saw at the beginning. Visually we have moved on, even though verbally such repetition implies stasis. An earlier image, which the commentary suggests is central to the film – a lorry passes a horse-drawn cart on the road

– is recalled implicitly as Siberia's location between past and future is echoed in conclusion. The commentary that breathed life into the corpses of the frozen earth towards the start of the film, and into the images, is inextricably linked to them throughout. But the images of *Lettre de Sibérie* also have a life of their own, which lies visibly beyond verbal recuperation.

Description d'un combat

Marker recounts how producer Wim van Leer (the 'Mike Todd of Mount Carmel') had approached him after he saw *Lettre de Sibérie* and suggested he make a corresponding film about Israel, *Lettre de Tel-Aviv* (Marker 1961: 125). *Description d'un combat* (1960) was the rather different result, the title of which comes from an early tale by Franz Kafka. Focused on the fledgling nation of Israel, the introduction that scrolls up on screen at the start tells of a country that has known struggle in all its forms, and ends with a statement that speaks for what *Description* seeks to approach and understand: 'Sous les images de la vie quotidienne en Israël, se livre à chaque instant ce combat intérieur, moins apparent que celui des armes, et peut-être le seul décisif.'[5] It wishes to probe beneath the surface of the images, to move beyond appearances, to focus on an interior struggle, which underlies day-to-day living. Over images of a crop-spraying plane later in the film, the commentary says that, to measure what has really happened in this land, we would need to x-ray it for it to tell its story. The film furnishes this radiographic vision and the implied exploration of the unconscious of the image, as it sets up a dialogue between word and image (distinct from the epistolary relation of *Lettre de Sibérie*), which foregrounds both the materiality and the transparency of signs. The struggle in which Israel engages is charted across a broad historical trajectory, and involves re-negotiating its fraught relation to itself as well as others.

Description features cameo appearances of the principal animals of Marker's bestiary – cats and owls – along with a reference to Agnès Varda ('Varda' figures on a sign and is the name of a hairdressing

[5] 'Beneath the images of daily life in Israel, this internal struggle is being fought at each moment, less apparent than that involving weapons, and perhaps the only decisive one.'

salon). Yet its playful asides, which suggest Marker's presence, and its wry humour do not undermine the serious engagement with Israel's current existence and pre-history. *Description* paints a picture of a land of myriad dreams and nightmares experienced over two thousand years. Partway through the film, bonfires burn on beaches: the enemies of the Jewish people are said to go up symbolically in flames, as Israel looks for a past that is different from resignation or martyrdom. Later, and with reference to the more recent past, extracts from *Les Illégaux* feature (shot by Meyer Levin and Bertrand Hesse of Pathé-Journal in 1947), which enable the commentary to introduce a general European culpability in forcing the various displacements of the Jewish population. Germany, France and England are singled out in particular. War and violence are never far away in the present and haunt even one of the more relaxed moments of the film: people at a Popular Culture Centre in Carmel drink, smoke and dance, while the voice-over announces deaths at the border. More positively, a busy Kibbutz meeting is filmed, and its form of governance and lifestyle is described in utopian terms as a limited but absolute form of democracy. Less rosily, the Arab minority is referred to briefly later on. We hear how desperately the Arab area needs improvement in terms of quality of life, and we are introduced to an Arab girl, Mouna, who raises her family single-handedly in a Nazareth slum, and who smiles continually against the odds. Towards the end of the film, the first wrinkles are said to appear on the face of relative peace. The commentary explains how the right to live that was bought by so much Jewish blood is now being hit by daily demons, the illnesses of happiness, like locusts. These biblical insects plague the images at this point, and block clear vision through their swarm. This swarm spills out of these images to question any unequivocally clear-sighted glance into the future. *Description*, more than any other film by Marker, has been haunted by future political events that cast Israel in a very different light from that presented in the film. After the Six-Day War, seven years after its release, Marker reportedly withdrew it from distribution and said that he did not want it screened publicly. But *Description*'s central encouragement to observe and understand suggests how we might continue to view it more peaceably.

The film begins with disparate fixed frame images. The commentary, read by Jean Vilar, announces that this land addresses us through signs. Israel is presented in all its diversity: from its rugged landscapes as well as built-up areas the length and breadth of the country; from the Red Sea in the south to the Dead Sea in the east, the Mediterranean to the west and the northern mountains; and from Tel Aviv through Eilat, Jerusalem and Nazareth to Haifa. Any dryness in the studious endeavour to read its numerous signs is immediately undercut at the outset by the appearance of a road sign indicating bumps and the slow-paced entry into the image, snout first, of a camel whose humps imitate it. Israel is introduced as being twelve-years-old, soon to be thirteen; a pregnant woman is filmed walking along a street, and the two million inhabitants are said soon to become three million. Signs, we are told, have a short life here: a tyre cemetery in Jaffa has already disappeared and a man standing on a raised mound in Lake Tiberias is said not to be there any more either. The bark of several tree trunks on the water's edge is filmed in close-up, and we hear that the only durable signs are on tree bark and human skin. The film cuts to a man's arm, followed by hands in the market place, exchanging coins then notes, and where everything from money to colours is understood as a sign. This area of Carmel is termed the rue Mouffetard of Tel Aviv, which establishes a link to the famous market street in the 5th arrondissement of Paris. Having shown us many 'signs', the commentary remarks that they are not only made for the eye: 'ils expriment un besoin vieux comme les juifs et neuf comme la soif – communiquer' (They express a need as old as the Jews and as new as thirst – to communicate). An ensuing discussion of communication also explains one of the formal principles of the film.

Communication is said to establish an order, a relation between things that are hostile or incomprehensible to one another. This definition is given over the image of an oscilloscope in the Weizmann Institute, the solitary action of which is thought to resemble that of contemplative animals. The film cuts to a shot of two owls, with a synthesised sound track, and then oscillates between the machine in the Institute and the birds. Over images of a university the commentary states that this is another privileged place in which the false symmetries of Israel crumble. The copulas of the synagogue and the planetarium are described as two halves rather than two enemies. Alternate shots of a man praying and people studying in a library illustrate a common silence. The editing of *Description* – by Eva Zora – functions according to the logic of communication that Marker's commentary describes: the juxtaposition of images here works to unravel, rather than reinforce, a binary model of signification. Thus, while through its choice of vocabulary (the omnipresent discussion of 'signs'), the film apparently ascribes to structuralist discourse, as Alter suggests (Alter 2006: 61–62), it subtly marks out its difference from this dominant critical paradigm of the time. Its juxtapositions deconstruct the very symmetrical oppositions upon which structuralism depends.

The structuralist approach to film was indebted to a broader trend within the humanities that involved rethinking the study of various subjects in terms provided principally by linguistics. Its period of influence was at its height in the 1950s and early 1960s. A Saussurean model of linguistics was at the root of this, which suggested that language is a system of differences without positive terms, and that signs signify according to binary oppositions and hierarchical difference from one another. The images – labelled 'signs' – of this film, as suggested above, do not follow this confrontational, oppositional logic in their correspondence with the system of communication that the commentary outlines. However, whereas communication implies a use of language that treats words as transparent in the service of what one wishes to communicate, the commentary's use of its key term serves a different purpose, which is central to the functioning of both word and image. The linguistic sign that is repeated most frequently in *Description* is the term 'signe' itself, but this has the effect of making the term more opaque, the more we hear it. Repetition serves to render the term itself visible and material – something we come to see rather than fail to notice. It is this requirement to look at, rather than see through, both word and image that the film insists upon through to the end, in order to understand what might otherwise resist or escape comprehension.

The final image of the film is a long take of a young girl who draws at an easel, seemingly oblivious to the camera's steady presence. We are told to look at her – an activity that the static position of the camera and duration of the image facilitates – to understand her, her innocence and the threats to which she is exposed, and perhaps talk to her. The commentary remarks that she will never be an Anne Frank but says that we need to remind her that injustice in Israel weighs more heavily than anywhere else. It concludes with the following words:

> Mais d'abord la regarder – jusqu'à l'énigme, comme ces mots qu'on répète sans cesse et que soudain on ne reconnaît plus – jusqu'à ce

qu'entre toutes les choses incompréhensibles de ce monde, la plus incompréhensible soit qu'elle est là, en face de nous, comme un oiseau et comme un chiffre – comme un signe.[6]

These words are self-reflexive with regard to the film's own strategy of repeating the term 'signe'. It is at this point that we have to look at the term again in the manner that we are being encouraged to look at this young girl who, as Lupton suggests appropriately, seems to be the same age as her homeland (Lupton 2005: 68). Without pausing the image, its stasis at this point registers a link to the future, rather than the past, to the possibility of learning how to read images afresh. The cinematography and photography of this film work thus to render life and a future visible in the images we see.

In addition to the graceful pans and tracking shots to which we were accustomed in *Les Statues meurent aussi* – albeit on a more restricted scale – Cloquet's camera in this film performs aerial acrobatics through which its viewing positions actually appear to have taken flight at some moments (for example, in the filming of crowds we see gathered for an outdoor ceremonial procession). At other moments, its mobility is valorised differently, as, for example, when a boy, Ali, is filmed in close-up, as he moves relatively quickly down a slope, and uses his delivery trolley to return home after he has finished his work. The camera remains level with him on the slopes of Mount Carmel for a while, and then drops back slightly, before it follows him finally, at speed. The commentary remarks that this is how sports are born, and dreams of Olympic glory are said to come from carrying out a daily profession. Cheers on the soundtrack accompany the rest of the descent. Yet Cloquet's camera is also frequently still as it films its varied subjects. With regard to the oscilloscope sequence discussed above, Guy Gauthier notes that it comprises many fixed shots and that one could think that this was a succession of photographs, which distance us from the art of cinema (Gauthier 1963: 40). In addition to many such static shots, the film features several photographic sequences. Rather than distance us from the cinematic, however, their succession brings us increasingly closer to the contemplative gaze upon the materialist sign that helps us to look again at what we see.

6 'But first of all to look at her – until she becomes enigmatic, like those words that one repeats ceaselessly and that one no longer recognises – until of all the incomprehensible things in this world, the most incomprehensible thing is that she is here, opposite us, like a bird and like a code – like a sign.'

There are many photographs in *Description*, some of which introduce humour (a series of tourist photographs of Israelis are shown to their subjects, with various reactions). Yet photographs of children are the most significant in drawing attention to the link that this film makes between contemplation and time. In the first such series, the ghettoes of Mea Shearim are described as the place where 'le temps se pétrifie' (time is frozen). A mobile camera focuses on details within each image. The concluding photographs of this sequence feature children, either on their own or in groups. The place where time has stood still and that these children inhabit can be contrasted with the children we see at the end of the film. *Description* comes to a close through alternating photographs and static film shots. The commentary remarks that children are born on the other side of fear. We see a series of photographs and are told that they come up to you in the streets and say 'Tsalemoti', which means 'take my picture'. The drawing class at the end of the film shows photographs in advance of fixed frame shots of each subject, and young boys appear before the final girl whose importance we noted above. Both the film footage and the photographs fix the frame of vision as *Description* draws to a close, but rather than place emphasis on time standing still, the stasis of the images works here in the service of Israel's future. Stillness helps us to focus on what materialises through the camera's gaze – otherwise incomprehensible signs that we, like Israel, need to look at and learn how to read time and again.

Cuba Si!

This chapter closes, as it opened, with a censored film. *Cuba Si!* (1961) is the final commentary published in *Commentaires*. Marker notes the symmetrical relation to *Les Statues meurent aussi* when he terms them 'deux zones d'ombre' (two shadow zones) (Marker 1961: 155). He comments dryly that the film obtained the Prix Terrenoire in 1961 (*ibid.*: 156), in reference to Louis Terrenoire, then Minister of Information, whose letter of censorship is published in the appendix to *Commentaires*. The film was banned because it was deemed a piece of ideological propaganda as well as an apology for the Castro regime. It was eventually released uncut in 1963. Produced by Pierre Braunberger, *Cuba Si!* presents the background to the Cuban revolution of

1959, and culminates with the failed Bay of Pigs invasion in April 1961. It sets itself in opposition to the wealth of misinformation that was appearing in the press at the time, especially in French news reports on Cuba. This counter-informational drive pre-empts Marker's work in the late 1960s and 1970s, for the *On vous parle* series in particular. *Cuba Si!* is the first of several of his films that relate to the Cuban revolution. Of all of them, this is the most celebratory, reflective of his self-confessed love affair with the country at the time (see Pays 1962: 5). Marker says that of his films to date, this one is the closest to his heart and that it attempts to communicate the 'rhythm' of a revolution that may prove a decisive moment in contemporary history (Marker 1961: 155). The published commentary strengthens the musical reference, since it labels each section with a different Italian musical notation – from Largos to Allegros, with Castro's interviews labelled Arias – to mark the various and frequent changes of pace. In their public defence of *Cuba Si!* against the retrograde French censors, Agnès Varda and Jacques Demy pick up on the rhythm too when they write that Marker: 'a filmé la Conga Brava, il a fait un film sur une révolution vivante' (filmed the Conga Brava, he has made a film on a living revolution) (Varda and Demy 1962: 39). (Varda was to use some of Marker's Cuban contacts a year later when she made *Salut les Cubains* (1963) (Varda 1994: 133).) This living revolution is fashioned from 16mm film shot by Marker on a visit to Cuba in January 1961, along with newsreel relating to the Bay of Pigs invasion, all of which is interspersed with photographs, posters and extracts from newspapers. The film has the same editor as *Description d'un combat*, Eva Zora. The entire collage is cut to the rhythm of life and indebted to a specific manner of reanimating stillness, enabled by assistance from the same members of the Arcady team who had worked previously on *Lettre de Sibérie*.

Cuba Si! comprises two parts. It begins in Havana in December 1960 with a carnival atmosphere among people in the streets. Everyone is celebrating the Day of Kings. Alongside images of men dressed up as magi talking on telephones to children about their Christmas wishlists, we hear that grown men and women have their own wise men. Images of leaders of the revolution succeed one another here: Che Guevara, Fidel Castro and Juan Almeida are said to have brought gifts of industrialisation, agrarian reform and alphabetisation. The collective revolutionary spirit is written throughout the film from images to commentary, initially in terms of solidarity among the people. The year of 1961 is that of alphabetisation and each literate person is responsible for an illiterate person. Although Havana is termed an Americanised graft onto Cuban skin, the film isolates a specifically Cuban way of doing everything as we see a traffic policeman sitting down in the middle of the road. Baseball is described as a great passion and the commentary reminds us that Castro himself led one team to victory. As the film cuts between images of the players and the crowd at one game in a manner which recalls *Olympia 52*, the voice-over reports that the crowd was under attack from the inside and the outside, and knew it, but that it would defend itself if the occasion arose.

A key innovation of *Cuba Si!* is the inclusion for the first time in one of Marker's films of direct interview footage – with a Cuban priest and Castro. Such contact with Castro quite literally brings him to life. The first time that we hear from him directly is preceded by his two-dimensional image on a board that is carried towards the camera and which is then replaced by images of him talking about the twelve men who initiated the revolutionary resistance of the Sierra Maestra in October 1958. Footage shows how they survived and armed themselves. Nicolas Yumatov, who reads the commentary of this film, will also feature as one of the voices in *Si j'avais quatre dromadaires* (1966). The latter work is a photo-film that uses the Sierra Maestra to characterise the dawning of a new era of tenderness and that utilises dynamic camerawork throughout to film its intricate photographic montage. *Cuba Si!* uses photographs within the Sierra Maestra footage to recall, reinvent and then explode a folkloric past. Castro is cast by the commentary as a Robin Hood figure but one who has read Marx. Interspersed with the footage of the revolutionaries in *Cuba Si!* are still images from a film on the famous outlaw of Sherwood Forest. As the Robin Hood myth is recast in a Cuban mould, the still images are subject to manipulation. Paul Grimault and William Guéry explain how the Robin Hood sequences were shot on the basis of photographs provided by Marker. Marker asked them to reproduce these, among other documents, using a mobile camera 'afin de donner un peu plus de vie' (in order to give a little more life), or to highlight a particular detail (Grimault and Guéry 1963: 57). The Robin Hood film was reanimated by them but in a very particular way. They filmed each individual photographic image to create a disjunctive kind of movement, which lends a comical edge to an otherwise serious alignment of Castro with the bandit who was on side of the poor and the good. The final image of the Robin Hood sequence is blown to pieces, as is the myth, however: the legend dies and the revolution takes its place.

The interview with the Cuban priest stresses his solidarity with the revolution, in spite of his religion. He deems its principles to be closer to Christianity than Batista's government that was in place beforehand. Footage of Batista appears at this point, accompanied by the people the commentary terms his entourage of gangsters. The voice-over then asks who Castro is. The film replies first of all with a montage of still images of him, in drawings, press cuttings and in a graphically similar image on a Greek vase, as everyone is said to have their own ideas, but it then turns to Castro himself. A fixed frame interview with him seated at a desk replaces the static images. He tells of how he became a revolutionary and intersperses references to a French past (to figures such as Marat, Danton and Robespierre) to make his own case more easily understandable to this audience. The talking head interview contrasts once again here with the varied static images of Castro that precede it, all the while suggesting the importance of both forms to the film, which enable Castro's revolutionary difference to be felt.

Towards the end of the first part of *Cuba Si!*, images of abject poverty sit alongside those of a millionaire existence in which we only see the gardens, but the statues, water features and grounds suggest wealth. We hear that nothing troubles the dreams of those who reside here, yet that elsewhere things were beginning to happen. The film cuts between increasingly disturbing and violent images, and the stillness of the enchanted gardens, and the commentary reports that Batista finally fled on 1 January 1959. For the first time in five centuries, Cuba is said to belong to the Cubans. The second part of the film begins with the word 'Libertad' written in capital white letters across the images. Statuesque muteness and tranquillity are associated with the dictatorship to which the revolution is opposed, as the film returns to the gardens and juxtaposes them contrastingly with life beyond. The US embargo is said to have had a devastating effect on the country, which proved how much it depended on America for survival. An advertisement hoarding goes by on the side of a motor vehicle which says 'Cuba sí, Yankees no!', and which indicates increasing animosity, while also giving the film its title. Castro speaks about the future birth of a new political system in Cuba, which will be institutionalised eventually; at the moment, he notes the proximity to Athenian democracy, but without slavery. This recalls the earlier resemblance of his image to that on the Greek vase and suggests how *Cuba Si!* rewrites the relation between the present and history, as well as myth, in line with Castro's vision. And this connects with the life injected into the film through its music and celebrations amidst the bloodier aspects of the history of this time.

The commentary announces the spontaneous eruption of a Conga Brava in the streets of Havana in January 1961. Shots of men with guns give way to an aerial view of a band as music with a drum accompaniment suddenly speeds up. People look into the camera, wave, smile, and everyone starts to dance. In a wholly negative commentary on the film, reviewer Michel Mardore is particularly critical of the fact that this is presented as a chance event, since Marker had pre-arranged it with the best conga player in Havana (Mardore 1964: 72–73). Yet even the staged conga is an authentic rhythmic incarnation of the spirit of the revolution. From this vantage point, the commentary questions what is going on in the rest of the world at this particular historical moment, and ranges through Algeria, France, the US, Congo and Laos. An apocalyptic climate is established in the build-up to the end of the film, which comprises footage sent to Marker from Cuba after he had left, relating to the Bay of Pigs invasion. Between radio broadcasts and newspaper reports, we see images from a moving vehicle as it travels through the streets, a pay toll and a long tunnel. The film cuts between this journey and crocodiles lying still in water and on land. The commentary declares that the attack failed on 20 April 1961 and that it would like to be able to announce this to the world. But it reports that the world prefers to believe only the dead witness and is prepared to slit the throat of the live witness, if need be, in order to trust their testimony. The final image of *Cuba Si!* is that of a man lying dead with his arm outstretched as we focus finally on his hand. This immobilised hand will be set in motion again in subsequent films, since, in its living form, it will become associated with a more defiant revolutionary gesture.

Through its quirky combination of stillness and animation, *Cuba Si!* joins with Castro to embody resistance and revolution as it rewrites a relation to past models and myths. The fascination for revolutionary politics, collective solidarity and a belief in the need to invent the future carry through to Marker's most recent film work to date. More immediately, however, the split between the filming of still images and direct interview footage will characterise two signal films of 1962, which for Marker represent a second start to his career and the possibility of a new beginning.

References

Alter, Nora M. (2006), *Chris Marker*, Urbana and Chicago, University of Illinois Press.

Bazin, André (1998), 'Chris Marker: Lettre de Sibérie', in *Le Cinéma français de la Libération à la Nouvelle Vague (1945–1958)*, Paris, Cahiers du cinéma, pp. 257–60; article orig. publ. in *France-Observateur* (1958), 30 October.

Cacérès, Bénigno (1982), *Les Deux Rivages: itinéraire d'un animateur d'éducation populaire*, Paris, Actes et mémoires du peuple/François Maspero.

Darke, Chris (2003), 'Eyesight', in *Film Comment* (May–June), pp. 48–50.

Dauman, Anatole (1989), *Argos Films: Souvenir Écran*, Paris, Éditions du Centre Pompidou.

Dubois, Philippe (2002), *Théorème 6: recherches sur Chris Marker*, Paris, Presses Sorbonne Nouvelle.

Gauthier, Guy (1963), 'Description d'un combat', in *Image et son*, 161–62 (April–May), pp. 38–41.

Giraudoux, Jean (1929), *Amphitryon 38*, Paris, Éditions Bernard Grasset.

Grimault, Paul and William Guéry (1963), '*Cuba Si*', in *Image et son*, 161–62 (April–May), p. 57.

Kämper, Birgit and Thomas Tode (eds) (1997), *Chris Marker: Filmessayist*, Munich, Institut Français de Munich.

Levinas, Emmanuel (1998), 'Reality and its Shadow', in Seán Hand (ed.), *The Levinas Reader*, Oxford, Blackwell; orig. publ. 1989, pp. 129–43; article orig. publ. in *Les Temps Modernes* (1948), 38, pp. 771–89.

Lupton, Catherine (2005), *Chris Marker: Memories of the Future*, London, Reaktion.

Mardore, Michel (1964), 'Conga no', in *Cahiers du cinéma*, 152 (February), pp. 72–73.

Marker, Chris (1952), *Giraudoux par lui-même*, Paris, Seuil.

Marker, Chris (1961), *Commentaires*, Paris, Seuil.

Naficy, Hamid (2001), *An Accented Cinema: Exilic and Diasporic Filmmaking*, Princeton, Princeton University Press.

Pays, Jean-Louis (1962), 'Des humanistes agissants', in *Miroir du Cinéma*, 2 (May), pp. 2–7.

Varda, Agnès and Jacques Demy (1962), 'La Photo du mois (en forme de vœux tardifs)', in *Cahiers du cinéma*, 128 (February), p. 39.

Varda, Agnès (1994), *Varda par Agnès*, Paris, Cahiers du cinéma.

2

A second beginning: 1962–1966

At the retrospective of his films held at the Cinémathèque Française in Paris in 1998, Marker was not prepared to show any work prior to 1962. The films of the previous chapter thereby enter a shadow zone of self-censorship created by their maker who considered them, in retrospect, to be stages in an apprenticeship not to be screened publicly (Marker 1998: 78). The decade of the 1960s, with the inaugural date of 1962, thus becomes his preferred starting point for his filmmaking career. Correspondingly, his critical book on Giraudoux was re-edited and the second edition places the text firmly in 1962 rather than 1952. The introduction is titled 'Giraudoux 62', the chronology at the back of the text runs through to 1962 and among the many illustrations there features a photograph from *La Jetée*, also of this year. In addition to his continuing collaborative work, he directed four films during this period, which will be the subject of this chapter: *Le Joli Mai* (1962), *La Jetée* (1962), *Le Mystère Koumiko* (1965), and *Si j'avais quatre dromadaires* (1966). The commentaries of the latter two works appear in the second volume of the Seuil publication, *Commentaires 2*, which also contains the script of the unmade film, *Soy Mexico* (1965), on the search for Mexican identity. The making of the first two films in 1962 is interwoven, but it is *Le Joli Mai* that builds most directly on a new technique already glimpsed in *Cuba Si!*.

Le Joli Mai

Le Joli Mai (1962) was released in France in May 1963, one year after the merry month of its title and the first springtime of peace that forms its subject. The allusion to peacetime at the start of the film corresponds with the end of the Algerian War through the signing of the Évian accords in March 1962. But the referendum for independence had yet to be held, and murderous acts were still perpetrated against Algerian citizens on a daily basis (see DiIorio 2003: 47). The memory of the war haunts the present time of filming, and will emerge in the film as part of the unconscious of everyday life that its probing style seeks to bring out. Based principally on interviews with a cross-section of the Parisian population, *Le Joli Mai* sets out to listen, first and foremost, to those it encounters, and to give them a voice. In this respect, it pre-empts Marker's links to the Medvedkin groups of the late 1960s and 1970s, which introduced film production to strata of society who were usually spoken for, and enabled them to have their own say. In keeping with sociological enquiries of the period, *Le Joli Mai* begins by exploring the extent to which those it interviews are happy. It also asks about their individual hopes and dreams, their awareness of socio-political events, along with their relations to other people. In this way, and in addition to listening, the film engages in a permanent questioning of its subjects, especially when individual happiness appears to be a wholly self-centred pursuit. Indeed, with only a few exceptions, *Le Joli Mai* shows how oblivious these individuals are to what lies beyond their own immediate concerns, and how easily they position themselves as the point of origin for the unravelling of time, memory and history without thinking of others. Occasionally, though, altruism also emerges as a potential problem when it leads to self-effacement. Consequently, the most unsettling aspect of this film – as well as being its strength, in so far as it avoids moralising – is that it does not present a clear stance on how people should be or behave: it just enters into a permanently interrogative relation to their lives. Dedicated to 'The Happy Many', *Le Joli Mai* looks for a happy medium between thinking too much about others and not enough.

This film benefited from technological developments in the 1950s and 1960s that made a new kind of filming possible. Lightweight 16mm cameras and other equipment permitted greater mobility and allowed the camera operator to get closer to his or her subjects than ever before. Synchronised sound accompanied these lighter cameras, the two being linked at first by a cord, but soon becoming cordless. In interview, Pierre Lhomme – chief camera operator for *Le Joli Mai* and credited as the film's co-director by Marker – speaks in detail about the shift from 35mm to 16mm film, and the more liberated techniques that the latter permitted. He discusses the state of 35mm stock at the time, which placed a barrier between camera operator and filmed subject because the operator was not able to pick up sound. In contrast, he explains that he was able to film *Le Joli Mai* wearing headphones (with sound engineer Antoine Bonfanti's assistance) and suggests that he partly forgot about the image and became very sensitive to what he heard (Lhomme 1964: 38–43). He terms *Le Joli Mai* a 'document sonore' (sound document) (*ibid.*: 40). Upon its release, initial reviews were generally positive, although some felt strongly and indignantly that it did not always listen with an empathetic ear. While for Guy Gauthier this film was without doubt the best document on France at that time (Gauthier 1963: 63), other critics had a less rosy vision. Louis Marcorelles notes that, through all of the individuals that we encounter, we get a strange picture of French life, selfishly closed in on itself and lacking in fraternal sentiment (Marcorelles 1963: 34). More critically, Michel Delahaye says that the people to whom we are introduced are all awful, but that this is because Marker's superior attitude portrays them so that we can only judge them thus (Delahaye 1963: 5). In the latter two critiques, a split emerges between seeing the people in negative terms because this is what they are actually like – troubling though this may be – and thinking that they are in fact different from the way that they are presented. Trust or doubt in the images we see and the filmmaker and camera operator who fashion them are what is at stake here, and these issues relate to the new style of filmmaking that the technological developments of the time facilitated.

Two styles came to the fore within this period: *cinéma vérité* and direct cinema. Marker favours the latter label for this film (Marker 2003a: 40), yet *Le Joli Mai*, as Geneviève van Cauwenberge points out, does not fall squarely into either category (van Cauwenberge 2002: 83–99). Although sometimes used interchangeably, the terms direct cinema and *cinéma vérité* are quite distinct. Direct cinema is a form of filming, mainly associated with productions in the United States, that attempts as far as possible to make the camera unnoticeable. This observational mode of documentary is different from the reflexive style of *cinéma vérité* that registers the presence of the camera, its operator and sometimes a crew. The key initial example of the latter is Jean Rouch and Edgar Morin's *Chronique d'un été* of 1960. In *Le Joli*

Mai Marker is audible at times, but he and Lhomme do not feature integrally within the images as Rouch and Morin do in *Chronique*. (Rouch and Morin appear fleetingly in Marker and Lhomme's film, as do Alain Resnais, Jean-Luc Godard and Jacques Rivette.) Correspondingly, some of the film's subjects talk or look directly into the camera: they thereby acknowledge rather than ignore its presence, as well as tacitly question the relation to direct cinema.

Le Joli Mai emerged in its original length of 165 minutes from fifty-five hours of rushes. Marker later shortened it to approximately 120 minutes and removed some of the Algerian material from the second half (DiIorio 2003 provides a useful discussion of this). The shortened version is the one to which this reading refers. The film divides into two parts: 'Prière sur la Tour Eiffel' (Prayer on the Eiffel Tower) and 'Le Retour de Fantômas' (The Return of Fantomas). Pride of place is given to the interviews with the people of Paris, yet an intermittent voice-over, provided by Yves Montand, is also present from the outset. Prior to the credits, and over images of the Paris skyline, a lyrical passage asks whether this is the most beautiful city in the world. The voice-over registers the desire to discover the city afresh: it describes how one would like to approach it without memory and try keys in locks to see whether they still fit. The subsequent mention of an owl and cat at this point is picked up again through images later in the film, and is one of several ways in which Marker's signatory presence is felt. After the credits, the first section begins with a Giraudoux passage, written on 1 May 1923, as we, like him forty years earlier, view Paris from the Eiffel Tower. The citation establishes a link between this area of the world and its past, through Descartes, Pascal, Corneille, Racine, Danton, Voltaire and Molière, among others. The move from discovering Paris, as if for the first time, to being immersed in one facet of its history is one that *Le Joli Mai* will retrace through the people it meets.

An early example of the style of questioning in which the film engages occurs outside the stock exchange. Two young men speak of their ambition and what money means to them – principally a means of procuring food, pleasure and entertainment. When pressed as to whether anything else in the world interests them beyond their careers, one of them says important events and one mentions Algeria. The persistence of the interviewer does not go entirely unchallenged: an older man objects to their being questioned in this way.

He intervenes on their behalf and then gets the chance to speak for himself, but only does so briefly. As another group of stock exchange workers discuss the situation in Algeria, their interest in the events is principally with a view to thinking about the impact on the French economy or questions of national sentiment, rather than on humanitarian grounds. Without passing explicit judgement, this scene is one of many in which the interviewed subjects are encouraged to think beyond themselves.

In addition to questions that challenge, the cinematography and montage serve a similar purpose and work to undercut what people say. When an inventor is interviewed he explains how he wants his name to be remembered by future generations. The camera focuses on a large spider, which crawls down his shirt, along the length of his tie and down his jacket. The interviewer picks up on the fact that the inventor says 'nous' (we/us), and asks whether he just thinks of himself or about others as well. He replies that he does think about others, but the response is not in an altruistic sense: he says that solitary inventors struggle more than those who are married, so it is better to have a wife. The need for others manifests itself here in a self-centred manner. In the final interview of the first part of the film, we are introduced to a young couple, a soldier and his girlfriend, who are twenty-one years old. They confirm that they have no other concerns than their personal happiness and, when asked whether they feel solidarity with others who perhaps are less contented, the woman says no. Intercut with their discussion of love and marriage are images of a riotous wedding party in which the bride does not look entirely happy. This undermines the final saying to which both Marker and the soldier allude: that after several years of marriage one is set for eternal happiness.

The second half of the film begins among the tombs of the Montmartre cemetery, which stretch under the rue Caulaincourt. The shadow of the Eiffel Tower in the first half is replaced by the invisible one of Fantômas, that elusive member of the underworld – a kind of human equivalent of T. S. Eliot's mystery cat Macavity – who served as inspiration for several of Louis Feuillade's films in the early twentieth century. In May 1962, Fantômas is said to move from his lair among the graves and to cast his immense shadow over Paris. The signs of this are equated with a bleak vision of a Paris seemingly on the brink of civil war. Over a succession of photographic images (which include that of a man by a burnt-out car, a building with smashed windows and tanks lined up in the streets), we are told in voice-over that during the past year, the French language had enriched itself with several words – 'putsch' is one of them – which were now common currency in May 1962. This term alludes to General Salan's attempt to overthrow the De Gaulle government in 1961. Other terms are said to be visible on the walls of the city, as we see a series of fixed frame film images, among which 'OAS=SS' appears under a prohibition to stick anything on the walls (the OAS was the right-wing terrorist group to which Salan belonged). We hear of the violent clashes between the forces of law and order with protesters, and the death of eight people in the Charonne metro station, crushed as they sought to take refuge there. The film features footage from the funeral on 13 February for which half a million people turned out to pay their respects.

The rest of the second half is focused more explicitly on political events, but a similar refrain recurs with regard to self–other relations. A man interviewed in an office condemns the use of torture by the French in the Algerian War. A group of women are asked about the trial of General Salan and whether they felt personally concerned by this, to which, in accordance with many other responses in the film, they respond negatively. An eccentric reclusive woman who lives alone with her cat (whom she dresses up and we see pictured in one of the homemade outfits) recounts how she is scared of people and confesses to her fears of being hurt. We also hear from a number of people whom the film takes very seriously: a priest who converted to communism, and others who have been victims of prejudice and colonial oppression, notably a black African student and a young Algerian man. It is the latter that serves to introduce a different form of questioning from that of so many of the other interviewees.

He speaks of the racial discrimination that he has faced in France. During this interview, the film cuts to images of men drilling in a street and the voice-over relates that Algerians frequently have the unhealthiest and lowest paid jobs. In 1962, in the euphoria of the Évian agreement, the commentary says that the last member of the proletariat of a colonising country always has someone lower than him in the proletariat of the colonised country and that this reality survives colonisation. The Algerian man explains that the future for him is in relation to Algeria: he hopes for a free Algeria that will be created through cooperation with France. He wants to bring up his family (he has six sisters, his father is old, and he is the only one who works) and is interested in teaching. When asked about his personal desires and what he wants for himself, he says that he has no time for love, is not thinking of marrying and has no plans. Here, in contrast to so many of these filmic encounters, the interviewer presses him in the opposite direction to think more about his own sense of happiness, rather than put himself solely in the service of others.

Towards the end of the film, time-lapse footage of vehicles around the Arc de Triomphe is accompanied by statistics relating to Paris in the month of May 1962, which range from the average temperature, through the amount of food, wine and milk consumed, to the main causes of death. Over an image of the Petite Roquette women's prison, we hear about the monotony of life there from one of the inmates. The relations between the prisoners replicate a more extreme sentiment that underlies the lack of human bonding within the film as a whole: an inmate says that it is the other women who make existence there unbearable. As the film draws to a close, the voice-over declares that they have discovered some people on their journey through Paris on whom the prisoner's gaze would remain incredulous, because they carry a prison around inside themselves. A succession of shots of peoples' faces appears at this point. Each looks preoccupied, as if they are seeing something that for us is invisible. The commentary questions what is wrong with each of them and, in conclusion, offers a tentative response:

> Est-ce, comme on le dit beaucoup, que vous pensez trop à vous? Ou n'est-ce pas plutôt qu'à votre insu vous pensez trop aux autres? Peut-être sentez-vous confusément que votre sort est lié à celui des autres, que le malheur et le bonheur sont deux sociétés secrètes, si secrètes que vous y êtes affiliés sans le savoir et que, sans l'entendre, vous abritez quelque part cette voix qui dit: tant que la misère existe, vous n'êtes pas riches, tant que la détresse existe, vous n'êtes pas heureux, tant que les prisons existent, vous n'êtes pas libres.[1]

---

[1] 'Do you, as is said frequently, think too much about yourself? Or is it rather that unwittingly you think too much about others? Perhaps you feel confusedly that your fate is linked to that of others, that unhappiness and happiness are two secret societies, so secret that you have affiliated yourself to them without knowing it and that, without hearing it, you are harbouring somewhere that voice which says: as long as misery exists, you are not rich, as long as distress exists, you are not happy, as long as prisons exist, you are not free.'

This unconscious connection to the time of others, which is felt distantly and hazily, is precisely what the interrogative style of the film aims to approach through those it encounters. It attempts to broaden out the perspective of each individual to events and to people beyond themselves, and it also registers the need to preserve a sense of self in the process. *Le Joli Mai* positions itself thus within a temporal progression that is mindful of the past and future, as well as being focused on the month of May 1962.

Marker says in interview that, while filming *Le Joli Mai* and on the crew's day off, he 'photographed a story (he) didn't completely understand' (Marker 2003a: 40). These photographs form the basis of *La Jetée*, in which an individual's relation to time undergoes a very different kind of expansion from that of *Le Joli Mai*.

La Jetée

The exploration of the relationship between time and the photographic image in Marker's filmic oeuvre finds an early and stunning apotheosis in *La Jetée* of 1962. This photo-roman, which lasts twenty-nine minutes and is comprised almost entirely of black and white still images, has assumed cult status and attracted an array of sophisticated and complex critical readings. It is Marker's best-known work and has inspired countless films, the most famous of which is arguably Terry Gilliam's remake *Twelve Monkeys* (1995). Marker himself will return to the concerns explored in *La Jetée* in *Sans Soleil* (1982), and *Level 5* (1996) has been read as his own remake of the early film (Francovich 1997: 36). These three works thereby constitute a loosely bound trilogy across the decades.

In the booklet accompanying the 2003 DVD release of *La Jetée* and *Sans Soleil*, Marker recounts how he made a film in his youth about his cat Riri using still images, which he screened to a school friend, Jonathan, who he thought would appreciate his work: 'Jonathan me ramena rapidement à la sobriété. "Mais idiot, le cinéma c'est des images qui bougent", dit-il. "On ne peut pas faire un film avec des images fixes." Trente ans passèrent. Puis je réalisai *La Jetée*'[2] (Marker

---

2 'Jonathan managed to get me sobered up. "Movies are supposed to move, stupid", he said. "Nobody can do a movie with still images." Thirty years passed. Then I made *La Jetée*' (Marker 2003b: n.p.).

2003b: n.p.). His friend Jonathan's reaction takes us back to the definition of film as a succession of images moving at the pace of twenty-four frames per second. In contrast, and as Peter Wollen suggests, the effect of *La Jetée*'s photographs is to show that 'movement is not a necessary feature of film' (Wollen 1989: n.p.). Marker does, however, introduce movement to the photographic image in other ways. Consequently, as we shall see, the photo-roman furnishes a distant echo of the introduction of mobility to stillness that has been evident in his earlier films, especially *Les Statues meurent aussi*. The connection between these two works in particular is cemented further by the fact that they also share the same narrator, Jean Négroni. The later work's images feature – and become equivalent to – statues that are to be brought back to life, to be reinserted into a different narrative, a different history. This (hi)story is that of cinema, as well as that of the man whose tale the photo-roman tells, but its crucial legacy is the photograph. The ontological connection between the photographic and the cinematic image, as discussed by Bazin, is implicated in Marker's manipulation of the static image, and is also reassessed. *La Jetée* takes us back in time to points of origin and departure – of cinema, of a man's life – that also turn out to be the locus of death. Yet time's arrow swerves into a loop in this photo-roman, as beginnings and endings collide to generate a hesitation between life and death. Haunted by death, and doubled by eternity, the male protagonist lives the temporal aspects of the photographic image as both boy and man. But *La Jetée* is concerned with the endurance of the photograph rather than its loss, in the shifts between youth, adulthood and the end of one human lifetime. Marker's delayed response to his childhood friend Jonathan's comments suggests the tenacious survival of a conviction relating photography to the 'movies'. As with *Dimanche à Pékin*, a thirty-year gap separates the youthful encounter with the still image from the adult filmmaker's return to it. Likewise, the Sunday that the earlier traveller spends in Peking is also the day on which we first meet our time traveller, as a young boy, in *La Jetée*.

The story begins on the pier at Orly airport, Paris, where parents used to take their children on a Sunday to watch the planes. The man who is to be the main protagonist in what follows is present here as a little boy, standing on some railings. The boy has a recollection of a woman's face and also of something else: we are told that it was only later on that he realised that he had seen a man die. Shortly after this,

World War Three breaks out. Paris, along with the rest of the world, is destroyed. The few survivors in Paris take refuge in the underground passages of Chaillot. They become prisoners who are subject to time travel experimentation by the camp guards, victors of the war. Since space has become uninhabitable, travel through time offers the only hope for the survival of the human race, and the guards attempt to send various people through loopholes in time, many of which trials end in madness or death, and all of which end in failure. Finally, they are drawn to the man whose story we have been following, whose capacity to recall a strong mental image from his past – of the woman at the end of the pier at Orly airport – suggests to them an ability to return there. After several attempts, he is able to make the desired return and also to find the woman of his mind's eye, located in the zone of uncertainty between memory, dream and fantasy. He is thrown back to her several times by the camp guards' experiments, and lives a fleeting, fragmented love affair, until the guards decide to stop sending him into the past and, instead, project him into the future. The men and women of the future, who greet him in a reconstructed Paris, give him what is necessary to set human industry in motion again before he returns to the camp. As he realises that the camp guards will not let him get out of there alive, he receives a visit from the people of the future who give him a route towards them. He requests, however, to go back to the past and to his childhood image of the woman at the end of the pier. He arrives there with the sense that the boy he once was will be there too; when he sees the woman, he also sees a camp guard who has followed him back from the future. The co-presence of these people from his past and future in the closing images is coupled with the realisation that he cannot escape time: the man's death that he saw as a boy turns out to be his own.

The voice-over narrative states that the man (played by Davos Hanich) is haunted by the memory of a fragment of time that has been lived twice. We may invert this, however, since what he 'lives' twice, in addition to the vision of the woman on the pier (played by Hélène Chatelain), is his own death. This coalescence of the living and the dead recurs in many different ways throughout and dovetails with what Emma Wilson speaks of as the hesitation between the two states in her striking reading of Alain Resnais's *L'Année dernière à Marienbad* (1961), one of the sources of inspiration for *La Jetée* (Wilson 2006: 81). The form of Marker's photo-roman is apparently perfectly matched with its subject matter. Raymond Bellour writes: 'If there are so many stilled images comprising an entire film, even a short one, it is because they all come together around a single image, the image of the main character's death' (Bellour 1990: 118). The still images and the story of *La Jetée* are indeed intimate with death, yet from the very outset there are stirrings of a different kind of intimacy through which the images are also linked inextricably to love and life.

The credit sequence begins with an aerial view of the pier at Orly, as we hear the roar of a plane's engine, before the choral music provided by the choir of the Russian Cathedral of Paris sets a poignant, minor key. The choir sings Kastalsky/Gontcharov's 'Tropaire en l'honneur de la Sainte Croix' – music that honours the Holy Cross – and thus introduces echoes of the crucifixion that will linger throughout, even as the soundtrack becomes lighter and more diverse. The static aerial view of the pier is set in motion through the mobility of the camera, which moves down its length before lingering on a view of the planes on either side as the credits succeed one another. This filming of the photographic image instates a dynamism that we have already encountered briefly in Marker's *Lettre de Sibérie* (1958) and that we will return to in his subsequent photo-films, *Si j'avais quatre dromadaires* (1966) and the co-directed *Le Souvenir d'un avenir* (2001). In *La Jetée* such motion appears through camera movements and through the transitions between images whose admittedly slow-paced editing is nonetheless akin to filmic form, with its equivalent straight cuts from one image to the next, its slow dissolves (which suggest gradual motion backwards and forwards in time, as well as dissolution), and fades to black. For Philippe Dubois, *La Jetée* is located between photography and cinema and he terms the units of this photo-roman 'cinématogrammes' (cinematogrammes) to register its hybrid form (Dubois 2002). The combination of mobility and immobility also suggests a bond between endings and beginnings, which is already implied in the temporal structure of the photo-roman, and which combines the life of the child and the death of the man in its opening and closing moments.

Just as the end of the narrative of this photo-roman is contained in the beginning, the static image, as well as being equated with the end of cinema, is also its point of origin, following Bazinian logic. This photo-roman tells a tale of origins on several different levels. Nestling among the almost exclusive succession of photographic images, is a moving filmic image, which emerges during one of the protagonist's return journeys to the past, significantly as he wonders whether he has invented the woman to whom he returns, or whether he is, in fact, dreaming. (Marker will revisit cinema as the site of dreams in *Sans Soleil*.) A succession of images of the woman in bed asleep increases gradually in pace, as the accompanying sound of birdsong gets louder, until it reaches its highest point and the woman opens her eyes. The speed of the montage catches up at this point with that of cinema, albeit momentarily. That this dawning moment is associated with a woman epitomises Marker's love of cinema, as he describes it in his CD-ROM *Immemory*: 'Pour cet enfant devenu grand, le cinéma et la femme sont restés deux notions absolument inséparables, et [...] un film sans femme lui est toujours aussi incompréhensible qu'un opéra sans musique.'[3] Through the protagonist's journey into an indistinct zone somewhere between his memories and his dreams, we encounter the opposite of stasis, and this photo-roman, as Daniel Frampton puts it, 'thoughtfully, finally, opens (our) eyes to what we forget we can experience everyday: movement' (Frampton 2006: 124). The protagonist's return to the past – which crystallises around the love of a woman and is accessed through the portal of her image – is a move that critics also link to an oedipal narrative, which connects the woman to the boy's mother (see Coates 1987 and Penley 1988). As we shift from the filmic back to the photographic image, our eyes are opened a second time to the fact that the previous awakening is the product of painful experimentation. The return to still images is made through a low-angle photograph of the head experimenter, who looks down on the protagonist and on us (he looks directly into the camera), as he removes the protagonist's padded eye covers. This reminds us that what we saw previously is a function of the experimentation that he has induced through the protagonist's attachment to a childhood image. It is significant that Jacques Ledoux plays the role of the head experimenter: as the then curator of the Belgian Cinémathèque he imbues the fiction with a connection to a broader temporal space, in terms of general and more specifically cinematic, history. The location of the experimenters' lair is important in both respects.

The victors' inhabitation of the underground passages and caves

[3] 'For this grown up child, the cinema and woman have remained two absolutely inseparable notions, and [...] a film without a woman is still just as incomprehensible to him as an opera without music.'

of Chaillot harks back to the Second World War. The passages were used by members of the French resistance, and, in keeping with the photo-roman's blending of opposites (movement–stasis, life–death), the space is inhabited here by torturers who whisper in German, thus pitting the resonance of resistance against the forces of occupation. At the start of the time travel experiments on the protagonist, we see his body writhe with pain from one image to the next, we hear a quickly pulsating heartbeat – that of Jean Ravel, the film's editor – which provides a fragile sign of life throughout these difficult sequences, but one that is nonetheless tense and fearful. As we are told earlier: 'Se réveiller dans un autre temps, c'était naître une seconde fois – adulte.'[4] The difficulty of being reborn as a man exchanges the miracle of religion for that of science: resurrection – that of Lazarus or Christ – is rewritten as re-birth through time travel. This thematic association with resurrection recalls remarks Barthes makes about the medium of photography in *La Chambre Claire* (Barthes 1980: 129). After successive shots of the protagonist biting on the strings of the hammock in which he lies, with his head thrown back in agony, we are told that memories begin to surge forth 'comme des aveux' (like confessions), forced out of him in spite of himself, as we see a succession of images of peacetime. There is a chilling recognition here of recent tortures in Algeria, which connects with *Le Joli Mai*'s preoccupations. Yet these tunnels and caves, these tortures past and present, are linked through the Palais de Chaillot (Trocadéro) to a different series of cultural memories. Constructed in 1937 for the World Exhibition – the last colonial exhibition in Paris (the French Empire being the second largest after Britain at that time) – the Palais now houses the Musée de la Marine, the Théâtre de Chaillot and the Musée de l'Homme, but was the location of the former Cinémathèque Française at the time that the photo-roman was made. Henri Langlois established the Cinémathèque Française in the 1930s. In the early 1960s, the Cinémathèque took up residence in the Palais de Chaillot, where it remained until 1997. The inaugural date of the early 1960s chimes, then, with the making and release of *La Jetée*. The fact that Chaillot is also the named setting for the experiments in time travel makes this a photo-roman about cinema as much as the history of its location.

The cinematic inter-texts of this photo-roman are numerous. The

4 'To wake up in another time meant to be born again – as an adult.' (All translations are taken from the English-language version.)

most obvious is Hitchcock's *Vertigo*, which is echoed in so many different ways, not least through the chignon of the woman's hair in some scenes, recalling that of Madeleine in the earlier film, and the sequoia cut that the lovers visit in Le Jardin des Plantes in Paris, which invokes that of Muir Woods in Hitchcock's film (the woman pronounces a foreign name that the man is said not to understand but that the commentary specifies as 'Hitchcock'). Bamchade Pourvali juxtaposes images from these two films, among others (from Eisenstein's *Battleship Potemkin* (1925) and Resnais's *Toute la mémoire du monde* (1956)), and shows the mise en scène of other films that the photo-roman is remembering, either unconsciously or consciously (Pourvali 2003: 21–29). Indeed, what the images themselves recall stretches out beyond cinema to broader historical realities. *La Jetée* was made at a time when the world was holding its breath with regard to the outcome of the Cuban missile crisis, with its threat of apocalyptic destruction. The scenario of a nuclear Third World War is born of such nightmares. For Réda Bensmaïa the dissolves of the photo-roman are the embodiment of conflicting drives towards fusion and destruction characteristic of an early stage of development in human subjectivity, and express the disintegration of the subject along with the horror of nuclear war (Bensmaïa 1988). As through the implicit reference to Algeria, the images and the form of their juxtaposition here recall traumatic historical moments, and the fact that this is all registered through the story of one man is significant. The experience of seeing a man die that registers unconsciously like a scar on the protagonist's memory at the start of the photo-roman, connects here with the political unconscious of *La Jetée*'s photographic images. A ghost-like, tacit but ever-present reminder of broader, less immediately personal, world-shaking events, haunts them throughout. In some respects, as Patrick ffrench suggests, the images register an affinity with documentary, rather than fiction (ffrench 2005); the final image of the man dying, for example, famously echoes the Robert Capa photograph of the Spanish Civil War Soldier falling to his death. The historical memories of the images of this photo-roman connect it to the history of cinema and the real, and it is precisely the relationship between cinema and reality that *La Jetée* also questions in philosophical and theoretical terms.

Like the ethical and political questioning of the status of the (African) artwork in *Les Statues meurent aussi*, wrested from the shadows of the museum case and set back into history, motion and life, *La Jetée* also situates the artwork on the side of reality and temporality rather than in the realm of the shadows of eternal stasis. In so doing, it turns one particular theoretical metaphor for cinema inside out. Sander Lee likens the cavernous space of the experimentation chamber to that of Plato's cave (Lee 2000). The myth of Plato's cave tells of chained-up prisoners who mistake shadows on the wall of the cave for the real; it takes one of them to be dragged outside to realise the distinction between representation and reality. When *La Jetée*'s protagonist is reborn in another time but as an adult, on the first journey that he makes back to his past, this suggests conformity with Luce Irigaray's reading of Plato's cave. She says that the male philosopher presents the cave as if it were a womb, and in order to access the light, world and knowledge, the prisoner must pass through a small passage and leave the mother's body behind (Irigaray 1985: 278–83). Yet the scrambled chronology and the oedipal bond of *La Jetée*, suggest that the mother is the permanent travelling companion of our protagonist, rather than being disregarded. The suggestive connection to the Platonic cave also harks back to one of the ways in which psychoanalytic film theory has conceptualised the space of cinema and the experience of spectatorship. In the work of Jean-Louis Baudry in particular, the cinema is likened to the space of the cave in which we see representations projected onto a wall (a screen), as in a dream. Marker's film, however, challenges the application of this Platonic theory to cinema. We will see how he engages with Plato's myth directly in his later work, *L'Héritage de la chouette* (1989). In *La Jetée*, the shadow realm of images stretches beyond mere escapism from a tortured present to provide access to something that is real. The first time that the protagonist successfully leaves the present of the camp, we see the images that are said to surge forth from him like confessions: a bedroom, a child, a flock of pigeons and tombs appear briefly and separately, each successively fading to black, but each described as real. The world of images becomes the protagonist's reality. Although he is said on several occasions to be uncertain whether what he sees is remembered, created or dreamt, all of these possibilities exist through the images that he sees and experiences as more than shadows on a wall.

The 'real' images that we are shown when the protagonist first returns to the past generate other images, which appear from a space said to be that of the museum of his memory. Statues, headless torsos and a crumbling face appear. Each image dissolves into the next, until the final image of a chipped stone head is replaced by the face of the protagonist wearing the white padded eye mask. This recalls an earlier moment in the photo-roman when we hear about the failures of the first experiments on other men: it cuts between images of statues, the experimenters' goggled faces and a man whose face is petrified. Bodies appear rigid with statuesque immobility, but material substance is disintegrating in keeping with the earlier series of dissolves, which portray Paris's material destruction above ground. The parity between stone and flesh recalls the bond established between the two in *Les Statues meurent aussi*. As in the earlier film, statuary and the material relic are subject to decimation here too: the juxtapositions suggest equity in their demise. If statues can die, then so can images but, as with the earlier film, entry into a museum (of the mind, or of memory in the case of *La Jetée*) is revivifying in the hands of Marker (and Resnais), and locates the statue on the side of life and the real – another example of the 'vrai' that sits among the protagonist's first peacetime images of birds, countryside and women. The statue re-enters time, alongside living beings, and an indistinguishable relation between the two materialises in the image, which does not deny the difference between life and death but which challenges our ability to distinguish between them in terms of either movement or stasis. We know full well that there is a difference between the two, that the men – victors and vanquished – are living and the statues are inert matter, yet both are equally immobile, shot in the same way and juxtaposed as clean-cut photographs, or separated only by the permeability of the haunting dissolves. This levelling gesture of the photograph might be read to render both equally dead through their stasis; similarly, however, one might read their parallel status in terms of a shared life. This is nowhere more possible than in the sequence of photographs taken in the Natural History Museum. To follow the theoretical association between death and the photograph is thus only part of the story that *La Jetée* tells. Rather than associate movement with cinema and life, it is photography that is rendered animate here – not through the mobility of the camera whose activity we registered earlier on, but through the porous membrane that the contents of individual images establish between the living and the dead.

The first time that the protagonist encounters the woman of his past, the fabric of the world overwhelms him. We see him fascinated by the materials around him, even though we do not see what he sees: glass, plastic and sponge-cloth are said to hold his attention to such an extent that, when he looks up again, the woman has gone. The experimenters send him back to the same point, and this time he is more focused and the two of them are able to speak. With no memories or plans they encounter one another in disparate places and times, he her ghost whose comings and goings she gradually accepts as natural. Towards the fiftieth day, they meet in a museum 'plein de bêtes éternelles' (full of ageless animals). The difference between the Natural History Museum and the contents (mainly stone statues) of the earlier museum of his memory is that the ageless animals were once living beings. The narrative description casts them as eternal, thus eliciting the other facet of the photographic image to which Bazin, in particular, is drawn, as this medium is deemed to embalm a moment forever. However, the explicitly eternal elements within the fiction of the images – the animals – are not so readily cut off from the progression of time, reality and life, and this reflects back on conceptions of time in relation to the photographic medium itself. The museum is the space of the lovers' longest encounter and the place in which the male protagonist is able to move around most freely, since the experimenters have their ultimate success at this point in projecting him perfectly into this series of moments. Giraffes, hippopotamuses, zebras, the bones of dinosaurs, various birds and wild cats, among other beasts, appear both in the open space of the museum floor and behind glass. What Bruce Kawin terms 'the overwhelming imagery of stasis' (Kawin 1982: 17) is lent a different kind of texture here from that of the humans or the statuary that has hitherto constituted the photo-roman's predominant focus. The man and woman are pictured looking at these ageless animals in rapt fascination, scrutiny, and occasionally laughing, visibly happy in this space together with the stuffed beasts that surround them. As if by association, through their proximity to the beasts within the images, the couple become part of this eternal space for the length of their visit, but the visual image serves to take us beyond the dual suspensions of both death and eternity.

The still museum images reproduce the frozen state of the animals, whereas they freeze the humans in their actions and poses. The visual appearance of both shows the difference between life and death, at times, to be invisible. Unblinking cats' eyes stare back at the couple; we view them from the perspective of the animals inside the glass cases, and, after one such point of view of the two lovers from the other side of the glass, we are told that the woman also seemed tamed ('apprivoisée'). She is positioned on the edge of a reflective glass case, which shows her and her image at this point, and suggests not only that she is both inside and outside the museum casing but that the transparent glass can also serve as a mirror. Her smiling face in a subsequent photograph is succeeded by that of a bird, the curl of its beak furnishing a visual imitation of the curve of her smile. Two such birds follow a photograph of the couple at an earlier moment, as these oscillations between the humans and the wildlife construct an uncanny hall of mirrors. The photograph stills life, yet here the camera's gaze is to work in reverse and to allow the beasts to materialise on a level with the humans who look at them, without recourse to the moving image, or even a mobile camera at this stage. Lifeless, and also apparently deathless in these photographic images, we see the humans no differently from the animals and birds, captured in their poses or stopped in their tracks, reinstated into the temporality of the lovers' encounter. As this sequence draws to a close, the woman points to something within a glass case on the wall, and all we see is her finger against the glass. In a subsequent image, her finger is photographed from a different angle, and this time it seems to be pointing out of a window, which is reflected in the glass from the opposite side of the museum hall. This gesticulation recalls the fingers of the man and woman in the image of the sequoia cut earlier in the film, when he uses the tree rings to designate that he is from a point outside of time. The exit from this museum space is through the woman's gesture. She points towards an elsewhere to which her male lover will return, his temporal position always differentiated from hers, even though the museum brought them both together through a common relation to the stuffed beasts, both inside and outside of time. Rather than stem the flow of life, the stillness within the images of the Natural History Museum reinvests the photograph with time and renders the borderline between the animate and the inanimate indistinct.

Both the man and the woman have brushed with death and eternity through this final sequence of the protagonist's time travel to the past. After his first visit and subsequent refusal to return to the people of the future, he chooses to go back to his childhood image.

As Orpheus looks back at Eurydice, the protagonist of *La Jetée* returns to the woman of his memory or dreams, yet it is he who pays for his final glance at her cherished image with his life. *La Jetée* is neither life nor death twenty-four frames per second. Nor is it simply the temporal stasis by which photography is often defined. This photo-roman projects photographs into the space of cinema, showing how 'movies' can be made from them but also how their stillness is never entirely static or lifeless, in spite of their difference from the filmic image. The photograph endures here beyond its status as the beginning and end of cinema, as the still image engenders time enough to live and love again.

Le Mystère Koumiko

In contrast to the Parisian-based focus of the two previous works, *Le Mystère Koumiko* (1965) takes Marker to Tokyo. This is the first of his films to be shot in Japan, and it is as concerned with the city of Tokyo as it is with the female subject of its title, Koumiko Muraoka. Marker explains in voice-over at the outset that he met her by chance at the Tokyo Olympics of 1964. After a first encounter in this context, much of the film is devoted to following her around the city and to exploring her thoughts in response to his questions. She is visible in the images, he invisible, while both are audible, among other voices, on the soundtrack. His relation to Koumiko is one of fascination and of incomprehension, both of which the film records in aural and visual terms as it gazes upon her attractions and mysteries. Writing of Koumiko's place in this film, Olaf Möller states that 'Japan is a woman (in mythological terms the Japanese might agree) with whom Marker falls in love' (Möller 2003: 36). This love affair is light and flirtatious but is also tinged with melancholia throughout, as Koumiko, along with the city through which she moves, drifts away from the filmmaker like so many fantasies and dreams. Melancholic for what it will never fully know, rather than what it has lost, this film recognises a love that leaves otherness intact within the asymmetries of desire.

The camera is first drawn magnetically to Koumiko, among thousands of other faces, in the Olympic stadium in Tokyo. She is introduced subsequently as a secretary who is over twenty and under thirty, born in Manchuria, and among her many likes and dislikes that Marker lists in voice-over, she is said to like Giraudoux (and later on, we hear, cats). This suggests a likeness between Marker and Koumiko at first, and such proximity carries over to the formal properties of the images themselves. Towards the start, Koumiko is filmed walking down the street in a black and white flecked fabric dress. We then view her standing still: she now wears neat black court shoes with a decorative strap and a smart bright green fitted woollen coat. These two colour schemes constitute the tones of her wardrobe for the majority of the film. The oscillation between the monochrome and more vibrant colours is worked through her clothing and into the film images in this early sequence and elsewhere, as colour and black and white footage are juxtaposed. Yet the film will also instate a more critical distance in recognising Marker's likes in Koumiko, or Koumiko in the form of the film. This distance is set out through a particular relation to French cinema.

In between filming, Marker explains in voice-over, Koumiko and he were able to talk. When he asks her about the difference between life in Japan as opposed to France or America, she replies that the air is damp in Japan. She walks past advertising hoardings and turns to look at one poster in particular, that of Jacques Demy's *Les Parapluies de Cherbourg* (1964). This introduces a prolonged lyrical sequence of people carrying umbrellas of all colours in the rain, accompanied by the theme tune, and key melody, of Demy's film. The published commentary labels this *Les Parapluies de Tokyo*. Michel Legrand originally composed the plaintive song that accompanies the images of Marker's brief tribute, but it is the well-known Japanese composer Toru Takemitsu who is responsible for the music in Marker's film (he and his work will also feature in Marker's *AK* (1985)). The presence of the melody links Marker's relation with Tokyo and Koumiko to the sad beauty of the French film in which two young lovers are separated by circumstances beyond their control and have to accept compromise by each marrying someone else. In spite of interweaving France and Japan here through this sequence, separation is implied through association with the earlier film. Koumiko's response (concerning the dampness of the Japanese air) that instigates this sequence is at first difficult for Marker to understand. This relates more broadly to her idiosyncratic use of the French language, which Marker speaks about at the outset, as he makes an indirect connection to another French film of the 1960s.

He remarks that conversation with Koumiko was challenging at times because of 'la façon charmante, mais un peu personnelle avec laquelle Koumiko manie la langue de Robbe-Grillet' (the charming but rather personal way in which Koumiko handles the language of Robbe-Grillet). By introducing her spoken French as being in the style of the twentieth-century writer Alain Robbe-Grillet, Marker links her to the cultural moment in which the *nouveau roman* was the literary talking point in France because of its formalist innovations. The new novel was the equivalent literary phenomenon to the innovations of the new wave in cinema. Lupton reads this film indeed as Marker's tribute to the Nouvelle Vague (Lupton 2005: 100). The reference to Robbe-Grillet has a direct cinematic corollary that is made explicit in a later sequence. In a questionnaire sent to Koumiko after he returned to Paris, Marker asks what men mean to her. She explains, in her tape-recorded responses, that men have been the mirrors in which she has seen her face and that she has lived in their eyes. As she continues to talk, the film cuts to a black and white still from Alain Resnais's *L'Année dernière à Marienbad* reproduced on a poster. The camera moves back slowly to show Koumiko who stands alongside the poster image. By referring earlier to the way in which she handles Robbe-Grillet's language, it is as if she has entered a fiction through Marker's film, scripted by the new novelist but manipulating his words in her unique way. Additionally, the love relation between a man and a woman in *Marienbad*, in which each lover escapes the other's possession, resonates throughout Marker's film.

Le Mystère Koumiko is concerned in different ways with how the West is fascinated by, and seeks to know, Japan. It is also aware of how Japan eludes its grasp without being constituted as unknowable per se: it is just that western epistemological frameworks are inadequate to the task. A female voice-over towards the start of the film says that a Harvard student, Peter Kassovitz, is undertaking a sociological study of the phenomenon of the telephone in Tokyo, and we hear numerous statistics that relate to surveys on quality of life and on religion over related images. Similar to these numbers that aim to pinpoint their subject, photographic images of Koumiko abound throughout the film and reveal a particular obsession with her face. Such a turn to stillness within the images occurs in an attempt to understand both muse and city.

At a late point in the film, footage of the streets of Tokyo is interspersed with black and white photographs, which show increasingly more violent scenes, somewhere between sadomasochism and torture. The still images flash up to the rhythm of a steady beat to be replaced by the everyday colour motion images, suggesting that they are the unconscious of daily life. Their pace is too quick to bear further contemplation, however. Koumiko talks briefly about violence; then a little later, in a different sequence, she speaks of tenderness. This initiates a succession of photographic images of her, which the camera peruses. Over the photographs, she states, in broken French: 'La tendresse, c'est l'intellect, la compréhension, quelque chose infini, sévère et délicat comme la sensation de la main qui découvre les cellules nerveuses. C'est une chose de plus beau, de plus profonde. C'est la seule raison de ma vie, espoir de ma vie, et on pourrait mourir pour cela.'[5] While she says this, the camera zooms in on her face in two separate photographic images, then down to her hand, while blurring her face, as she mentions tactile sensation. The film cuts to a photograph of her holding a white dog, and the camera moves up its body to show its nose on her face. What Koumiko says she could die for is brought out through the filming of photographs here. The tender treatment of her frozen images respects their subject, as the static image, like its filmic counterpart, and her dialogue, preserve, rather than reveal, the mysteries of their muse. The attempt to freeze time and then scrutinise the surface of images, in order to know her at a different pace of temporal progression, fails to pin her down.

The closing sequence of the film is lengthy and suggestive of endless journeying. We see through the windscreen of a car as it drives along motorways in the rain, and then through the windows of a monorail train as it proceeds along its tracks. Marker explains that he had one final question to ask Koumiko. There is a quick montage of television footage from Vietnam, as he asks her what she thinks about what was happening there and whether it could have an effect on her. Her extended sphinx-like response, which is accompanied by orchestral music, suggests that everything reaches her at some point. Marker reiterates her last words, 'jusqu'à moi' (to me), over a colour close-up shot of her face. He then reports blandly, in conclusion, that

5 'Tenderness is intellect, understanding, something infinite, severe, delicate, like the sensation in the hand, which discovers its nerves. It is something more beautiful and profound. It is my only reason for living, my life's hope, and one could die for it.'

there are fifty million women in Japan, and one and a half billion on earth. Like the western researchers earlier, he too resorts finally to statistics, which slide off their subject rather than holding on to her. And like an early Robbe-Grillet novel, or the gardens of *L'Année dernière à Marienbad*, in which ordered geometrical precision prevails but which are riddled with labyrinthine complexity and uncertainty, Koumiko escapes capture through the filmmaker's structures or apparatus, leaving her enigmatic grace intact.

Si j'avais quatre dromadaires

The succession of photographic images that accompanied Koumiko's reflection on tenderness heralds the form and utopian drive of Marker's subsequent black and white photo-film, *Si j'avais quatre dromadaires* (1966). Marker notes that the photographs were taken in twenty-six countries between 1955 and 1965, and that the 'film' was composed entirely on a banc-titre (Marker 1967: 86). The 49-minute work does not entirely correspond to the script published in *Commentaires 2*, which is longer overall with additional photographs, and suggests the existence of more material than we see in the photo-film. It takes stock of the vast array of photographs Marker has in his possession. Yet *Dromadaires* is far more than the mere presentation of this personal archive. The title comes from the final line of a poem by Guillaume Apollinaire, 'Le Dromadaire', which features in his poetic book of beasts, *Bestiaire, ou Cortège d'Orphée* (1911). The subject matter of *Dromadaires* is announced in the following terms: 'Un photographe amateur et deux de ses amis commentent des images prises un peu partout dans le monde' (An amateur photographer and two of his friends comment on images taken almost everywhere around the world). Marker thus hands over his photographs to someone else and introduces the staged encounter that furnishes the film's plurivocal commentary: the amateur photographer's voice is that of Pierre Vaneck and his two friends' voices are provided by Nicolas Yumatov and Catherine Le Couey.

The title of Apollinaire's book appears first of all, followed by the individual lines of his poem, in which an aspiring traveller tells of how he would voyage around the world admiringly, if he had four dromedaries. In one respect, the photo-film grants and develops the traveller's wish: by transposing it from 1911 to 1966 and from poetry to celluloid, the filmed photographs record past years of travel. The grammatical structure of the title invites a conditional clause to follow it, however ('if I had four dromedaries, this is what I *would* do', rather than 'this is what I have done'), and thereby introduces a complication to the temporality of this photographic record of past travels. Skilfully, Marker uses the interrelation between the images and commentary to create a photo-film in which these documents of the real give access to a possible future and enable us to glimpse something that *could* be, but has yet to be conjured from within our visual imaginary. The connection between the past and future constructed by *Dromadaires* is different from the future anterior tense that Barthes speaks about in relation to photography. The power and significance of this photo-film lie in seeing beyond the spectre of death, to think a more conditional relation between time and the still image.

As with Marker's filming of photographs elsewhere, his approach is dynamic. The transitions between photographs are made through dissolves, as well as straight cuts, at varying rhythmic paces, sometimes in keeping with the soundtrack (produced by Antoine Bonfanti). A mobile gaze focuses on details within images, scanning, panning, while never allowing one photograph to delay it too long. The order and pace that the film imposes is something that Susan Sontag praises for its 'visual legibility and emotional impact' (Sontag 1979: 5). In the conversational sections, the photographs act largely as the catalyst for the commentary. The photographic theory by which the film operates is set up through the opening frames and dialogue and is located implicitly closer to Bazin than Barthes. Pierre states: 'La photo, c'est la chasse, c'est l'instinct de la chasse sans l'envie de tuer. [...] On traque, on vise, on tire et – clac! Au lieu d'un mort, on fait un éternel.'[6] The 'shot' here plays on the dual sense of the term, which applies to both a camera and a gun, but here death is transcended. Allied with eternal preservation rather than obliteration, the succession of images continues as we hear that the photographer, according to Pierre, renders eternal his own gaze with the gaze of the person he captures. We are taken closer to the statue of a face at this point, to look directly into its eyes while it looks back at us. Eternity lies within

6 'The photograph is the hunt, it is the instinct of the hunt without the desire to kill. [...] One tracks, one aims, one fires and – click! Instead of killing someone, one makes them eternal.'

this point of contact between two gazes, and it is immaterial that the figure that stares back at us is made of stone. The animated relation to statuary, so important to *Les Statues meurent aussi*, is echoed here and extended to reflect on photography as an art form. Pierre notes that photography is an art in that it belongs to the world of the double rather than life. Over a succession of photographic close-ups of people's faces, he states: 'Si tu participes à quelque chose, c'est à leur vie et à leur mort d'images ...' (If you participate in anything, it is their life and death as images ...). Images also die, then, but an eternalising gaze re-animates photographs of anyone and anything without, however, participating in the reality from which these instants were taken. The life and death of images is what this photo-film will be concerned with, as the imaginary takes on a life of its own, but one that does, ultimately, connect back to ours.

The photo-film divides into two parts: 'Le Château' (The Castle) and 'Le Jardin' (The Garden). Pierre, the photographer, is initially the most authoritative of the three voices. He begins by talking his interlocutors through photographs that he took in France, Sweden, Havana, Japan and Russia. Catherine and Nicolas interject intermittently to discuss what they see. Pierre's vocal delivery alternates between a conversational tone, a more formal voice-over and the musings of an internal monologue. He asks why he loves Russians so much as he reflects on the photographs that he took in Russia, along with the signs of the times that they reveal. In a subsequent internal monologue, Nicolas criticises Pierre's loquaciousness, and then reflects differently on what we have just seen and heard, as he looks now at other images from his position as a Russian exile. Nicolas's intervention draws attention to the biased stance of the photographer, whose European gaze is apparent in the images and commentary (as we will see, this acknowledgement and critique of the European gaze is missing from Marker's *Sans Soleil*, a similar work of taking stock of past images). Pierre's authority is somewhat undercut, and the voice whose theories and pronouncements seemed the most authoritative to begin with stands as just one position among others. It is Catherine who clarifies the meaning of the title of the first part of the film, through reference to a statement by Castro: 'Trahir les pauvres, c'est trahir le Christ' (To betray the poor is to betray Christ). 'Le Château' is said to represent the gulf between the rich and the poor. In one of Pierre's subsequent interventions, over images of people celebrating, he explains that one day he saw happy poor people in Nanterre on the first day of Algerian independence. Catherine's cautionary corrective underlines that this instant of happiness came at a price of seven years of war and one million dead. This section concludes on a pessimistic note as she speaks of the continuing existence of the castle, and says that the poor still exist and we continue to betray them.

'Le Jardin', in contrast, offers a different series of possibilities. It begins with images of animals and then children at play. Pierre comments that the jungle of the animal kingdom is the castle of the human world. The garden, however, in which animals and humans, especially children, build a relation of trust with each other, is something from which he says we can learn. The garden is set up as something to be discovered, though, and this section turns first of all on difficulties and unrest. Catherine speaks of the children of the world, and notes the impossibility of uniting the rich and poor. Then moving principally between images of Korea (many of which appear in Marker's book *Coréennes*) and Cuba, Pierre talks as the camera focuses on the hands of those in the Cuban photographs we are shown. This recalls tacitly the contrasting bloodier, murderous shot of the hand at the end of *Cuba Si!*. He creates an imaginary narrative around an elderly Cuban woman in a crowd at a protest meeting against the Bay of Pigs invasion. A note of disillusionment is sounded as he extends his sense of what this woman has lived through to what millions of militants throughout the world have faced: 'Le monde socialiste n'était plus le lieu d'une seule fidélité et d'une seule fraternité' (The socialist world was no longer the place of a single faith and fraternity). Images of protest against the Vietnam War follow this, in China, Tokyo and Oslo, which leads Pierre to an extended meditation on Scandinavian utopia. A close-up of the face of a Scandinavian man is contrasted with a range of others from around the world and is described as having everything that all of the others could want – everything except immortality. This introduces the theme of death, which brings with it two significant echoes of *La Jetée*.

Pierre says that he once met a man in Moscow who had survived his own death. He was Hungarian and among those who should have been shot by a firing squad in Budapest, but he survived and now toured democracies with the propaganda pamphlets that proclaimed his death. This is recounted over images of the man whose eyes, finally, engage our own. Later on, Catherine speaks about mortality and lingers on the suggestion that women have a special relationship with death. A series of images of paintings and statues succeed one another through dissolves, before we see photographs of women. One Russian woman's face (which Marker will return to in subsequent films), is photographed in close-up and recurs through a series of dissolves, until the image appears to move and she smiles at us. As with *La Jetée*, however, this photo-film relies overall on the photographic, rather than the filmic, to establish a sustained link to life and love.

Towards the end, the commentary of the three friends is slowed, voices are distorted, and, after a pause, their words become the chatter and cries of chimpanzees. This move from the human voice to the animal fits with Pierre's ensuing explanation that the garden – the subject of the latter half of the film – exists within us: 'Et qu'il existe à travers notre part la plus irréfutable, notre part animale. [...] Il y a bien une Loi du Jardin, qui s'exprime par des gestes très simples, par les gestes les plus simples.'[7] As he says this, we see a succession of images of people holding hands, linking arms, women together, men and women together, and animals either alongside or touching one another. Pierre speaks of the dawning of an era of grace, with a hint of the revolution as he terms it a 'Sierra Maestra' of tenderness: 'quelque chose qui avance ... à travers nous, malgré nous, grâce à nous, quand nous avons la ... grâce ... et qui annonce, pour on ne sait pas quand, la survivance des plus aimés.'[8] What the commentary envisages is already discernible in the gestures of togetherness in the final photographs we see.

This photo-film takes us through its castle and out into its garden to play, like animals and children, but then turns the interior and the exterior inside out, since the revolutionary potential for a change in the field of vision lies within ourselves. *Dromadaires* looks differently at photography and sees beyond the death or eternal isolation of the manifold subjects it captures, to imbue these images with the breath of life that moves forwards in time. The photographed subjects will not

---

7 'And that it exists through the most irrefutable part of ourselves, our animal side. [...] There is indeed a Law of the Garden, which expresses itself through very simple gestures, through the simplest of gestures.'

8 'something which is advancing ... through us, in spite of us, thanks to us, when we have ... grace ... and which heralds, for an unknown time, the survival of the most loved.'

venture here – they die, as Barthes suggests, but have been embalmed, as Bazin contends. Yet this rich photo-film establishes connections that exceed the individualist focus of these photographic theories. Life, love and survival emerge here through hands that touch, arms that enlace and bodies, which, although static, are gesturing together in the uncertain direction of someone else's future, which lies beyond their own certain death.

Si j'avais quatre dromadaires was not released until 1974. Its resultant dual placement in the 1960s and 1970s is fitting. Its photographic form and reflection on tenderness relate it to *La Jetée* and *Le Mystère Koumiko* respectively; and the coining of the 'Sierra Maestra' refers back to the revolution of *Cuba Si!*. These revolutionary stirrings gain in vitality in the subsequent decade. Cuba is one country among many whose history undergoes unprecedented shifts, which Marker and his collaborators record on film.

References

Barthes, Roland (1980), *La Chambre Claire: note sur la photographie*, Paris, Seuil.

Bellour, Raymond (1990), 'The Film Stilled', in *Camera Obscura*, 24 (September), pp. 99–123.

Bensmaïa, Réda (1988), 'Du photogramme au pictogramme: à propos de *La Jetée* de Chris Marker', in *Iris*, 8, pp. 8–31.

Coates, Paul (1987), 'Chris Marker and the Cinema as Time Machine', in *Science-Fiction Studies*, 14:3 (November), pp. 307–15.

Delahaye, Michel (1963), 'La Chasse à l'I', in *Cahiers du cinéma*, 146 (August), pp. 5–17.

DiIorio, Sam (2003), 'The Truth About Paris: Reconsidering *Le Joli Mai*'s Investigation of French Social Attitudes in the Early Sixties', in *Film Comment* (May–June), pp. 46–47.

Dubois, Philippe (2002), '*La Jetée* ou le cinématogramme de la conscience', in Philippe Dubois (ed.), *Théorème 6: recherches sur Chris Marker*, Paris, Presses Sorbonne Nouvelle, pp. 8–45.

Frampton, Daniel (2006), *Filmosophy*, London, Wallflower Press.

Francovich, Allan (1997), 'The Mind's Eye: Chris Marker's *Level Five*', in *Vertigo*, 7 (Autumn), pp. 35–37.

ffrench, Patrick (2005), 'The Memory of the Image in Chris Marker's *La Jetée*', in *French Studies*, LIX: 1 (January), pp. 31–37.

Gauthier, Guy (1963), 'Le Joli Mai', in *Image et son*, 161–62 (April–May), pp. 62–63.

Irigaray, Luce (1985), *Speculum of the Other Woman*, New York, Cornell

University Press; orig. publ. (1974), Paris, Minuit.

Kawin, Bruce (1982), 'Time and Stasis in *La Jetée*', in *Film Quarterly* (Fall), pp. 15–20.

Lee, Sander (2000), 'Platonic Themes in Chris Marker's *La Jetée*', www.sensesofcinema.com, 4 (March) [accessed 30 November 2006].

Lhomme, Pierre (1964), 'Interview', in *Image et son*, 173 (May), pp. 38–43.

Lupton, Catherine (2005), *Chris Marker: Memories of the Future*, London, Reaktion.

Marcorelles, Louis (1963), 'La Foire aux vérités', in *Cahiers du cinéma*, 143 (May), pp. 26–34.

Marker, Chris (1967), *Commentaires 2*, Paris, Seuil.

Marker, Chris (1998), 'Marker mémoire (Cinémathèque Française, 7 janvier–1er février 1998)', in *Images documentaries*, 31, pp. 75–85.

Marker, Chris (2003a), 'Marker Direct', in *Film Comment* (May–June), pp. 38–41.

Marker, Chris (2003b), '*La Jetée, Sans Soleil*: deux films de Chris Marker', Paris, Argos Films/Arte, no page numbers.

Möller, Olaf (2003), 'Ghost World: Japan through the Looking Glass', in *Film Comment* (July–August), pp. 35–37.

Penley, Constance (1988), 'Time Travel, Primal Scene, and the Critical Dystopia', in *Camera Obscura*, 15, pp. 66–84.

Pourvali, Bamchade (2003), *Chris Marker*, Paris, Cahiers du cinéma.

Sontag, Susan (1979), *On Photography*, London, Penguin; orig. publ. 1971.

Van Cauwenberge, Geneviève (2002), 'Le Point de vue documentaire dans *Le Joli Mai*', in Philippe Dubois (ed.), *Théorème 6: recherches sur Chris Marker*, Paris, Presses Sorbonne Nouvelle, pp. 83–99.

Wilson, Emma (2006), *Alain Resnais*, Manchester, Manchester University Press.

Wollen, Peter (1989), 'Fire and Ice', in John X. Berger and Olivier Richon (eds), *Other than Itself: Writing Photography*, Manchester, Cornerhouse Publications, no page numbers.

1 A repeated image: workers levelling a road surface in *Lettre de Sibérie*

2 Aerial vision and the land of Israel in *Description d' un combat*

3 Fidel Castro in *Cuba Si!*

4 The enshrined cats of happiness in *Sans Soleil*

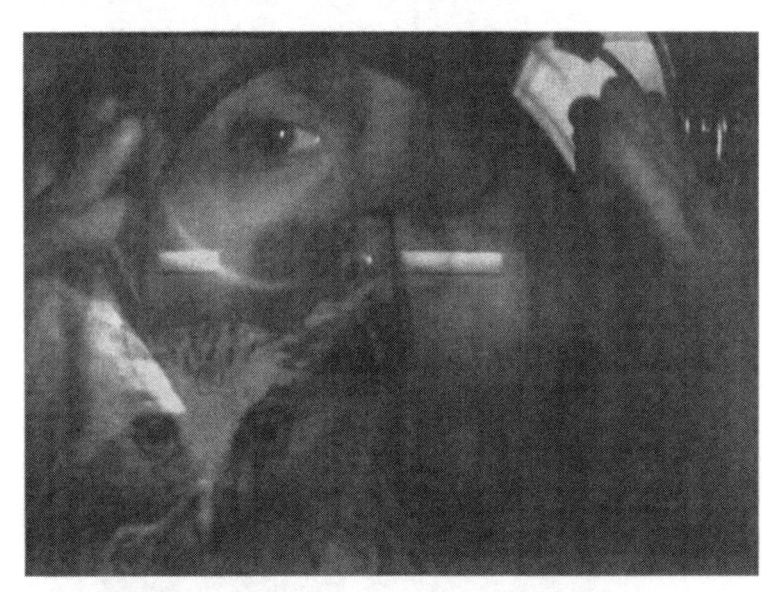

5 Laura and the O.W.L. in *Level 5*

6 Memory's scar in *La Jetée*

7 Life and love, death and eternity in *La Jetée*

8 Bloody encounters in *La Sixième Face du Pentagone* and *Le Fond de l' air est rouge*

9 The montage cat of *Le Tombeau d' Alexandre*

10 The way of all flesh in *Les Statues meurent aussi*

11 Metaphysical tracking and the circular insert in *Une Journée d' Andrei Arsenevitch*

12 The graffiti cats of Paris in *Chats perchés*

13 Collective protest in *Chats perchés*

3

Collective endeavour: 1967–1977

From 1967 until 1977, Marker veils his individual signature as a film director. While he continues to produce his own work, these years place increased emphasis on collective projects. He also plays a crucial behind-the-scenes role in facilitating recognition of other people's work. Although his filmmaking has been politically engaged from the outset, this is a period of heightened militancy. It begins and ends with critical reflections on the Vietnam War and charts major upheavals in regimes around the world, as revolutions are fought against repressive forces. A key collective was established in 1967, termed SLON (the Russian word for elephant, but which stood for: Société Pour le Lancement des Œuvres Nouvelles; Society for Launching New Works). This organisation was responsible for producing *Loin du Viêt-Nam* that same year. As Min Lee emphasises, SLON was a production and distribution cooperative that existed independently of Marker (Lee 2003: 38), yet he played a key participatory role in it in a number of different capacities relating to film production. The collective organisation was registered in Belgium to begin with, because it was less restrictive there than in France, but in 1974 it became a French company called ISKRA (the title of Lenin's newspaper, which is reworked as the acronym for: Images Son Kinescope Réalisation Audiovisuelle). ISKRA is still fully functioning today. One of Marker's main roles as enabler during the late 1960s and 1970s was born of the co-directed film *À bientôt j'espère* (1968) on the strike at the Rhodiaceta factory in Besançon. This SLON film spawned the idea for the Medvedkin groups – factory workers initially based in Besançon and then also in Sochaux who made their own films. In addition to these involvements, Marker's filmmaking bears witness to the general mistrust of the media that swept through

France in the wake of May 1968. His most significant contribution to a more widespread challenge to mainstream reporting was in a series titled *On vous parle* for which he made five episodes. These sit among his various other films in this decade, all of which cast a critical eye on the status quo; indeed, during this decade, film itself becomes a valuable weapon with which to promote or even fight revolutionary causes throughout the world.

Loin du Viêt-Nam, *La Sixième Face du Pentagone* and *À bientôt j'espère*

Although different in terms of their conception, making and subjects, these three films of 1967 and 1968 are a pivotal group in terms of their focus on filmmaking as a collaborative endeavour, which sets the predominant tone for this particular ten-year chapter of Marker's work.

Marker wrote the commentary, edited and was the initial impetus behind *Loin du Viêt-Nam* (1967). This collective work comprises twelve sections and was filmed by a range of established names within cinema, including Jean-Luc Godard, Joris Ivens, William Klein, Claude Lelouch and Alain Resnais. Agnès Varda's name features in the credits in order to acknowledge that she was integral to the shaping of the project, but her filming was not ultimately part of the final version. Marker stresses how their collaborations were strictly non-hierarchical and explains that they arrived at this collective response to the Vietnam War because none of them felt able to resolve the problems individually (Marker 1968: 66). An intertitle at the start declares the filmmakers' solidarity with the Vietnamese people. The rich 115-minute film that follows is multi-layered in its treatment of the war, using newsreel footage and documentary segments, as well as fiction. It features pro- and anti-war demonstrations (the latter prefigures the focus of *La Sixième Face du Pentagone* and some of the footage that will feature in *Le Fond de l'air est rouge*); it makes the resistance of the Vietnamese apparent throughout, along with their tragedies; and it also includes sequences that are variously philosophical and self-reflexive on war and filmmaking. An aural connection to previous wars is woven throughout in the presence of Hanns Eisler's score for Resnais's *Nuit et brouillard* (1956). This film, on which

Marker collaborated, warned of the risks of forgetting the atrocities of the Second World War, and was made in the political climate of the Algerian War. In its own way, *Loin du Viêt-Nam* serves to counter an amnesiac relation to the past with reference to colonialism. An early flashback recalls French colonial rule in Vietnam. The film thus remembers this period of French imperialism, while constituting a clear protest against the American military presence in the 1960s and coming out on the side of the Vietnamese throughout. Such anti-war sentiment is central to Marker's next work, co-directed with François Reichenbach.

The refrain of a protest song – 'it takes a real man to say no' – opens and closes *La Sixième Face du Pentagone* (1968). This 28-minute film focuses on the march on the Pentagon on 21 October 1967, which harnessed the collective outrage that had gathered by that time in the US against the war. Featuring footage shot principally by Marker and Reichenbach, the credits also list other camera operators along with a broader team as part of this SLON production. The film begins with a Zen proverb: 'Si les cinq faces du Pentagone te paraissent imprenables, attaque par la sixième' (If the five sides of the Pentagon seem impregnable, attack by the sixth). The Pentagon, described by the commentary as the nerve centre of American defence and the current personification of the Vietnam War, is imaged in a black and white aerial photograph. Its sixth side, invisible of course in this image of the building, comes into being in the ensuing film – in colour and black and white, photography and moving footage – in the form of around 100,000 marchers, and through a mixture of protest and confrontational 'direct action'.

After showing us the preparations in the lead-up to the march, the filming of the protest begins with a minute's silence in memory of Che Guevara, led by black activist John Wilson. The day's events include speeches, mini dramatic performances and songs, all of which register the solidarity of the crowd with the oppressed, and which are interrupted only occasionally by the dissenting voices of young Nazis and an anti-communist priest. Throughout the film, we hear of men who have either destroyed or returned their call-up papers. A group of hippies provide a note of humour, as the commentary describes how they asked the Pentagon for permission to levitate the building to the height of three hundred metres in order to exorcise the demons. The levitation was authorised to the lower height of ten metres. Cordons of military police form human barriers around the Pentagon, but one group of protesters finds an unprotected area of the perimeter. Handheld camera footage captures them as they break into a run and then records the resultant bloody clash between them and the police who lash out violently.

In the midst of the conflict, the film cuts to a black and white photograph (taken by Marc Riboud) of a woman, who stands in front of a line of military police and holds up a flower in front of her with both of her hands as she faces their guns. In the next photograph, she has dropped the flower and she stands staring at them with her arms opened out wide, as if daring one of them to pick it up. From the first to the last images of this film, photographs abound, capturing power as well as its opposite in such frozen moments of defiance as those taken by Riboud. When dawn breaks, the people who have lived through this night are described as having moved from a political attitude to a political gesture. A suite of photographs closes the film, many of which show protesters who spent the night in prison – writer Norman Mailer and filmmaker Shirley Clarke were two of the more famous figures who were arrested during the protests and who appear in these closing images. The final photograph of the film is of a more anonymous group of students. As the camera moves in slowly to focus on the face of one student, the voice-over declares that the least it can say of the fraction of this young generation who protested in Washington is summed by the words of one fifteen-year-old girl who announces, 'j'ai changé' (I have changed), after a night on the steps of the Pentagon. As this film moves from the fifth to the sixth side of the Pentagon, the photographs register political entrenchment as well as its subversion. They work thus in tune with the rest of the footage to construct a vision that counters political stasis with change. Marker's subsequent film, co-directed with Mario Marret and shot in black and white, makes different but related use of a combination of photography and film.

Marker recounts how he was in the middle of editing *Loin du Viêt-Nam* in March 1967 when he received a letter from two teachers at a popular culture centre in Besançon informing him that the workers at the Rhodiaceta factory had gone on strike. They asked him whether he could supply some 16mm film and suggested he bring it himself so that he could see what was happening there. He explains how the resultant trip to Besançon (in the company of sound engineer and friend Antoine Bonfanti) was the first step towards the making of *À bientôt j'espère* (1968), as well as being key to SLON (and, later, ISKRA) and to the formation of the Medvedkin groups (Marker 2006: 14). *À bientôt j'espère* is included on the invaluable ISKRA 2006 release of a DVD box set of the militant films of the Medvedkin groups. Members of the SLON group explain in interview that, although their moment of inception was 1967, which coincided with the release of *Loin du Viêt-Nam*, they felt that *À bientôt* marked the true beginning of their endeavours, since it was less dependent on a collection of individual points of view (Hennebelle 1973: 36).

Mario Marret became an immediate part of every subsequent trip made by Marker to Besançon and participated in all of the filming. *À bientôt* begins in front of the Rhodiaceta factory at Christmas in 1967, but footage dates back to the time of Marker's first trip to Besançon. Marker provides the voice-over and a broader context for the strike at the start. His vocal presence is intermittent throughout the film, though, since the principal aim is to give voice to the workers and their struggle. The film comprises footage of meetings and speeches rallying the workers and good-humoured discussions with groups of them, as well as more intimate interviews with husbands and wives. It also features several montages of photographs. The first move from film to photography is by way of a travelling shot of a wall, on which the words 'Grève Rhodia Liberté D'Hommes' (Rhodia Strike Men's Freedom) are written. The mobile filming of the graffiti on the wall tracks its stasis and sets it in motion. The movement of the film is thereby united with the political protest it records. The photographs that ensue proceed by means of straight cuts, the pace of which work in line with the politicised motion of *À bientôt*. Over this sequence, a worker explains in voice-over that during the strike, the men experienced collective existence for the first time. This combination of photography and moving images, which run into one another seamlessly as workers speak in voice-over, is repeated later. And a further travelling shot of graffiti on another wall – 'Rhodia Nous Gagnerons' (Rhodia We Will Win) – continues to support the militant drive of both form and subject.

The warmth and candour of the workers' testimony is apparent throughout, even as they talk less positively about their jobs in the interview sequences. The repetitiveness and boredom of their daily tasks is described and juxtaposed at times with the workings of the machines that they usually operate. We hear about the impact of eight-hour shift rotations on family life and the strain that this places on relationships, along with people's health. Although those who are asked their ages are in their late thirties, most look older than their years. The smiling and articulate unionist Georges Maurivard 'Yoyo' is a central voice throughout and he galvanises the workers into action. As Marker's closing voice-over notes the failure of the strikes in 1967, Yoyo's final defiant intervention, addressed to the employers, is to say that he hopes to see them soon. This statement of hope for a different encounter with them in the future gives the film its title.

Marker says of Marret: 'C'est à lui qu'on doit, à travers À bientôt j'espère, cette ambiance de parfaite égalité entre filmeurs et filmés que je n'aurais sûrement pas été capable d'établir à moi seul'[1] (Marker 2006: 15). Upon viewing the film, the workers felt that there was still an ethnographic element to the filmmakers' presence, however (Hennebelle 1973: 36). One further critique focused on the treatment of women who often also had factory jobs but who appear secondary to the men in the film. In one interview sequence, with husband and wife Claude and Suzanne Zedet, for example, Claude is virtually the only person who speaks. The camera focuses on Suzanne several times, on her silence, as she listens to her husband's description of their lives and those of other people, only intervening once. The Medvedkin groups (named after Russian director Alexander Medvedkin, at Marker's suggestion) arose in response to these and other criticisms. The first group of worker-filmmakers was established in Besançon and, when one of them – Pol Cèbe – moved to Sochaux, a different group was formed there. The inaugural film of the Besançon group was *Classe de Lutte* (1968), which focuses mainly on Suzanne Zedet's role as worker and militant. In this film, she is able to give her side of the story, which was absent from À bientôt.

The words on a sticker that we glimpse briefly during one of the rallies in À bientôt say: 'Seul tu ne peux rien, ensemble tout est possible' (Alone you can do nothing, together everything is possible). Such camaraderie was registered in the initial spirit of *Loin du Viêt-Nam* and carried through the mass marches of *La Sixième Face du Pentagone* into the fight of the workers of Besançon. Solidarity that

[1] 'It's to him that we owe that atmosphere of perfect equality throughout À bientôt j'espère between filmmakers and filmed subjects, which I'm sure I wouldn't have been able to establish myself.'

gestures beyond the individual in the name of an ongoing revolution will be a thread that runs through subsequent works.

On vous parle du Brésil: Tortures

This film is the first of Marker's five contributions to the *On vous parle* series. Prior to this, Marker had suggested the idea for the *Ciné-Tracts* (1968) series of very brief anonymous films made by different directors. These were silent and filmed on 16mm black and white stock. They took account of current affairs as they happened and also served a counter-informational drive against the mainstream media. Correspondingly, the *On vous parle* series labels itself a magazine of counter-information in its strident generic introduction. The title appears in capital white letters on a black screen, each word interspersed with faint still images, accompanied by the slow, steady beat of a drum. The additional sound of a siren gets increasingly higher in pitch as the images progress and culminates at its highest point to place us in a state of alert for the hard-hitting contents of each film. Each is made in black and white on 16mm stock and lasts between fifteen and thirty minutes. In spite of the fact that these films belong to the period in which Marker's individual presence as filmmaker blends into the collective identity of SLON, some of the images of the opening to the series are recognisably his. We see the Russian woman whose face becomes animated briefly as a result of fast-paced dissolves in *Si j'avais quatre dromadaires* (her photograph will reappear several times in *Le Train en marche*, too). We also see a better-known image of Marker whose face is half-concealed behind a Rolleiflex camera. His stamp on the overall series, his vocal presence or role as camera operator in some of his own contributions, and his editing serve to reinforce his alignment with the revolutionary subjects he treats.

On vous parle du Brésil: Tortures (1969) is number three in the series. It deals principally with the institutionalisation of torture by the military dictatorship of Brazil, which assumed power in 1964 and which used brutality as a means of countering political subversion to devastating effect. At the start of the film, over newspaper extracts, drawings, photographs and archive film footage, the commentary recounts the abduction of the then US ambassador to Brazil by a group of revolutionaries on 4 September 1969. In return for the release of the ambassador, they demanded the release of fifteen political prisoners who had been imprisoned under the repressive Brazilian regime. They also asked for their anti-imperialist manifesto to be published in the press. Their conditions were met and the ambassador was freed. The released prisoners were flown first to Mexico and some made the journey on to Cuba. This latter group is then interviewed in the closed space of an anonymous room in Cuba in which each will tell their individual tale. Most of the ensuing film is based on their accounts of the tortures they underwent during their respective periods of imprisonment.

The revolutionaries come from different professional backgrounds: the group includes an architect, a student, a doctor and a lawyer, among others. Each has their specific tale of woe, but the processes and instruments that they describe are very similar: electric shocks applied to sensitive parts of the body; strategic, repetitive beatings; being suspended from various kinds of equipment; and psychological torture (being woken at dawn and left in a room; watching other people being tortured, especially family members). In addition to focusing on each witness's face as they recount what they went through, the film also shows the others listening: they either look at the speaker or stare straight ahead, locked behind inscrutable gazes.

The commentary reports that in spite of worldwide condemnation of the tortures that were brought to light through the kinds of testimony presented here, the Brazilian dictatorship was undaunted. The film cuts briefly to images of a demonstration and then back to the face of one of the interviewees, as the commentary affirms that this time it will not be possible for people to say that they do not know what is going on there. *On vous parle du Brésil: Tortures* is a powerful beginning to Marker's *On vous parle* films, which are as uncompromising in their portrayal of the horrors of dictatorial regimes as they are unstinting in their support of the revolutionary activity that aims continually to undermine them.

On vous parle du Brésil: Carlos Marighela

The Brazilian focus is continued in the next film. *Carlos Marighela* (1970) does not feature the generic introduction that characterises the other *On vous parle* episodes, but its subject matter and treatment bear the unmistakeable hallmarks of the counter-informational thrust of the series. At the start, a television presenter declares: 'Lorsque la télévision donnera aux choses et aux gens leur vraie place, on y entendra par exemple ceci ...' (When television accords things and people their true place, we will, for example, hear this ...). Similar to *Détour Ceaucescu*, a later short film that appears in Marker's installation *Zapping Zone*, which accuses television of treating its spectators as if they were idiots, this film uses the television set as an initial point of access to exposing deeper and harsher realities of which the public need also to be made aware. *Carlos Marighela* is a posthumous portrait of the revolutionary leader who was assassinated on 4 November 1969 by the Brazilian government. One year on, the film reflects back on Marighela's life and the violent phase of history that he traversed, particularly in the struggles of the 1960s. It includes testimony supplied by one of his comrades, news photographs and archive film footage of demonstrations.

Marighela's comrade is visible only as a hazy silhouette in a faint and shadowy image on the television set, which returns throughout the film. The interview was recorded in Cuba, where many Brazilian exiles live, and his anonymity is respected. He speaks highly and warmly of Marighela who is said to have given stability during difficult times. *Carlos Marighela* cuts between this interview, dynamic filming of photographic images and archive footage. These combine to give visual testimony to the mass uprising against the repressive military dictatorship in the 1960s, which united students, workers and broader swathes of the population, and drew together Catholics and communists in a common struggle. The images also bear witness to the violent suppression of their protests. In 1966, the voice-over explains, Marighela resigns from the Executive Committee of the Brazilian Communist Party. His letter of resignation, which is read out as part of the commentary, registers his strong sense of the need for armed struggle against the State powers. This thereby aligns his revolutionary beliefs implicitly with those of Che Guevara, for whom armed combat was the way to counter repressive and imperialist forces. In 1968, the commentary describes how Marighela launched the Action for National Liberation, which advocated urban guerrilla warfare in the first instance, before moving into rural areas. Again, this was matched by violent countermeasures from the dictatorship. The end of the film returns to the subject of *On vous parle du Brésil:*

Tortures, and focuses on the kidnap of the American ambassador in 1969 by Brazilian revolutionaries. For Marighela, the kidnapping was important, we are told, since it showed how different revolutionary groups could work together. The importance of this collaboration across separate groups will repeat itself throughout the *On vous parle* series. The film draws to a close with news of Marighela's murder by the dictatorship, but his idea of action had already been taken up by a large number of people by that time, which made it difficult to suppress. Marighela's comrade explains that Che Guevara became a revolutionary flag for the Latin American people and that Marighela represents something similar for the country of Brazil.

Marighela's photographic image appears on screen periodically in the film as a reminder of its absent subject, and the direct gaze of his facial pose suggests the Barthesian temporal paradox of a death that has already happened and has yet to occur. Yet, as Salvador Allende will reiterate powerfully at the end of *On vous parle du Chili* (1973), the death of one revolutionary leader, however tragic and immeasurable a loss this may be, does not mark the end of the revolution. The need to think beyond the death of the individual subject is written into the revolutionary struggle from the outset, whether as a mark of defiance against repressive or murderous actions of dictatorships, or as a sign of solidarity beyond individualism within the ranks of the revolutionaries. *Carlos Marighela* gives form to the struggle against repression, as still and moving images combine to keep the revolutionary spirit alive long after Marighela's death.

On vous parle de Paris: Maspero, les mots ont un sens

Marker's next contribution to the *On vous parle series* (number five), is a portrait of the left-wing publisher François Maspero. *On vous parle de Paris* (1970) is based principally around interviews with Maspero, and has a voice-over commentary from Marker. It furnishes candid reflections on the problems that beset the editor in the selection and publication of books, along with discussion of his profession in relation to broader revolutionary struggles. He is an engaging interlocutor from the outset, lucid in his political vision and his professional choices. The film opens with the name of François Maspero on the front cover of a book. A page from a dictionary appears, masked out for the most part, with the term 'Citation' left visible. After a brief citation from Gramsci, which registers the need for optimism of the will in the face of the pessimism of reason, the film subdivides into an Introduction and five chapters, each introduced by the same masking: Selection, Definition, Information, Recuperation and Contradiction.

Maspero presents publishing as a profession in which everything is imperfect but in which everything drives towards perfection. He appears briefly with a colleague as they discuss the errors in a book that has just come out. He states in voice-over that the thirty-second sense of euphoria he experiences each time a book is published quickly disappears as they discover its imperfections. He describes how he has benefited from the benevolence of anonymous donors when in financial difficulties, but explains that this is offset against the people who steal from him on a regular basis. He is clear that he does not think that everything they have published has been good. Furthermore, he reports that they would never have survived if they had not taken the risks of publishing material that turned out to be of poor quality, or if they had not turned down work of quality because it duplicated subjects on which they had already published. Marker notes that Maspero's publishing house was indispensable if one wanted to know what was going on inside the head of a Cuban revolutionary or a black American militant. A young male reader in one of Maspero's Left Bank bookshops explains that he came to the publishers because it was the main means of finding out about Algeria. He mentions Henri Alleg's *La Question*, which was banned during the Algerian war but which was available there.

Marker explains how all the contradictory strands of revolutionary thinking exist alongside one another here: Marx against Michaux, Che Guevara next to Giraudoux. In line with establishing unities across the boundaries of difference, the film juxtaposes images of the covers of books by contrasting authors, and creates through montage the combinations that Maspero covets and his readers praise. This filmic performance of the publisher's beliefs is continued through a succession of still photographs and posters at a later stage. Maspero describes militancy and revolution as struggles of global proportions which need to unite people across individual countries. He says that this is especially true with regard to the unequal distribution of the world's wealth, and notes that the authors of the books that he publishes concur that there can only really be a global economy. The film cuts from one still image to the next at this point. A mobile camera focuses on details of posters and photographs that variously show starving and desolate children, a Bank of America advertisement, a militiaman, a James Bond poster, among other images, before arriving finally at a photographic image of an emaciated elderly figure. Maspero affirms that the unequal distribution of wealth affects everyone everywhere. Essentially Marxist, rather than explicitly altruistic, politics acquires an ethical dimension here nonetheless, as he reiterates that this concerns everyone. The film gives form to the problems Maspero speaks of and the change of thinking his vision necessitates. The montage of photographs and posters stresses the apparent disparities between what each depicts, along with the need for relational thinking beyond the limitations of the static individual image.

To the 'authentic' revolutionaries who refuse to make any concessions and who think that to publish books in a capitalist society is to be an uncritical part of it, Maspero's reply is to flag the importance of working against the system from within. This warm portrait of a man with whom Marker has obvious affinities shows how essential Maspero's own revolutionary political struggle is to the wider counter-informational network of challenge.

La Bataille des dix millions

Marker's next film, *La Bataille des dix millions* (1970), takes him beyond the confines of the *On vous parle* series and returns him to Cuba. With Valérie Mayoux, Marker edited together some of his own material with television and newsreel footage, along with extracts from films by Santiago Alvarez, photographs and cartoon animation. Mayoux relates her trepidation when Marker went away and left her in charge of editing particular sequences of this film without leaving her any instructions, even though she praises the freedom she was granted through such an approach (Mayoux 1997: 95). *Bataille* builds on Marker's love of Cuba, already registered in *Cuba Si!*, and the rhythm of revolution is still to be heard through the film's music. Yet here we focus on Fidel Castro's self-criticism with regard to one particularly vast socialist project that failed, and the countrywide efforts of the Cuban population who tried to make it work.

Bataille begins with Castro's address to his people from a television studio on 9 February 1970. In order for the Cuban economy to establish itself, the voice-over explains, a ten million ton sugar cane harvest was announced on 14 July 1969 as the target to be reached in 1970. Castro reports that the *safra* – the name given to this harvest – was apparently working well in the western provinces but that problems were beginning to appear in the east. He asks for volunteers from the entire population to help the country meet its goal and has confidence that everyone will do what is necessary to harvest the ten million tonnes. The film then cuts to images of Cuban daily life. It focuses on disparate people before it shows never-ending queues, the struggle to get the most basic of provisions and signs that say that there is nothing left. Several of the film's images in this sequence are frozen and interrupt the progression, as the voice-over declares that Cuba is not fashionable this year. Europeans are said to love populations who are fighting but only if they are martyrs or victims: the struggles of everyday life fail to capture the attention of the wider world. A variant of this attitude is described as a refusal to see reality in disturbing images, or to claim that showing such images is to play into the adversary's hands. In the face of these alternatives – turning away, looking without seeing or fuelling the enemy's criticisms – the frozen images are deliberate in wanting to give pause, to slow the flow of the film, albeit momentarily, to get us to linger over what might disturb rather than turn away. From the outset, *Bataille* deploys its moments of stillness in the name of establishing solidarity with Castro and the Cuban people.

Photographic images serve a similar purpose in a later sequence and extend this connection beyond Cuba to other countries in Latin America. We are shown film footage of Cuban people (and Castro among them) giving blood for victims of a devastating earthquake in Peru. As the commentary tells of their common struggle against underdevelopment and American imperialism, a succession of photographs appears from Cuba, Bolivia, Brazil and Guatemala. This montage conveys a revolutionary connection across Latin America. However, these bonds never distract from the fact that Cuba is responsible for its own specific struggle. The battle of the *safra* is the focus of the rest of the film, which moves forwards and backwards in time after the moment of its inception. It alternates principally between footage from Castro's legendary speeches to the masses, encounters with individuals among them and the work involved in the colossal harvest.

Castro takes to the podium for Lenin's one-hundredth anniversary and adjusts each of his many microphones in turn (a habit to which *Le Fond de l'air est rouge* will return, humorously). Filmed from a fixed position, this sequence registers the importance of the Soviet Union for the Cuban revolutionary movement. *Bataille* makes use of interviews, here and elsewhere, to establish closer contact with the Cuban people. Cubans are asked individually what they would say to Lenin if he were alive today. The voice-over commentator says that what would interest him is a dialogue between Castro and Lenin, and film footage of each man is edited back to back. The final interviewee says that he would take Lenin fishing and perhaps teach him something he did not know. The commentary reminds us that it is with people like this that the battle of the ten million was fought, as footage appears of the harvest in action. However, the strain on existing machinery proves to be too great to accomplish the task and the production problems multiply as the film progresses. A further setback is introduced through animated cartoon imagery, in the form of a CIA-instigated kidnap of the crew of two Cuban fishing boats. We see a photograph of the fishermen, who are eventually liberated. Castro's angry verdict on this situation is that the enemy just used the problems of the *safra* to create this incident, but he is adamant that if anyone is to blame for the problems of the *safra* it is the Cuban people and their leader.

The last stages of the battle are introduced through a succession of photographic images of workers from one province who worked gruelling days for eleven months in an attempt to meet the target. The voice-over explains that, when Castro speaks on 26 July 1970, it is these people whom he addresses first and foremost. The total of the harvest was eight and a half million tonnes: a record-breaking amount, but still not enough. The immense effort put into producing the required amount of sugar had set other areas of production out of line. Cutting then between images of Castro on the podium, workers at their machinery and interviews with people who listened to him that day, the climax of the film is testimony to the stirring power of Castro's speeches and the magnetism of his leadership. He praises the proletariat for worrying about production problems above all else and he takes as much blame as anyone for the failure of the *safra*. In spite of these difficulties, socialism is still registered as the only route, their only choice, and is seen as the possibility of best using the country's resources for the people. Castro's concession to his critics is that they have been right about everything other than the belief that there is an alternative to the revolution for the Cuban people, and *Bataille* ends with him thanking the people for their confidence.

The scattered use of photographs throughout this film, the frozen moments at the start, along with slowed footage elsewhere, work in tune with Castro's desire for a unified fraternal struggle in the face of adversity, rather than serving as grist to the mill of the adversary. To pause on images that reveal problems in the revolutionary socialist project is to be open to the very criticism Castro endorses throughout in the name of progress. Complicit with Castro's vision, *Bataille* embraces the self-criticism of socialism readily, as a sign of strength rather than weakness. It will not be until *Le Fond de l'air est rouge* that Marker will take more distance from the stance and pronouncements of this rousing Cuban leader.

On vous parle de Prague: le deuxième procès d'Artur London

Marker's next film returns him to the *On vous parle* series. *On vous parle de Prague: le deuxième procès d'Artur London* (1971), number six in the series, is a complex reflection on what it means to be a true communist. It focuses on Artur London, a founding member of the Czechoslovakian Communist Party who was arrested in 1951 under orders from Stalin. He was imprisoned, tortured and then given a false confession to deliver at the Slansky trial in Prague in November 1952. He was tried alongside thirteen others, who were also said to be traitors to the communist cause. Rudolf Slansky (former Secretary General of the Czech Communist Party) and ten others were condemned to death, while London and the remaining two were sentenced to life imprisonment. London was freed, however, in 1956. His book, *The Confession*, is a vivid account of living under Stalinist rule, which filmmaker Constantin Costa-Gavras decided to make into a film, *L'Aveu* (1970). *On vous parle de Prague* moves between newsreel footage of the Slansky trial of 1952 and footage shot on the film set of *L'Aveu*, which includes interviews with Costa-Gavras, the main actors in his film (Yves Montand and Simone Signoret), the writer Jorge Semprun and Artur London himself. The film of the book was deemed highly controversial. Indeed, the second trial to which the subtitle of *On vous parle de Prague* refers is the result of a deceptively simple but risky decision to adapt a text for the screen.

On vous parle de Prague begins with archive footage of the Slansky trial, as the voice-over points up its wild theatricality, even though the whole performance is painfully and tragically real. Moving from the trial to Costa-Gavras's film set, there are several shots of hands busying themselves operating cameras, winding film reel, gesticulating, resting or smoking, as Marker's voice-over says that they have been living for nine weeks in the closed world of *L'Aveu*. Marker was employed as the on-set still photographer for *L'Aveu*, and his photographs, along with other still images, are interspersed throughout this film. We also see silent filming of scenes from the making of *L'Aveu*, some of which material forms the short film *Jour de tournage* of 1969. He says that this world of solitude and silence is full of people with intelligent hands, who work in a manner closer to pottery than to automation in the so-called industry that is cinema. The film cuts to hands in handcuffs as a very haggard-looking Montand (who plays London) is interviewed.

Montand explains that he has lost a great deal of weight and that he is more tired than he has ever been in his life but that, in comparison to what London himself went through, this is nothing (London, when he comes on set, is particularly struck by Montand's countenance). More than just an explicit concern to get into character, Montand's suffering appears a form of penance for believing so religiously in the past in the incorruptibility of socialism. His conviction now is that people need to read about and see the flaws, especially of the Stalinist regime, and other interviewees share this view. One question returns as a refrain in all of the interviews, as Marker asks whether exposing the cracks within socialism just adds grist to the mill of the adversary. Jorge Semprun responds that if anybody fuelled the anti-communist cause, it was those who ran the trials from the 1930s onwards. Filmed in fixed frame close-up to emphasise the importance of his words, London quotes Gramsci's statement that the truth is always revolutionary. He states the need for socialists themselves to analyse faults and problems within socialism, in order to restore to it a human face. Speaking more generally about the value of *L'Aveu*, Signoret (who plays Lise, London's wife) replies that if the film shakes up people's thinking, then it is doing some good. Marker's commentary takes this even further later on, when he affirms that *L'Aveu* is not simply a film: it is, above all, a political act, which aims to have an effect on reality.

The initial impact of the film confirms that it does indeed achieve this aim.

The end of *On vous parle de Prague* returns to the 1952 trial but is overlaid by a broadcast from Radio Prague in 1970, the year in which *L'Aveu* was released. The radio broadcast along with some newspapers repeat the accusations of the 1950s. In addition to this trial by media, London is stripped of his Czech nationality for the second time. Yet the repetition of history is paused at this point. The difference between the 1950s and the 1970s is that those who remained silent in the earlier decade now speak out in defence of London, whom they feel is being wrongly accused again and are now able to say so. The final image of the film is still: an aerial shot of a tank in a street with people at the roadside. The camera focuses in on the grainy figure of a man with a clenched fist raised in the air. This frozen temporal moment of defiance mimes the break in the exact repetition of a history of wrongs, and symbolises the delayed emergence of the truth that *On vous parle de Prague* is finally able to record.

Le Train en marche

Marker's next two films are not part of the *On vous parle* series. The first focuses on the early work of Russian director Alexander Medvedkin. On Marker's invitation, Medvedkin came to Paris in 1971 and this visit is the basis of *Le Train en marche* (1971). Described by Richard Roud as 'a little masterpiece' (Roud 1973: 83), *Le Train en marche* registers the importance of this filmmaker's work to SLON and the worker-filmmakers of Besançon and Sochaux, as well as to Marker. Marker first met Medvedkin in 1967 at the International Festival of Documentary Film in Leipzig. He had already seen Medvedkin's *Happiness* (1934) at a Soviet Cinema retrospective in Brussels, which he greatly admired. He thereby echoed Sergei Eisenstein's reaction some thirty years earlier, who had declared this film to be among the greatest of that period in Soviet film history. A long-standing friendship ensued after Marker's first encounter with Medvedkin, followed up most immediately by this trip to Paris in 1971, and by a subsequent exchange of letters. Their epistolary relationship lasted over twenty years until the Russian filmmaker's death in 1989, although Marker's *Le Tombeau d'Alexandre* (1993) extends this bond posthumously. Marker invited

Medvedkin to come and talk to the worker-filmmakers of Besançon and Sochaux about the extraordinary experiment of the 'film-train' in the 1930s. The film-train travelled the length and breadth of Russia; its crew met and filmed workers with a view to improving their productivity in line with revolutionary objectives. *Le Train en marche* has a lengthy introduction, with a female voice-over, which features photographs and archive footage, and brings together the subjects of train transportation and cinema in relation to the Russian revolution. The introductory section then gives way to the more specific focus on the film-train. This is narrated by a male voice-over, and is constructed principally around an interview with Medvedkin in a train depot in Noisy-le-Sec, just outside of Paris. Medvedkin explains the constitution and purpose of the film-train, along with the story of *Happiness*, which was inspired by its many journeys.

The opening section of *Le Train en marche* interweaves stillness and movement in an intricate manner both formally and thematically. Archive footage of trains in motion leads to contemplation of the Russian gaze, captured in photographic and film images, as Lenin's pronouncement on cinema being the most important art form is stated in voice-over. Footage of Lenin's immobile body in its coffin is accompanied by a commentary that registers a progression from looking to filming: 'D'abord le regard, ensuite le cinéma, qui est l'imprimerie du regard' (First the gaze, then cinema, which is the printing works of the gaze). The importance of using cinema to look at things in a superior manner to that permitted by the human eye is related to Dziga Vertov's 'kino-eye'. Transcending the earlier film images of his death, Lenin's voice echoes over other photographs of Russian people, many of whose gazes look piercingly into the camera. The Russian woman's gaze, which is animated in *Si j'avais quatre dromadaires* and which features as a static image in the generic introduction to the *On vous parle* series, appears a couple of times. This image and many of the other photographs that figure in this opening section are filmed in the dynamic manner to which we have become accustomed in Marker's approach to stasis in other films. Pioneering Russian filmmakers who are said to have seen and captured everything on camera in these early years feature in photographic images. We are introduced to Mikhail Kaufman, Vertov and Eisenstein, as well as to a young member of the Red Cavalry – Medvedkin – who is pictured in uniform. Several different photographs of Medvedkin feature in this first section, in contrast with his later appearance in the interview footage from 1971. This suggests that the photograph is associated with a certain past, which the motion of the film images necessarily builds on or contests. With the launch of the first five-year plan in 1928, the commentary announces hard times. The train system furnished the network that linked everything together in the first part of the twentieth century, and trains are said to have disseminated messages of the revolution and also, occasionally, to have brought cinema to the people. However, this is described as the filmmakers' cinema, brought down to the people from on high. Medvedkin's film-train was to bring to the people filmmaking of a different kind.

In accordance with the blend of stillness and movement encountered in the film's introduction, the ensuing interview with Medvedkin is filmed with a handheld camera with him mainly walking and talking in front of a motionless train in the Noisy-le-Sec depot. Occasionally, he speaks from a seated position in the doorway of one of the carriages. Pol Cèbe notes how Medvedkin talked non-stop during his week-long stay in France, and that Marker had to find a fourth interpreter to help the three who were already taking it in turns to keep pace with everything that the Russian director said (Cèbe 1971: 9). As Medvedkin explains in detail, the film-train was a collective endeavour, which involved thirty-two men. They had been given three old train wagons, which they converted to provide a laboratory, an editing room, an animation table and a small projection room, leaving one square metre of living space for each of the filmmaking team who would travel on the train for the next 294 days across Russia. It left Moscow for the first time on 25 January 1932 and met the country's disparate workforces. Its mission was to address problems with the revolution frontally by filming what the workers did and then screening this back to them *in situ*. It is easy to see why this would appeal to SLON and the worker-filmmakers of Besançon and Sochaux: filmmaking was thereby handed over to the people and the films could be signed by the workers themselves who were the real actors on both sides of the camera. Medvedkin details how they would place examples of good and bad practice alongside one another, which would provoke animated discussion among each workforce and serve as a corrective aimed at improvement. Whenever they encountered denial of bad or counter-productive work on the part of members of any workforce, Medvedkin explains that film served as an incontestable document to dispute this. Of the original film-train team, we are informed that only eight of them were still alive in 1971, as we are shown a photograph of the crew. The voice-over tells of Medvedkin's simple yet far-reaching idea at the centre of all this: he thought that seeing oneself or one's friends in a photograph was always an emotive event that could provide leverage for communal action. This is explained over a series of photographic images of groups of people posed before the camera.

Apart from a few photographs, many of which feature in this film, no images taken from the film-train's journeys remain. The testimony of Medvedkin, therefore, makes *Le Train en marche* a valuable document in itself. *Happiness*, which did however survive, was inspired by the journeys of the film-train: its fiction was based on observation of fact. As initial French reviews of this film confirm, the French release of *Happiness* was accompanied by *Le Train en marche*, which was described as an indispensable preface to Medvedkin's film. The story is based on a peasant who enters the collective work environment of the kolkhoz but is unhappy there. The film charts his quest for contentment and, after many failures, he eventually finds, through collective existence and assistance from various people, something that approximates a good enough idea of happiness. Brief extracts from *Happiness* are interspersed with Medvedkin's descriptions. The film-train, Medvedkin explains, nourished him with many ideas and he came to love the people he filmed. Picking up on this, the commentator remarks that it had a similar effect on other people, and mentions the Medvedkin groups: the film-train is said to be a valuable reminder to workers that cinema is a weapon for them, which teaches them how to look. This recalls Lenin's declaration that cinema is the most important of the arts, along with the female voice-over's words which focused attention on the gaze from the outset of the film. The effect of filming Medvedkin walking around a depot of immobile trains, and of seeing images related to the earlier era of his film-train alongside the setting of Noisy-le-Sec, is to bring together different temporalities and places. This is not to collapse the differences between them but to learn from what this past experience in another country can teach the present and give to the future.

As the film draws to a close, the voice-over states that it is as if the film-train had escaped its original place and time and become identified with everything that moves forwards. The film-train is dubbed the train of revolution and of history: the commentary declares that the biggest error is to think that it has stopped. These words are spoken over footage of the wheels of a train that spin fast on their axis as it travels along its tracks. Abruptly, the film then just cuts to black. The mythical train's movement is aligned with revolutionary progress towards the future, yet the photographs throughout the film preserve precious visual testimony of the film-train and complement Medvedkin's rich reminiscences. Located thus between motion and stasis, document and change, *Le Train en marche* – through the title's suggestion of a present tense – is poised between the past and the future. This particular film may end but the train rolls on.

Vive la baleine

In spite of the apparent contrast in subject of Marker's next film, *Vive la baleine* (1972) relates centrally to the highly politicised treatment of death and surviving that runs throughout this decade of filmmaking. Co-directed with Mario Ruspoli and produced by Argos Films, *Vive la baleine* is a hard-hitting, critical study of the history and current state of the global whaling industry at the time of filming. It features footage from Ruspoli's *Les Hommes de la baleine* of 1956 (for which Marker wrote the commentary, under the pseudonym of Jacopo Berenizi). As Lupton remarks, the later work is a 'sharply politicized re-take' on the earlier anthropological undertaking (Lupton 2005: 130). Marker's fascination with animals is apparent throughout his films, but this one in particular raises explicit ecological issues as they impact on a dying species. Additionally, though, it broadens out to include humanity beyond the mammals of the world's seas and oceans whose existence and disappearance it charts. At the start of the film, the voice-over of Louis Casamayor gives factual details about various species of whale and the traditional weapons used to kill them, all of which are pictured on annotated colour posters. The camera pans along them, as if taking visitors on a tour through the documentation of a marine centre. Audible in parallel to Casamayor's expository tone, or set off by particular terms that he uses and emerging through the gaps of his own discourse, is the more personal, reflective and interrogative voice of Valérie Mayoux, who laments the fact that some species are already extinct and others are disappearing fast.

(Roland Barthes gets an unlikely cameo mention here, since one of the whales is said to resemble him in a rhyme that involves his name.) Mayoux asks how humanity will see in the darkness without these and other beasts, once they have all gone. With these words she registers a concern for the human race in relation to other animals on the planet in a way that connects with Marker's most recent film to date, *Chats perchés*. For the most part, *Vive la baleine*'s worry for the future is articulated through still images of various kinds: black and white drawings, colour paintings, sepia and colour photographs, feature alongside posters, woodcuts and engravings. Moving image footage does however surface towards the end, as the entire filmic collage explores the question of survival.

Mayoux's voice is the only one we hear after the introductory section. A recurrent refrain, 'baleines, je vous aime' ('whales, I love you'), establishes her poetic narrative as a direct address to these creatures from the outset. The initial colour posters give way to drawings of ships and whales and then to photographs of Eskimos who began the trade of whale hunting. The Japanese also figure at this early point in the history of whaling through painted scenes, which show whales in pastel blue seas, partially covered by netting and impaled by several spears. In relation to the Dutch, another early whaling nation, we are told that the rich actually took painters with them on their ships to record the scenes as they happened. The camera adds mobility to the painted images it films. Although the range of static images used here broadens beyond the photographic dimension, the temporality of photography is connected to that of painting nonetheless through the commentary, as the painterly and other still images are said to survive the creatures they capture. Whereas the temporal link to death and eternity in photographic theory may be extended to lend immortality to the whales, the loss of the whales pictured in the individual images is read to signify the loss of the entire species. In a morbid reversal of the logic of solidarity that we have witnessed in the *On vous parle* series in the shift from the individual to the collective, here the loss of the individual whale pictured in an image, whether painted or photographed, gives way to a future vision of collective death.

At the end of the nineteenth century, nations across the globe were said to have whaling fleets whose size matched the country's relative power and status. America is singled out through its large share in this Empire of the seas (Hermann Melville is cited more positively for singing the praises of the whale), while Britain and France are also mentioned. Over shots of paintings linked by straight cuts and dissolves, Mayoux's voice-over tells of attack and slaughter, along with some heartrending attempts made by the whales to save themselves. Suddenly amidst the painted images, film footage of a whale's tail appears momentarily, thrashing out of the sea, accompanied by an eerie sound effect of its cry. This colour film footage serves further to vivify the slaughter that we have seen up until now mainly in paintings. In spite of a hunting ban imposed in 1962 by The International Whaling Commission, Japan and the USSR continued, saying that their industries depended on this trade. Over film footage of a whale in the water surrounded by blood, the voice-over comments that when all of the whales have disappeared, their industries will have to find other solutions. The graphic footage shows blood-red water as the life drains out of the whales, which are harpooned until they no longer move. Mayoux's voice-over reports that for centuries, humans and whales have occupied enemy camps and fought on the neutral ground of nature. In a cautionary tone she continues that the clash now occurs between those who defend themselves by defending nature and those who, in destroying nature, are also destroying themselves. She concludes: 'Cette fois les hommes et la baleine sont dans le même camp, et chaque baleine qui meurt nous lègue, comme une prophésie, l'image de notre propre mort.'[2] This worry for the future of the planet, which echoes across the film's final images of dead whales, reveals the spectre of humanity's own demise. The temporal future of these images, whether still or moving, is read as that of our own death. 'Long live the whale', the slogan of the film's title, thus extends to include a wish for the survival of the planet, the responsibility for which, as ever, lies in human hands.

On vous parle du Chili: ce que disait Allende

Two years after his previous contribution to the *On vous parle* series, Marker's final episode focuses on Chile and is the first of three films devoted to the political situation in this country in 1973. *On vous parle du Chili: ce que disait Allende* (1973) is number ten in the series. The film

2 'This time man and whale are in the same camp, and each whale that dies bequeaths us, like a prophecy, the image of our own death.'

is based on extracts of a conversation between the left-wing writer and militant, Régis Debray, and the then newly elected President of Chile, Salvador Allende. The extracts are taken from Chilean filmmaker Miguel Littin's *Compañero Presidente* (1971). Marker's edited version of this film focuses on key details of Allende's political project, as well as the reactionary forces that he came up against, which eventually took his life.

Debray explains in voice-over at the start that, in January 1971, he had just been released from prison in Bolivia. Allende had been President of Chile for four months when he and Debray met. From the outset, Allende's style of governance is marked out as different from other revolutionary struggles in Latin America: Debray emphasises that Allende privileged democratic electoral means over the armed route championed by Che Guevara. He adds that the two men knew and respected one another but that what he did not know at the time was that they would share the same assassin (*Le Fond de l'air est rouge* will re-label Allende's assassination a suicide). Delaying this event in Allende's case, however, the film cuts to his conversations with Debray. Allende shows him a book, which Che Guevara gave to him, with an affectionate dedication to Allende who he understood to be striving to achieve the same thing as him by other means.

Debray's and Allende's discussions are filmed in various locations. Allende explains that the struggle for economic independence and political freedom is the priority for Chile, through an anti-imperialist drive to nationalise the country's wealth. The backbone of this revolution and its motor force is the working class, and the goal is to create a national, democratic government of the people, which opens up a pathway to socialism. With the first mention of the workers and the masses, the film cuts to an aerial view of thousands of people gathered together and then focuses at a lower level on individual faces. Allende replies affirmatively to Debray's question of whether those who were yesterday's instruments of oppression (the judiciary, police and the armed forces) can be transformed into today's defenders of the oppressed. We see still images of soldiers and members of the public caught up together in demonstrations, all of which are cut to the strong rhythm of the soundtrack. These are followed by film footage of similar scenes, which is slowed in the latter half of the brief sequence. This sequence leads tellingly to the closing questions of the film, which address Allende's personal safety. Explaining that

COLLECTIVE ENDEAVOUR 97

his death is not a major preoccupation for him but that he does not wish to make it easy for someone to kill him, he eloquently reinforces his belief in collective life. He says that the bourgeoisie have made the individual the essential factor in a process that is actually social. Instead, he orients attention towards society and the masses. His conception is that the people will go on and that the loss of one man cannot stop things. The last images that we see are of him smartly dressed, meeting and greeting the military and walking among the people. The ability of the military to be turned so easily in the direction of the ruling powers haunts these final images in the light of impending events, even though they show Allende alive, well and engaged in his presidential duties.

Allende died in a violent *coup d'état* on 11 September 1973, which was backed by the CIA and led by General Augusto Pinochet who instated a cruel military dictatorship thereafter. By concluding with Allende's pragmatism about death, the film's images refuse to collude with the assassination that had already happened by the time it was made, as suggested by Debray's earlier allusions. This film harnesses the spirit of Allende's revolutionary politics, which reaches out to others beyond his death, and, by that token, proves far more difficult to kill.

L'Ambassade

Made in the same year as *On vous parle du Chili* and just prior to *La Solitude du chanteur de fond*, the subject of *L'Ambassade* suggests initially that this will be a direct reflection on the political situation in Chile after the horrific events of 11 September 1973. On screen at the outset, we are informed that this is a Super 8mm film found in an embassy. Lasting only twenty minutes, it focuses on the aftermath of a violent *coup d'état* and the arrival of political refugees in an embassy run by an ambassador and his wife. They welcome the refugees and give them shelter for a week, during which time we hear about what they have seen or suffered, and also witness how everyone occupies themselves in the confines of this besieged abode. Yet the assumed relationship to the Chilean context turns out to be allegorical at best. At the end of the film, the refugees leave in small groups to make their journeys into exile, and, after one group climbs into the back of a van, there is a shot of a city skyline in which the Eiffel Tower is clearly discernible. *L'Ambassade* thereby reveals itself to be a fiction staged as a documentary, since it confirms that the setting was Paris all along.

The people who enter the embassy are described in voice-over as left-wing militants whom the camera operator had seen at protests and meetings. They hid in a school first of all, but had to flee for fear of being caught and shot. Marco, a young student, led them to the embassy. The camera captures the anguish on peoples' faces, which only lifts every now and again. Everyone finds something to do: the ambassador vacuums and others play cards or chess, talk, help with the meals or read. The children brought their tortoises with them, which are said to fascinate the adults because they are the only living things that have been able to resist being crushed. In one of the rare views outside the embassy, a man is seen running towards it, but he is shot before he gets there. In another, military security buildings are visible from the embassy terrace: two floors are still lit. As news from the outside world gradually starts to filter through, the refugees hear that thousands of people have been rounded up in a stadium and that every evening there are executions (a further allusion to the Chilean context). When the television is restored, the new fascist rulers explain that their aim was to get rid of the 'Marxist cancer' in order to save the country. The commentary notes how this discourse rarely changes. The rulers impose a ban forthwith on all political parties and all unions, and they say that a new constitution is to be set. A fierce political debate erupts among the refugees after they see the television broadcast, which is said to reopen old wounds that had never truly healed. Prior to the departure of the refugees from the embassy, the commentator notes that his camera had started to annoy those whose suffering it filmed. It captures a woman through the crack of a door, who sits in the dim light of a bedside lamp, turns to the camera with a look of consternation, a bruised eye apparent, and raises her hand as if to discourage him from filming any further. Handheld and intrusive, while also a necessary witness among these refugees, the camera's place and that of its operator are negotiated explicitly from the outset.

The male voice-over commentary (spoken in French with a foreign accent) opens with a disclaimer: he explains that this is not a film but notes taken from day to day, and, instead of a commentary, his voice-over just supplies further notes made when he was not filming. He is demonstrating the capabilities of Super 8mm filming, and says that he would have been just as happy to have done this somewhere other than in an embassy with different subjects from these political refugees. This feigned arbitrariness of the subject matter of this film serves to emphasise the importance of its formal properties. Super 8mm film was used extensively within experimental cinema of the 1970s for financial and aesthetic reasons. This is Marker's first use of such film. The colour footage has a hazy quality in which everything appears a little uncertain, and the mobility of the handheld camera adds disorientation to this along with a sense of claustrophobia from filming within the embassy rooms. Although we see the refugees, albeit in this blurry and partial manner, our only contact with their experiences is through the cameraman's voice-over, which relates what they have been through. The footage is shot in silence, as if an eerie animation of photographic muteness: we cannot hear the refugees and are shut out from their experiences as if viewing them through misted, soundproof glass. At one point in the film, the commentator and camera focus on a man called Mike, a photographer, who is taking still images of this existence under siege. Since there is no photographic laboratory in the embassy, his images are said to remain 'en sursis, comme nous' (suspended, like us). The delayed development of the photographic image also speaks for the relation that this film bears to time. For Cyril Bhégin it is time, as well as the cinematic image, that trembles through the handheld camerawork of this film (Bhégin 2002: 165), as form and subject matter are tightly interwoven.

The terminology used to describe the suspended image is suggestive of a juridical suspended sentence. This connection is confirmed when the refugees are likened to prisoners by the commentator, as they talk of how things used to be: 'comme dans toutes les prisons, on s'imagine parler d'ailleurs en parlant d'avant' (as in all prisons, one imagines speaking of an elsewhere as one speaks of the past). Another time is figured here in terms of another place and this parallel is repeated later on. After listening to Jeanne, one of the refugees, who sings and plays the guitar, the commentator reports that, only a week ago, she was performing her songs to thousands of people. He says that this was the evening he understood that this would never happen again, and notes: 'Le passé, c'est comme l'étranger: ce n'est pas une question de distance, c'est le passage d'une frontière' (The past is like a foreign country: it is not a question of distance, but the crossing of a border). Marker takes up this quotation again in his book on Japan, *Le Dépays*, of 1982, as he photographs a cat in Tokyo, which reminds him of a cat he used to see in Paris, and he notes the appropriateness of having written such a sentence (Marker 1982: Section 1, n.p.). The quotation bears a similarity to L. P. Hartley's declaration in *The Go-Between* of 1952 ('The past is a foreign country; they do things differently there'). Yet the border crossing of which Marker speaks maps one time onto another, one place onto another, as well as time onto place. Where *La Jetée* privileged the merging of different times in the twist of its conclusion, *L'Ambassade* merges different places: Paris is the retrospective layer applied to the assumed Chilean focus of the preceding film. Suddenly, we are not where we thought we were, in temporal or geographical terms or in relation to fiction or documentary. Nonetheless, the fictive setting remains haunted by the chilling resonance with the historical facts of Chile. The fragile border between the here and there, the now and then, does not allow these events to be entirely cordoned off as something that only happens elsewhere and to others. It is presented as something that concerns everyone and that could indeed happen anywhere, albeit differently. The film hints at this early on as the commentator introduces a placid woman called Maria who smiles faintly and is described as the calmest of anyone there. He adds that this is the third time that she has found herself in this position in the three different countries in which she has lived.

The first and last images of the film are of white trails of a plane in the sky, viewed from the ground, seemingly static when seen from this angle, even though crossing borders and time zones at rapid speed in the air. The similarity between these images suggests circularity, repetition and stasis. Both space and time contract and overlay one another in the passage from Chile to Paris, then to now, history to fiction, as muted visual echoes from someone else's past sit as a suspended warning for everyone's future.

La Solitude du chanteur de fond

La Solitude du chanteur de fond was released in 1974 together with *Si j'avais quatre dromadaires*, and many of the initial reviews paired the two films because of this. In keeping with Marker's other films of the 1970s, *La Solitude du chanteur de fond* has a strong political backbone.

It focuses primarily on Yves Montand's rehearsals and preparations in the week leading up to his one-man show on 12 February 1974 at the Olympia Music Hall in Paris in aid of Chilean refugees. Through this observational documentary portrait of a popular entertainer in France, the link is retained to the political situation in Chile that informs the previous two films. Indeed, Montand's show is more than just a performance in which he takes on different guises for the range of songs that he sings: it is a record of how actions and gestures can speak as loudly as words in engaging an audience through music. Whereas in *Si j'avais quatre dromadaires*, the simplest of gestures – that of a gentle touch or caressing embrace – heralded the dawning of a new era of tenderness, here the performative gestures of one man's hands join with his words to communicate protest against injustice in song. This continues a fascination with hands and protest, already evident in *Cuba Si!* and also apparent in the photographs of Cuba in *Si j'avais quatre dromadaires*, thereby establishing a subtle connection to struggle, across Latin America in particular, that will be broadened out across the globe in *Le Fond de l'air est rouge* of 1977. In this film, however, what Lupton aptly terms 'the ballet of Montand's hands' (Lupton 2005: 136) is linked to carrying on the struggle through less bloody means.

La Solitude du chanteur de fond begins with an echo of the title of the English book and film from which its own title is adapted – *The Loneliness of the Long-Distance Runner*, by Alan Sillitoe, 1959 and Tony Richardson, 1962 respectively – as Montand is filmed in jogging gear running through the grounds of his estate in Auteuil. *Solitude* cuts between him exercising and his presence on the theatrical stage, before we see him in the rehearsal space in his home with his pianist Bob Castella. From this moment onwards, it moves between the rehearsal – in his private space as well as the Olympia – and the final performance. The montage lessens the temporal distance that separates the two, showing the run-throughs and the ultimate outcome alongside one another. Although the concert marks Montand's return to the stage after a six-year period of absence, there is never any sign of apprehension or lack of confidence on his part about making this theatrical come-back. Indeed, with his composure and sense of certainty, it is as if he has never been away. He gives detailed explanations of how he runs his performances, and he takes out his exacting brand of professionalism on his pianist in a row over the rhythm and melody of one song. He shares some candid views on politics, revolution, women (he says that on a number of points – his self-confessed male arrogance does not allow him to say all points – men do not measure up to women), as well as select autobiographical information (he speaks about his immigrant Italian family background and explains how he has always identified with the working classes).

Filmed with key members of the image-sound team who were involved in making *Le Joli Mai* – namely Pierre Lhomme and Antoine Bonfanti – *Solitude* also exploits the flexibility of using 16mm stock (which is blown up subsequently to 35mm) to capture Montand in action. Montand is heard intermittently in voice-over as well as through direct sound. The handheld camerawork focuses in close-up on his expressive gestures, which extend what he sings about and says. During the course of the film, he performs a full range of songs, some of which are jaunty and funny, while others are sensuous or have a politically serious tone. At an early point, he talks through the choices he is faced with when wanting to perform powerful and rich texts. He recites the words of one such text – a poem by Nazim Hikmet – at an oblique angle to the camera. He then explains in voice-over (while we still see him whisper the words) that he received it in a telegram while touring the USSR in 1956–57. At the mention of Russia, a sepia-coloured photographic image irises out to show him and Simone Signoret in Leningrad in 1956. The poem is concerned with the misery there is in the world and of how people are complicit in their own unhappiness, in that they allow themselves to be worked by the system. In the rehearsal space, he explains that he always has to make a decision between whispering and speaking this kind of text, because it is rather like moralising to people. The film cuts here to an image of a spotlight on stage and Montand is heard whispering the text. In the rehearsal space he makes a downward gesture with his arm as he sings of people being squeezed like grapes, and explains how this movement is instinctive, initially unplanned, but that once it happens it will always happen at that point. As far as he is concerned, this move signifies the difference between being inside the song, and experiencing it, rather than just performing it. Performing the song's sentiment thus through gesture, we see Montand do this on stage, before we focus again on his fist in the rehearsal space. He works with few props: a beret for a song about a bourgeois man called Monsieur Ducon, and a yellow hat for a song about planting coffee in the blazing heat. Montand's actions throughout are convincing and engaging: they involve the film viewer in what feels like a private concert. His emotions, captured in close-up, are palpably different in each song, and allow us to feel rather than just see and hear his performance: the passion that he communicates is real rather than a mere theatrical creation. The link between life, performance and politics is made in other ways throughout the film, both in relation to Montand himself and in connection to the Chilean refugee cause.

Interspersed with Montand's rehearsal and performance are extracts from films in which he has acted. Sepia footage of him on stage in America in the 1950s also features. Much of this earlier film and stage material is slowed without being stilled, and registers a different, almost dreamy time through its more languorous speed. More nightmarishly, though, and as a stark reminder of the reason for his one-man concert, the film features archive footage from Chile, before and after the military coup, which is also slowed down. Montand's past stage and film performances are thus presented in the same manner as the more recent history of Chile, and the formal parity thereby established between these other places and times chimes with the very combination of performance and protest that inspired the concert. The image of Victor Jara, the Chilean national singer, is particularly poignant in this respect: a female voice-over explains how he was arrested, tortured and then shot. Jara's melancholic song serves as a grim counterpoint to Montand's zestfulness, and the Chilean context associates itself with some sobering reflections on Montand's part with regard to politics and change. The rehearsal and the show itself reveal how he lives the varied songs through his body as much as his voice, and his heartfelt horror at the events in Chile is registered unequivocally in voice-over. What he also notes towards the end of the film, however, is a sense of disillusionment in political transformation. Over images of his performance on stage, he comments on how impotent one can feel because so many terrible things are happening all over the world. Yet, paraphrasing words of Scott Fitzgerald, he explains how it is important to understand that things are hopeless but to still want to change them. He says that even if you realise that everything you have believed in for years suddenly turns out to be utopian or impossible, it is important nonetheless to keep making sparks here and there. Montand's concert can be seen as one such spark made in the darkness of the Olympia stage – his performance a physical manifestation of his ongoing belief in the possibility of future change, all the more valuable because it is born of generosity in spite of disenchantment.

The final film of this era reflects on the historical events that feature in Marker's work, and in the world beyond, between 1967 and 1977. It is both an immense stocktaking exercise and a reflection on the continuing possibilities for revolution.

Le Fond de l'air est rouge: scènes de la troisième guerre mondiale 1967–1977

First released in 1977, with a running time of 240 minutes, *Le Fond de l'air est rouge* is a breathtaking montage film which takes a long look back at ten years of political revolution across the globe. The film exists in several different forms; this reading will focus on the shortened three-hour 1993 version, but will consider it within its initial context. (There is an English-language version: *A Grin without a Cat*. While the English title invokes Lewis Carroll's Cheshire cat, the French is a wordplay, which translates very approximately as 'there's red in the air'.) Simone Signoret's voice is heard at the start over excerpts from Eisenstein's *Battleship Potemkin*, which correspond to the parts of it that she remembers. Images from *Potemkin* are then interspersed within the opening credit sequence (accompanied by Luciano Berio's rousing title music), juxtaposed with footage from diverse protests and clashes. The opening culminates with an image of a female interpreter being interviewed on the Odessa steps in Russia, the location of one of the most famous scenes of Eisenstein's fiction. The reference to this film, which recurs throughout, traces the roots of subsequent revolutionary activity back to the Soviet Union in 1917. Additionally, the juxtapositions by which *Le Fond* will advance, although not always as jarring as Eisenstein's theory of montage in the 1920s, provoke thought in a manner not too dissimilar to the shock tactic combinations of the Soviet master. Marker's aim was to reinstate history's polyphony, not through gratuitous rapprochements nor malicious exposure of people's contradictions but by creating space for an additional voice beyond those we hear. In the introduction to the published script, he writes:

Chaque pas de ce dialogue imaginaire vise à créer une troisième voix produite par la rencontre des deux premières et distincte d'elles ... Après tout, c'est peut-être bien ça la dialectique? Je ne me vante pas d'avoir réussi un film dialectique. Mais j'ai essayé pour une fois (ayant en mon temps passablement abusé de l'exercice du pouvoir par le commentaire-dirigeant) de rendre au spectateur, par le montage, 'son' commentaire, c'est-à-dire son pouvoir[3] (Marker 1978: 7).

This empowered third voice that Marker wishes to enable will emerge from a frequently painful confrontation with what he refers to in the film's subtitle as 'scenes of the Third World War'. The colour of the revolution is connected viscerally to that of blood, and the association with death runs throughout. However, while it charts disillusionment, along with the fatal fault lines that caused the political left ultimately to founder in these years, *Le Fond* also registers how the revolutionary spirit lives on – in material, rather than ethereal, form.

The first part of the film, 'Les Mains Fragiles' (Fragile Hands), is subdivided into two sections: the first runs from the Vietnam war to the execution of Che Guevara in Bolivia in 1967 and the second focuses on the events of May 1968. The second part of the film 'Les Mains Coupées' (Severed Hands) comprises sections three and four. The third section is centered on the Prague Spring in 1968, and the fourth is introduced with an open-ended question, 'Du Chili à ... quoi, au fait?' (From Chile to ... what, in fact?), which asks where the events in Chile 1973 lead or leave us. The symbolism of hands that we have traced visually through several of Marker's films of revolution, from *Cuba Si!* onwards, is also central to *Le Fond*. Some of the film footage embodies in its form the frailty that the first part takes as its title. Trembling hands introduce the first images of the second section, as we see sepia footage of the streets of May 1968 interspersed with white writing on a black background, which asks: 'Pourquoi / (why) quelquefois / (sometimes) les images / (do images) se mettent-elles / (begin) à trembler (to tremble)?' Marker announces that this happened to him in Paris 1968 on Boulevard St Michel. Similar shaky images

---

3 'Each step of this imaginary dialogue aims to create a third voice produced by the encounter of the first two and distinct from them ... After all, perhaps that is dialectics? I am not boasting that I have succeeded in making a dialectical film. But I have tried for once (having in my time frequently abused the power of the directive commentary) to give back to the spectator, through the montage, "his" commentary, that is, his power.'

from Prague in 1968 follow this as the film records the nervousness of the operator, who cannot hold the camera steady. The title of the first part of *Le Fond* – 'Les Mains Fragiles' – comes from a French banner that we see at the close of the first section, and which refers to how the workers will take up the flag of struggle from the fragile hands of the students. The film broadens out this French reference to May 1968, however, and it is human fragility of a different kind that we see at the outset, through an encounter with imperialist power in images that are difficult to watch.

The first archive footage is of an American fighter pilot flying his plane, talking to the camera and explaining excitedly how we will see bombs and napalm on this particular flight. After the strike, he describes it as an outstanding target, as the Vietnamese people who are still able to move run for their lives. The pilot continues to talk, and we hear him state in voice-over that he would like to go in with the army on the ground to see just how effective these air strikes are. This is said over footage of victims of such an air raid – we see disfigured faces, bodies clinging to life because flesh is burnt through to the bone, and a woman who is missing the lower part of both legs. Later in this first section, footage of US anti-war protests from *La Sixième Face du Pentagone* is juxtaposed with other US groups who support the bombing of Hanoi. In a subsequent interview, Paul Vergès (Secretary General of the Reunion Communist Party), explains that Vietnam unites masses across the world, and points out that one population has never been placed by history in such a position of convergence of all global contradictions. Such visual juxtapositions, which variously echo, reinforce or undermine one another, give the measure of just some of the ways in which the disjunctions of *Le Fond* will give voice to the polyphony of history.

Through montage later in the first part of the film, a US military soldier, Major Shilton, is shown to agree tacitly with the Secretary General of the Communist Party in Bolivia. Both explain from their radically different ideological positions that the biggest error of the guerrilla war in Bolivia was for Che Guevara not to have obtained the agreement of the communist party when he arrived there. At the beginning of the second part, the repetitions and missed opportunities of history are brought out through Marker's dexterous editing. French and Soviet newsreel footage of Prague in the Second World War is placed together as the city is described as one of the first victims of Hitler, and then liberated by Soviet tanks. Further newsreel footage of Soviet tanks entering the streets of Prague registers the occupation of 1968. The film records the opportunity Castro had to break with the USSR as a result of the occupation, along with his failure to do so. It accompanies his contorted speech about the situation in Czechoslovakia, which he gave in Havana on 23 August with a discordant soundtrack. A later humorous montage focuses on Castro's habit of bending microphones during his speeches: it is a line of Soviet microphones that refuses to move, in contrast to all the other sets. These montage sequences, like many others, allow the images and their direct sound or musical soundtrack to speak for themselves. Yet the voices of the commentary that interject occasionally are a significant, eloquent presence in taking stock of what they and we see.

Signoret's voice refers to Vietnam and confesses that she did not realise at the time that this war could be for the Americans what Indochina was for 'nous' (us). This reference reveals how, on a number of counts, the film deals with the experience of a particular generation. In a roundtable discussion of *Le Fond* for *Cahiers du cinéma* shortly after its release, Jean-Paul Fargier says that he finds this a very personal film, and that the 'nous' used in the commentary is recognition of the fact that Marker felt close to the people who accompanied him through these years – those we hear on the soundtrack (Fargier 1978: 47). In addition to Signoret, the published commentary lists the voices of Marker, Sandra Scarnati, Jorge Semprun, Yves Montand, François Maspero, Davos Hanich, François Périer and Laurence Cuvillier, many of whom are familiar from other Marker films. The personalised element of *Le Fond* also accounts for some other criticisms it received upon release. It takes stock of a wealth of events around the globe, but for some critics, in spite of the range of events featured, *Le Fond* was not quite representative enough: Palestine, Cambodia and Angola in particular are singled out as notable omissions (see Fargier 1978). Accurate though these observations are, this objection registers the difficulty of assembling an all-inclusive film. The focus of *Le Fond* reveals an admittedly partial take on the ten-year history of revolutionary struggle, since it is filtered through Marker's perception. The broad span of revolution across various geographical spaces is, however, apparent in the focus on 1968.

The struggles of the students and the workers in France 1968 are placed side by side, and interwoven, even though their solidarity sometimes ruptured – we hear of students who ran away when required to fight. The barricades and uprooted paving stones of Paris feature with an accompanying soundtrack of mixed reactions to the protests. Concerned to broaden out the focus on 1968 across the world, the film includes footage from cities where there was similar unrest, although in Japan in particular the authorities are said not to have vacillated: we see violent repressions of the masses at this point. The film cuts from Paris to Italy, India and Ireland, where protesters are seen throwing things at the forces of law and order. Here and elsewhere, the problematic reduction of all struggles to the same one is avoided through respect for their specificity: it is a sense of solidarity rather than an ahistorical sameness that unites them across their geo-political differences. By this point in Marker's filmic oeuvre, even through the eclipse of his overt signatory presence during the SLON/ISKRA years, we have become accustomed to the non-linear progression of historical time within his work. *Le Fond* emphasises this concern with temporality in particular, as it doubles back on events, and shows their ripples across different geographical spaces as the film rolls on through montage. Stasis does feature, however, and is associated explicitly with the representation of death. Archive film footage of a student protester's funeral – Gilles Tautin, killed by the Paris police on 10 June 1968 – appears prior to photographic images taken from a *Ciné-Tract* of his funeral on 15 June. Masses of the population turn out with images of Tautin on posters; the *Ciné-Tract* images show views of a coffin, fists, raised hands and people in tears. The commemorative pause does not slow the pace of the editing and the still images are approached in keeping with the other footage, as the film spirals downwards towards the political disappointments that characterise the end of this era. Over images of the public vilification of Jean Vilar, Signoret's voice remarks that it is a strange continuation of the spirit of 1968 to despair of things so quickly. The recourse to still images to represent Tautin's funeral links, however, to other moments when death is an explicit subject.

At the end of the third section of *Le Fond*, midway through 'Les Mains Coupées', colour footage of the streets of Prague on 25 January 1969 features in which everyone and everything has come to a halt. Although this is moving image footage, it films silence and stillness. As the people of Prague come to life again, we see a monument with candles and a photograph, too distant to see its subject, but this commemoration is confirmed subsequently as being for Jan Palach, the Czech man who set light to himself in protest against the occupation of Czechoslovakia by Soviet forces. In voice-over, a young woman explains that he did this courageously for everyone and that it was not an act of suicide. The film then cuts to an interview with her in the street: she says that everyone there feels guilty now that they did not do more at an earlier time. She labels the procession 'le cortège de la culpabilité' (the cortege of guilt). For critic Laurent Roth, reviewing the 1993 re-release, both the form and subjects of the image at this point use stillness to mark time and reflect on the contradictions and crimes upon which historical temporal progression has depended (Roth 1996: 16). The film does not pause to reflect on death when it returns as a subject later on but animates the stillness with which it is associated, refusing to let its grip take hold.

Among the selection of archive material in *Le Fond*, Marker intersperses relevant footage from his productions of the late 1960s and early 1970s. He also includes extracts from earlier films, most notably *Cuba Si!* and *Olympia 52*, which are revisited in this different context. This recontextualisation and re-examination of history through film speaks for the broader trajectory of *Le Fond*. It is the subject of the Olympics that reintroduces the spectre of death. Marker returns to *Olympia 52* after footage of an interview with Emil Zátopek in the context of the Soviet invasion and occupation of Czechoslovakia in 1968 in the second half of the film. Over images of the crowds cheering and Zátopek lapping the Olympic stadium, Marker speaks in voice-over and says how the games were a breath of fresh air, an island of peace, in the Cold War. He notes that in following the show jumping of the Chilean team, he thought he was just filming a horse rider: this man by the name of Mendoza would become one of Pinochet's junta. He states: 'On ne sait jamais ce qu'on filme' (One never knows what one films). *Le Fond* then moves back first to the Munich Olympics of 1972 and the murder of the Israeli hostages in the midst of the games; it turns subsequently to Mexico in 1968 where Marker says he saw two hundred people massacred prior to the start of the games. The film cuts to Mexican papier-mâché statues of skeletons on stands in a gallery space at this point, filmed at close proximity and accompanied by discordant sounds. One statue carries the Olympic flame, another holds a discus, two are entwined, seemingly wrestling with one another, and disparate other representations of the games are shot in fast-paced dynamic fashion, which animates these otherwise static figures, who entwine sporting Olympic activity with death. *Le Fond* does not deny these and other morbid links. It does seek, however, to drive forwards, to reanimate and ultimately to avoid closure on the stasis with which death is conventionally associated.

When Beatriz Allende, Salvador Allende's daughter, addresses the Cuban masses from a lectern in Havana in September 1973, to tell them what happened in the Chilean presidential palace on 11 September, she terms Cuba a brother country. She thereby picks up on a thread that runs from the opening citation of *Potemkin* throughout the film: 'Frères!' (Brothers). *Le Fond* returns to one of its points of departure with this word, as fraternal solidarity is again evoked in conclusion. Interspersed with her speech are two intertitles, though: the first announces that she will commit suicide on 13 October 1977, and the second says that this is what her father did four years earlier. Aware that the cost of revolution is death, but refusing to let it have the final word in this sequence, we see archive footage of Allende in a parade, in slow motion, and hear him in voice-over. *Le Fond* depicts him still alive (as with the episode from the *On vous parle* series devoted to him), rather than dwelling on the intertitle that announces his death.

The 1993 voice-over asks us to imagine that the person who put together this montage of images returns to them after an interval of fifteen years. It explains that he could meditate on the historical changes just by looking at the words that would have made no sense to the people of the 1960s: ayatollah, perestroika, AIDS and the boat people are listed as some examples. The voice-over registers the collapse of communism, and capitalism is said to have won a battle, if not the war. *Le Fond* draws to a close with images of death, yet the commentary still marks a clear note of defiance. It shows wolves being shot from a helicopter, both as a demonstration of firepower and an attempt to limit their number. The commentary confirms that, fifteen years later, some wolves still survive. The implied relation between human revolutionaries and these luckless beasts harks back to an earlier link to cats and children, who were among the first victims of mercury poisoning in Minamata, Japan, caused by chemical discharges by the Chisso Corporation into the water. However, the death of the sailor in *Potemkin*, which began *Le Fond*, and the deaths of the wolves in conclusion serve to mark out that the revolution is not dead. This may be of little consolation to those who suffered the multiple losses and disappointments of these years. Similarly, it cannot bring back the wolves that have been slaughtered. But in affirming that the struggle continues beyond these deaths, albeit in different forms, it suggests that they did not all occur in vain. The loss of revolutionary romanticism is something to which *Sans Soleil* will return. For the time being, this film declares that there is still a hint of red in the air, as palpable as the grin of Lewis Carroll's capricious cat.

References

Béghin, Cyril (2002), 'Des images en sursis: *L'Ambassade* de Chris Marker', in Philippe Dubois (ed.), *Théorème 6: recherches sur Chris Marker*, Paris, Presses Sorbonne Nouvelle, pp. 159–65.

Cèbe, Pol (1971), 'Rencontre avec Medvedkine', in *L'Avant-Scène cinéma*, 120 (December), p. 9.

Fargier, Jean-Paul, Thérèse Giraud, Serge le Péron and Jean Narboni (1978), 'Table ronde sur *Le Fond de l'air est rouge*', in *Cahiers du cinéma*, 284 (January), pp. 46–51.

Hennebelle, Guy (1973), 'Brève rencontre avec le groupe SLON', in *Écran*, 73: 13 (March), pp. 36–38.

Lee, Min (2003), 'Red Skies: Joining Forces with the Militant Collective Slon', in *Film Comment* (July–August), pp. 38–41.

Lupton, Catherine (2005), *Chris Marker: Memories of the Future*, London, Reaktion.

Marker, Chris (1968) 'Interview with Chris Marker', in *Image et son*, 213 (February), pp. 66–69.

Marker, Chris (1978), *Le Fond de l'air est rouge: scènes de la troisième guerre mondiale 1967–1977* (textes et description d'un film de Chris Marker), Paris, François Maspero.

Marker, Chris (1982), *Le Dépays*, Paris, Éditions Herscher.

Marker, Chris (2006), 'Pour Mario', in *Les Groupes Medvedkine: le film est une arme*, Paris, ISKRA, pp. 11–19.

Mayoux, Valérie (1997), 'Témoignages: Valérie Mayoux, monteuse', in *Positif*, Dossier Chris Marker, 433 (March), pp. 93–95.

Roth, Laurent (1996), 'Rouge vertige', in *Cahiers du cinéma*, 502 (May), p. 16.

Roud, Richard (1973), 'SLON: Marker and Medvedkin', in *Sight and Sound*, 42: 2 (Spring), pp. 82–83.

4

Continuity and change: the 1980s

Marker's filmmaking of the 1980s is prefaced in 1978 by his first foray into installation work. The two-screen *Quand le siècle a pris forme* (1978) passes images of the First World War and the Russian Revolution through a synthesiser, and thus presages some of the effects that his subsequent films will also deploy. The new computer technology opens windows onto new image worlds, which are explored in different ways in *Sans Soleil* (1982), *2084* (1984), and *L'Héritage de la chouette* (1989). Additionally, the latter, a television series, constitutes Marker's first sustained use of video in his filmmaking. Yet these, and especially the other films of this period (*Junkopia* (1981), *AK* (1985), and *Mémoires pour Simone* (1986)), retain their connection to earlier media technologies. Marker's work of the 1980s is located thus between continuity and change.

Junkopia

Marker filmed *Junkopia* (1981) with two colleagues – Frank Simeone and John Chapman – while in San Francisco in July 1981, shooting for *Sans Soleil*. The film comprises a collage of images and a distinctive soundtrack with no commentary. It won a César for Best Documentary Short in 1983. Barely six minutes in length, *Junkopia* focuses on sculptures made from driftwood and other disparate objects that the Pacific tide has washed onto the shore of Emeryville Beach. This geographical place is presented in rather less conventional terms, however, at the outset. Intertitles register a position of latitude 37° 45´ north and longitude 122° 27´ west without specifying that this refers to somewhere in San Francisco. Indeed, the title of the film and location of shooting (although aural and visual confirmation does appear in the second half) are provided only in the closing credits. The delayed identification of the place by its name keeps us guessing where we are, and this questioning of precise location is also a function of this film's form. Latitude and longitude are angles that uniquely designate points on a sphere: when combined, the co-ordinates pinpoint any place on the planet. In keeping with such exactitude, *Junkopia* consists of a succession of fixed frame shots, filmed from a variety of positions by a static camera from very precise angles.

A montage of shots builds up a fragmented vision of a coastal no-man's land for the first three minutes of the film's running time and suggests that this space, with its creative use of junk made in imitation of familiar objects and life forms from our planet, exists in isolation. It begins and ends at high tide. In the opening long shot, objects are seen floating centre-frame off the coast. Upon a closer view, it is possible to make out a model red plane suspended on a wooden pole, another pole alongside it and a small white ship. The otherworldliness of the soundtrack features some recognisable noises: a ship's foghorn, seagulls, creaking wood, breaking glass and a human voice can be made out at times. On land, and in the creeks separated by grassy banks at low tide, a range of objects is visible: a train, a bicycle, a painted lady, a space ship, animals and even a brightly painted fish. The only signs of life beyond this in the first half of the film are vegetation and birds.

The angles from which these objects have been viewed then shift significantly, if only by a few degrees, to give a different perspective in the latter half of the film. This reveals proximity to a more identifiably human world, although strangely untouchable and distant, which speeds by indifferently in motor vehicles, or is there as an implied presence in far-off high-rise buildings. Moving traffic is reflected in water, before some of the objects from the first half of the film are seen again. This time, though, elements of this wider world feature in the frame. A mixture of radio broadcasts can be heard over an image of a suspension bridge, faintly visible in the distance, and the location is designated aurally and visually at this point. A hazy shot of San Francisco appears before the images return finally to the white ship and red plane of the opening shots, which reveal the city skyline in the background this time.

This film takes us closer to the structures of 'junkopia' than to the surrounding world, as this liminal, watery space registers the passage of time and tide to which the human world, although oblivious here in its sturdy substantiality, is also subject. The passage of time and its effects on this place are not, however, registered through the succession of images. *Junkopia* ends at high tide with an image of the same objects with which it began, suggesting the cyclical flow of the tides, yet there is no indication that the first and last images were filmed in sequence. The light remains the same neutral tone throughout, suggestive of simultaneity rather than temporal succession. The form of the film is more interested in points of view on this strange world than in recording processes of transformation, evolution or decay. The static positions and varied angles that the camera adopts suspend this documentary short between photography and film: *Junkopia* is located formally between the image of stasis and duration, with a crucial emphasis on the precision of placement from the outset. Viewed first of all as a distinct space and then in relation to San Francisco, the location of this place on the planet overrides concerns with temporality. *Sans Soleil* will develop this concern with place and time but will reverse the priority in favour of time in dazzling ways.

Sans Soleil

Hailed as Marker's masterpiece, and also taken to be the quintessential essay film, *Sans Soleil* (1982) continues to attract the degree of critical attention that *La Jetée* also enjoys. This shared acclaim is fitting, since the later film relates intimately to the concerns with time that were already apparent in *La Jetée* twenty years earlier and extends them in important ways. The 2003 release of both films (in the French and English versions) on the same DVD under the Arte label secures the bond between them. *Sans Soleil* privileges the use of 35mm film footage, rather than photographs, but frozen film images and stills are interspersed occasionally throughout. As with *La Jetée*, our main protagonist is male: an imaginary cameraman by the name of Sandor Krasna who has travelled around the globe filming for the past twenty years. The celluloid fruits of his travel encounters are what we see. This is a film that takes stock of the passing of time over these decades, and, in one respect, *Sans Soleil* stands as a filmic montage equivalent of the survey of collected photographs in *Si j'avais quatre dromadaires*. From *Sans Soleil*'s epigraph onwards (taken from Racine's 'Seconde préface à Bajazet' in the French version and T. S. Eliot's 'Ash-Wednesday' in English), a concern with time is promoted over space and place. Our cameraman moves through a range of different places on his travels towards the impossible dream of being able to journey outside of time. Filming is the means of striving for this aim. Although, like the protagonist of *La Jetée*, Krasna is caught within the web of time and brought up against the inevitability of death, he finds through film a way of challenging the end that death usually represents. *Sans Soleil* expands the notion of what it means to 'film': it becomes the spreading of a fine enveloping and impressionable membrane over the surfaces of whatever and whomever the camera encounters. The fabrication of what amounts to a second skin through the act of filming causes even the impermanent and the immaterial to materialise. Marker's gloss on the film in English is the 'Dreams of the Human Race'. *Sans Soleil* brings us into contact with the ethereal realm of sleep from which its images are said to emerge, and to which they necessarily return in the end, as Krasna fashions himself in celluloid in order to breach the ultimate limit of an individual human lifetime.

Krasna has written a series of letters on his travels to a woman who becomes the film's narrator – Florence Delay (in the French language version), Alexandra Stewart (in English) (German and Japanese versions are also in existence, for which the narrators are Charlotte Kerr and Riyoko Ikeda respectively). She reads the letters out by way of a commentary, which reflects both obliquely and directly on the images we see. The narrator is not given an assumed name, a tactic that establishes the voice as that of documentary commentator, even though her gender and the letter-based style breaks up the expository, authoritative aspects of this somewhat. (Stella Bruzzi has written eloquently on the female voice of this film (Bruzzi 2000: 57–65)). Extracts of other filmmakers' work feature throughout (for example, Alfred Hitchcock, Danièle Tessier, Haroun Tazieff), as do some of Krasna's film images that have been altered synthetically by a Japanese friend of his, Hayao Yamaneko. In addition to the commentary, diegetic and non-diegetic sound contribute to the contrapuntal texture, through radio and television broadcasts, recorded music, unaccompanied voices and music altered synthetically (the sound is attributed to Michel Krasna who along with Sandor Krasna and Hayao Yamaneko constitute a trio of alter egos for Marker). The film comprises footage from Japan, Okinawa, Africa (namely Guinea-Bissau), the Cape Verde Islands, Iceland, San Francisco and France, mainly from the 1960s through to the 1980s. Fascinated by islands along with mainland coastal areas, one of the only landlocked places that features here is the Île-de-France, the departmental area that includes and surrounds Paris. With no land-based geographical links to other countries, the watery shores isolate these islands; but a filmic continuum indebted to Soviet montage theory and a series of graphic matches, along with other visual and aural correspondences, creates a sense of continuity across the globe. The formal strategies of this film are set up early on, one of the most important principles being the avoidance of a contrastive technique, as it charts the extremes of the desert and the post-industrial cityscape without privileging one over the other. Krasna, through the narrator, states: 'Mon perpétuel va-et-vient n'est pas une recherche de contrastes, c'est un voyage aux deux pôles extrêmes de la survie.'[1] Marker's editing in *Sans Soleil* functions as a bridge that joins one land to another and also juxtaposes different times.

To return momentarily to comments made by Pierre Lhomme with regard to *Le Joli Mai*, one of the drawbacks of filming with 35mm stock in the 1960s, in his view, was the technical lack of connection to sound. He remarks that with 35mm, at that time, one was concerned with an image above all else (Lhomme 1964: 38–43). In spite of some eruptions of diegetic sound from within the images of *Sans Soleil*, the image track proceeds at one remove from what we hear and thereby disjoins us slightly from what we see. Krasna's description of watching a young Takenoko dancer perform in Tokyo could readily apply to the experience of watching *Sans Soleil*: he speaks of an invisible aquarium wall which separates him from the scene he observes and which seems to take place in a parallel time sphere. Observation in the present thus takes on the qualities of looking at a different time, and the film stock apparently enables the kind of separation of the image that Lhomme bemoaned in the 1960s. It is significant that the first image of the film (of three young girls on a road in Iceland)

[1] 'My constant comings and goings are not a search for contrasts. They are a journey to the two extreme poles of survival.' (All translations come from the English-language version of the film.)

was taken in 1965, since the 1960s is a key point of return on more than merely formal grounds. Through its glances back to this era, Catherine Russell terms *Sans Soleil* melancholic for a historical period of militancy that no longer exists (Russell 1999: 303). This film of loss is, however, one of reinvention too, as it looks backwards in order to move forwards in a different way.

Political struggles of the 1960s in Japan, in which peasants defended their land against the construction of an airport in Narita, are juxtaposed with similar footage of the present, which records the fact that the airport was built in spite of their actions. At a later point, the film dwells on the historical and political underpinnings of the failed attempt to unite Guinea-Bissau and the Cape Verde Islands. Krasna charts the revolutionary struggle from its beginnings in 1959, in which Amilcar Cabral, leader of the PAIGC (a joint party uniting both countries), led guerrilla warfare against the Portuguese in the fight for independence. This is followed up by news of his assassination in 1973 by members of his own party and his being replaced by his half-brother Luis. Footage of a political ceremony in February 1980 concludes this episode, in which the man who was to overthrow Luis the following year, João 'Nino' Vieira, is pictured in tears because, the commentary reports, he has not been raised high enough above his fellow men. We are told that behind each of the faces we see lies a memory, but that rather than form a collective memory these remain individual and fragmented in relation to the shared historical experience. Such individualism runs counter to the thrust of Marker's revolutionary films of the 1960s and 1970s, in which the emphasis was on the collective and on solidarity with others. In both of the aforementioned cases, *Sans Soleil* attempts to intervene in the historical occurrences to change something: through synthesising images of the past in Narita, it aims to move beyond the stasis of images that do not change in the present. It also contributes to the attempted reconciliation of Guinea-Bissau and Cape Verde early on by screening images of Bissau accompanied by Cape Verde music. Yet these efforts alone cannot alter the passage of time or the historical events (*Level 5* will engage with this dilemma again through the historical tragedy of Okinawa, which also features in *Sans Soleil*). In the face of a loss of revolutionary connection to others, *Sans Soleil* does, however, offer a post-revolutionary vision of connectedness, centred on the figure of Krasna and his relation to what he films.

In Guinea-Bissau, in Cape Verde, in Japan, Krasna films people's faces, particularly those of women who either look back at him or attempt to avoid his gaze. In the first instance, our cameraman is a voyeur, an uninvited observer who steals images and passes over the surface of the people he encounters without even attempting to know them in any more detail. This is not a painstaking ethnography and his contact with others seems fleetingly possessive rather than generous: this is about Krasna, his journeys, his memories and his revisiting of history. On a superficial level, this is his film and no one else's – a mere variant of the individualism discussed above. Similarly, a fascination with the exotic and the erotic makes him just another belated Orientalist, unapologetic about his desiring gaze, the origins of which he otherwise wishes to disguise. The French-, English- and German-language versions of the film place Krasna differently in that his points of reference are French in the first (a Platini goal, La Samaritaine), American in the second (a Dodgers pennant, Macy's), and German in the third (a Rummenigge goal, Karstadt). With his reference points, Krasna is positioned as Euro-American in spite of the fact that he never defines himself explicitly, and this runs the risk of concealing a biased perspective and a potentially neo-colonialist or imperialist stance. The legacy of Euro-American dominance is inscribed in his cultural markers, but he refuses to explore his position, geopolitical or otherwise, beyond this. Kaja Silverman argues that *Sans Soleil* is penetrated by other people's memories to the extent that it remembers in the voice of the other and encourages spectators to do the same (Silverman 1996: 186–93). In view of Krasna's implicit geopolitical position, there is a risk that such an act of remembering may also re-colonise a space that is not his own. Yet the film does build more positive fundamental links to others, nonetheless. These relations extend beyond humans to animals and places. Krasna relates to and connects the human and the non-human, the animate and the inanimate in the same way. Consequently, even the main cityscape of the film, which is Tokyo, is brought to life.

Tokyo constitutes the principal place of return for the traveller who confesses to having never known the simple joys of going home to a country or a family. He relates that the twelve million inhabitants provide him with this on one of his journeys to the city. When he does not understand what he sees around him or on television, this heightens his enjoyment. We see the television screen and the programmes that he watches in Japan, the majority of which are screened as still images. As a space of adopted homecoming and anonymous encounter, the foreign city furnishes a home, but one that actually turns out to be illusory. The cityscape is fleshed out before it becomes a stage for the fabrication of memories and dreams, a place of life and substance, and also the locus of access to the insubstantial. Krasna's return to Tokyo is narrated over images of the city's motorways, which in terms of visuals and the electronic sound effects hark back to Andrei Tarkovsky's filming of this city in *Solaris* (1972). Further on in the same sequence in *Sans Soleil*, Tokyo is described as criss-crossed by trains, tied together with electric wires and showing her veins. The formal grammatical convention by which pronouns that refer to the city gender it feminine is made more substantial here, as the trains and wires that circulate become the blood stream of a woman's body. A different *Solaris* is also relevant to this discussion: that of Steven Soderbergh, of 2002, who makes the love story between Chris Kelvin and Rheya (not Hari, as in the Tarkovsky original) the modified sole focus of the film. Rheya's non-human reincarnation recalls the memories of her lifetime double, now dead, but she is unable to remember the experiences that generated them. Her body did not live the past that her head remembers and which she sees in her mind's eye in flashback. This visual contact with a memory cut off from its point of origin in experience is something that links to Krasna, since images, for him, take the form of his memories, which come to matter through celluloid and its myriad distortions.

In a sequence of the film that proceeds by way of straight cuts from the Island of Sal (part of the Cape Verde group), spliced with cityscape images, to the Île-de-France, to Tokyo, we move almost imperceptibly between desolate, arid landscape, lush green watery undergrowth and densely populated city spaces. This is an indicator of the formal moves by which one area is related to another throughout the film. Furthermore, these images are described by the commentary in a particular way with reference to Krasna's memory. Time dilates and space is diminished as the film refers back to the place where Krasna is at the time of writing this particular letter. In straightforward terms, he is on the Island of Sal listening to radio Hong Kong, thinking back to when he was in Tokyo in winter, subject to these and other images that return unbidden through association with his present. We are beyond distanced contemplation of images that may or may not have been filmed by him, but we are also beyond flashback, neither seeing through his mind's eye nor seeing images as testimony to his memory: rather, we are told that the images *are* his memory. (This sense that camera images replace the cameraman's memory of Tokyo is taken up again by Wim Wenders in *Tokyo Ga* (1985), which pays homage to *Sans Soleil*.) Time is more important than place, movement than stagnation, in this film that spirals vertiginously down memory's path, with concentric memories growing face on face, like a series of tree rings. Later on, indeed, *Sans Soleil* features stills from *Vertigo*, one of which shows the sequoia cut in Muir Woods, and then film footage of the similar cut in the Jardin des Plantes in Paris, which figures in *La Jetée*. As in *La Jetée* this is an impossible memory, the only difference being the introduction of moving images, and the fact that Krasna does not feature within them to be looked at as the protagonist of *La Jetée* does. These memory images may well function thus to point back to Krasna's location at the time of writing, but this position is constructed in the film as a visual and aural absence – Krasna is never seen or heard directly. Yet Krasna's memory, fashioned by film in every sense, opens out beyond himself in the absence of his physical presence.

As the film progresses, the montage and/or voice-over refers back to things that have already been mentioned or seen. This forms a self-reflexive enclosure that identifies the spectator with a point of view that actually ends up being as distant from Krasna's experience as it is from the spectator's own. Not only did Krasna not film many of the images of *Sans Soleil*, even the ones that could be labelled his take on a life of their own. They refer now to other filmic images, rather than a pre-existing historical or psychical reality. And this is where Krasna's perspective becomes less self-centred. The move beyond the filming self does not take place through an ostensible openness to the manifold subjects he films, as Silverman has it. Rather, this occurs from within the very perspective of the images at this point, not what they show, or how they are put together. This film that flashes over those people and places it encounters, getting to know no one in particular, no others in their singularity, also creates a space in which people and places are positioned beyond the viewing self's perspective rather than being contained within it from the outset. As such, what is documented here is a reworking of documentary's relation to the real and to experience, through the profound calling into question of the viewing self. This different relation to the real is founded in an altered connection to the index and time, which passes through a dream space before it enters the 'Zone'. This latter space marks a return to Tarkovsky – this time to a later film, *Stalker* (1979).

Tarkovsky's 'Zone' is a space that does not function according to physical laws and is therefore an appropriate term to designate a form of filmic manipulation or experimentation that similarly contests the laws of the physical world. In Wenders's *Tokyo Ga*, the voice-over commentary states that, as he views his images filmed in Tokyo, the city now seems like a dream. We approach Marker's dream space in terms that bring us into contact with a texture. For the psychoanalytic theorist Didier Anzieu, the dream is a 'pellicule' (film) in the sense that it is a fine membrane, which envelops and protects certain parts of organisms, yet it is also like photographic film, which supports the sensitive layer that will be marked during sleep. He writes: 'La pellicule peut être mauvaise, la bobine se coincer ou prendre le jour et le rêve est effacé. Si tout se passe bien, on peut au réveil développer le film, le visionner, en refaire le montage, voire le projeter sous forme d'un récit qu'on en fait à autrui'[2] (Anzieu 1995: 238). The film of the dream is open to internal and external stimuli and could break at any moment. The dream is given materiality through analogy with, and expression in terms of, film, which works well with reference to the kind of film that is impressed upon indexically, celluloid and not digital technology. The psychical life takes on a consistency here, through a skin or membrane that is also a photographic film: it comes to matter and be tangible through dreams. In *Sans Soleil* this has material resonance, as Krasna's impossible and illusory celluloid memories also become the film – in both senses of the term, following Anzieu – of dreams.

Tokyo's cityscape passes through analogy with the comic strip (the walls of buildings are drawn over with images, which are described as 'voyeurising the voyeur') before it becomes a dreamscape. Krasna asks whether he is dreaming all of this or whether he is part of everyone else's dreams in which the images he sees are just a projection. Cinema, the factory of dreams, in its exploration of the boundaries

2 'The film may be defective, the reel may get stuck or let in light and the dream is erased. If everything goes well, we can on waking develop the film, view it, re-edit it or even project it in the form of a narrative told to another person' (Anzieu 1995, trans: 211).

between the imaginary and the real, presents us here with the light of Krasna's mind, melancholic and sunless, imaginary and real, yet we feel and touch as well as see in the darkness. Having removed the black sun that Gérard de Nerval and latterly Julia Kristeva use to figure melancholia, Marker turns to music – a Mussorgsky song cycle – for the film's title. The land of the rising sun that features throughout is ridded of its very defining object, and this enables us better to understand the dreamscape in which one never sees the sun, even though what one may dream of is flooded with light. As we enter the most explicit dream sequence of the film, the images take us underground to Tokyo's department stores. Krasna muses first of all whether he could pick up one of the telephones and hear the beating of Sei Shonagon's heart, the eleventh-century lady-in-waiting to Princess Sadako in the Heian period whose passion for listing things that quicken the heart he finds such a good criterion for filming. Time travel back through the ages becomes merely a matter of picking up the phone. People are then seen filing through ticket turnstiles as they go towards their trains. When the commuters are on the trains, the camera focuses in particular on those who are asleep and intercuts images from television sequences that were shown earlier. The impossible dream of this film is that it wants to distort or to escape the things that make its very being possible: the image and time. It has to fail in this, of course, but in failing it achieves a move beyond the constraints of an ontological and ethnocentric vision. It steps into eternity through an electronic fabric woven from the contact Krasna has had with other places, people and times. Anzieu once again suggests how this impossible dream might materialise.

In a fictional fantasy text, *L'Épiderme Nomade* of 1990, Anzieu's protagonist dons the skin of those he likes or desires, as they do his, in order to know one another intimately, quite literally placing each other in the position of being able to film their interior life (Anzieu 1999: 13). His ultimate move into eternity is secured through his fabrication of a shroud made of pieces of the skin of all those he has known: 'Il me suffira d'avoir pour linceul, sur ma peau mortelle, cette seconde peau incorruptible tirée d'une multitude de gens que j'aurai connus et qui m'accompagneront pour toujours'[3] (Anzieu 1999: 26). This skin

---

3 'For my shroud it will suffice for me to have on my mortal skin, the second incorruptible skin taken from the multitude of people that I have known and who will then accompany me forever.'

is a film, a permeable layer through which he enters into epidermal contact with the other's desire, and wears it, along with his own. It is this final move into a timeless dimension that is relevant here, narrated as the tactile experience of carrying the skin of others with him into eternity. Krasna engages with death in order to transcend it, and the second skin that he fabricates is a function of the contact he has with everything and everyone he films.

Death as an end beyond which we cannot see is the focal point for one lengthy sequence of *Sans Soleil*, which chooses to look beyond this end point by means of the different cultures it focuses on. It also takes the concerns of two key interfilmic reference points – *Vertigo* and *La Jetée* – one step further. The segment begins by establishing a difference between Japan and Guinea-Bissau in terms of their responses to death. Shot sequences splice the ritual mourning ceremony for the death of a panda in Japan into the killing of a giraffe in the African savannah (this is footage shot by Danièle Tessier). Continuity across spatial disparity is assured thus through montage, but a sense of difference between the two is retained. The Japanese funeral rite lays flowers on the slaughtered giraffe in the African savannah. We attempt to see through the very thin partition that we are told death represents from the Japanese point of view. We are then taken on a journey through the Bijagós archipelago off the coast of Guinea-Bissau in which travel between islands ends on a note of death as departure: the dead walk the land of the living to get to a boat that will take them into the beyond. Earlier in the film we are told of the magical function of the eye at the centre of all things, even when it works against Krasna at times – notably when he tries to film the women of Bissau. Here, though, an eye is being gouged out by birds of prey in the filming of the death of a giraffe. The ocular focus then proceeds in more human terms, to refer to the vertiginous spiral of time, contained in the eye, in Hitchcock's opening credit sequence. We, following the Japanese children earlier in this montage sequence, are tempted by the thought of what lies on the other side – of the eye, of life, of time – but the camera can only take us to what we can see. It binds us to a time of its own making, as it reflects on *Vertigo*'s impossible memory and the madness of love – extracts from the film being present only as still images, while Krasna retraces Scottie's steps in moving images. It then brings in the time travel of *La Jetée*. Both filmic intertexts emphasise, however, that there is no escape from time: Scottie needs a re-run with Madeleine's alter ego to play out what *La Jetée* does with one person split between two separate times. The Jardin des Plantes appears, and marks out an indirect reference to *La Jetée* (the photo-roman also features obliquely earlier on in the film in images from the Japanese bar in Shinjuku named after it). *Sans Soleil*, like the other two films, attempts to escape temporal constraint but does so differently as it turns in on itself and alters its own images. While the temporality of *Sans Soleil* reflects back to past moments, it is also future-directed in its attempt to escape time altogether. This forward-looking thrust is associated with the survival of the filming self; his dependence on filming conditions the possibility of his future existence, even though his own image is nowhere to be seen.

Krasna's points of reference are rendered in material terms: forgetting is described as the lining of memory, and, as we have already observed, Tokyo shows her veins, memories become celluloid images and the indexical mark on the reel of film is transformed into an unreal dreamscape. Verbal imagery has its counterpart in what we see (even though the commentary does not always match the actual images before us) and in the manipulation the images themselves undergo. Krasna uses this peculiar contact with others through these images to enter eternity. Both the filmic and the still image contribute to this passage, yet the stilled moment, extracted from the flow of time, is not permitted to delay the film's relentless pace unduly. Several images are frozen towards the start of the film, and stills feature throughout but, as the commentary remarks, memories drift. To stop a moment would cause it to burn 'comme l'image d'un film bloquée devant la fournaise du projecteur' (like a frame of film stuck in the projector): the frozen image will burn like ice. Krasna's 'memories' – the memory bank of films that he has seen merge with the images that have since been cut off from his experience – become subject to material distortion. Montage is assured through straight cuts but also in dissolves or fades; film stills are used, as stated above; black leader is inserted between shots, as with the children from Iceland at the very beginning; the television is filmed, and images from Japanese television are also stilled, before being shown frame by frame in a manner akin to slide projection; and, finally, images are passed through an electronic synthesiser, as is the soundtrack at times. This ultimate passage through the synthesiser, credited to Hayao Yamaneko, which emerges early on in the film, but to which it returns in the end, is an entry into the Tarkovsky-inspired 'Zone'. The images within this realm that also flag up their status as non-images are described as having the only texture that can convey sentiment, memory and imagination and as the only eternity we have left. An early image of a woman from the Praia market, whose initial glance lasted only the length of a film frame, one twenty-fourth of a second, is fixed as a synthesised image in conclusion, before the pin that controls it is removed, the image is unfixed and the commentary asks whether there will be a final letter. Krasna has donned all these images – without incorporating them, and beyond their mental presence in his mind's eye – as a second skin, and he is thus fashioned by film in every sense. To film other people, animals, places and times, is, for Krasna, to be impressed upon by the experience, and to wear this as the skin of his and others' memories, fabricated through celluloid as the impossible dream of stepping outside of time. As with Anzieu's dream skin, Krasna's move into eternity involves mind and matter. The relation with others that fashions Krasna serves as the multivalent film of consolation for losing touch with the conscious world. These celluloid dreams surface from, and return us to, the sleep that surrounds our lives.

2084

2084 (1984) is a brief but important work that occupies a pivotal place among Marker's films of the 1980s. The ten-minute short was made in response to an invitation from the CFDT union to commemorate one hundred years of trade unionism in France. Filmed in collaboration with the CFDT Audiovisual Group, *2084* projects this anniversary a century forwards in time. A woman's voice-over announces that the robot-presenter of an inter-galactic television channel was programmed to celebrate this occasion. A computerised image of a robot's face accompanies her words, before her voice is replaced with that of actor François Périer. He informs us that in view of the difficulty of saying how things stand currently with trade unionism, the decision was taken to explore the possible future directions that it could take. Three filmmakers/computer programmers are visible in the darkness of a studio, surrounded by computer and television screens, along with film editing equipment. A familiar Marker image of a black cat's face features in a photograph in the background of a couple of shots. Some of the screens show text-based and numerical programming, others random images, and some of these are passed through an electronic synthesiser (Hayao Yamaneko is credited with this technical experimentation, as in *Sans Soleil*). The film sketches out three hypotheses for the future of trade unions on the basis of fixed frame interviews with various people.

Each hypothesis is given a colour: grey, black and blue. The first two hypotheses are formed on the basis of the interviewees' dislikes. The grey hypothesis suggests that society will continue exactly as it is because nobody has any energy to create an alternative: the unions just help to maintain the status quo. The black hypothesis is worse, however. In this scenario, technology takes the place of ideologies and the government furnishes the directors of techno-totalitarianism. The unions serve first just to oil the state machinery. They then cease to function entirely in 2000 and exist in name only. The blue hypothesis is the most positive of the three. It cultivates collective doubt and questions the status quo; it envisages the transformation of the world through struggle and promotes solidarity. There is still a note of caution suggested insofar as the computer age may hold as many fearful surprises as others, and it is made clear that the hypotheses explored are three among many options, some of which could be worse, and some better. Yet the film ends hopefully as we are told that the future remains to be created, rather than being programmed in advance.

2084 is poised between celluloid, electronic and digital culture: the filmmaker-programmers edit strips of negatives, watch solarised and other images, and also work with figures and text on their computers. During the description of the blue hypothesis, one woman sits in front of a screen and seems to radiate multi-coloured electronic beams, as the commentator speaks of the fabulous transformation of the world that technology could permit when placed in the right hands. However, in its predilection for fixed frame shooting, *2084* also records a hesitation between the cinematic and the photographic frame. Indeed, the film's thematic concern with looking into images of the past in order to look forwards fits with its formal preoccupations, as well as its central relation to Marker's other work. While the presence of the synthesised images recalls *Sans Soleil*, the manner in which other images are projected and the filmmaker-programmers are viewed pre-empts techniques used in *L'Héritage de la chouette* and

Level 5 where people are reflected in or actually become the screen for images. The filmmaker-programmers are visible as reflections in their computer screens, and they also serve as screens for some of the images we see, which are projected onto their flesh. Images shroud the filmmaker-programmers, coating their skin, and this once again recalls *Sans Soleil*, but with a notable shift. More visibly than was the case for the imaginary Sandor Krasna, the surface of their skin (faces and hands) becomes a host for the images we see. The visions of the past that they screen for us take us into predictions of the future; the filmmaker-programmers remain part of the images as the layering of the two membranes is quite literally fleshed out. We read the different layers of time within images, and between them, which has implications for spatial montage techniques in Marker's later work.

2084 embodies the technological vision that it advocates: its collaboratively produced prediction of solidarity depends on harnessing technology to build ever-new collective relations in the future. Through its manipulation of time (both within and between images) and a multivalent sense of projection (looking to the future and the projection of images onto screens and bodies), its Janus-faced position between images of the past and future also reflects its forward- and backward-looking place in Marker's work. It lies between the photographic and the cinematic, old and new media, the celluloid and the digital era. This in-between position, in spite of Marker's adoption of the new technologies at his disposal in his future projects, is one that he continues to occupy, fittingly unable to part with the past while moving into the future.

One of the few mobile camera moments within a shot in this film focuses on wild horses projected onto a woman's hand. The horse will occupy a central place in Marker's next film, *AK*.

AK

Consisting mainly of footage shot on location among the foothills of Mount Fuji in 1984, Marker's *AK* (1985) charts the making of select scenes from Akira Kurosawa's *Ran*. Both films share the same French producer – Serge Silberman – and both were released in 1985. The relationship between *Ran* and *AK* is one that the documentary interrogates sensitively throughout. *AK* is a conscious reflection on how to make a film about the making of another film. The documentary cuts occasionally from the location footage to a video recorder and screen on which television images appear, along with scenes from Kurosawa's other films. There is also a section of archive footage of a Japanese earthquake in 1923, which has significance for Kurosawa's filmmaking and his early ability to confront horror. *AK* features music by Toru Takemitsu who composed the score for *Ran*. Additionally, a mini-cassette recorder appears at the start of the film to signal the only access that *AK* will have to Kurosawa's thoughts: extracts from conversations recorded by friends of the director. Kurosawa's opening statement remarks on the importance of memory to creation, and *AK* explores what this means for *Ran* as well as for its own status as a documentary.

Kurosawa's first words are translated as follows: 'Je dis toujours à mon équipe: créer, c'est se souvenir. La mémoire est la base de tout.'[4] The motif of one's memory containing one's future knowledge is present elsewhere in Marker's work, but here memory is broadened out beyond the creating self. In *AK* it has little to do with the self-centred focus of Platonic anamnesis in which life is a voyage of remembering and re-discovering knowledge that one is born with and instantly forgets. Rather, in Kurosawa's understanding, creation becomes a matter of remembering something that lies outside one's own personal history – literary history and somebody else's work – and of modifying it through a new interpretation. This makes sense when we remember that *Ran* is a version of *King Lear*. The voice-over (provided by François Maspero) terms the film Lear's echo, which reverberates across the castle walls built by Kurosawa. Kurosawa transposes Shakespeare's tragedy into the medium of film and the time of feudal sixteenth-century Japan. The time-line that connects the self to others through this film is to be found in the individual creator's link to a broader pre-history. In view of the proximity between Kurosawa's and Marker's interest in memory, the challenge for Marker is how not to make the other filmmaker's creative act of remembering his own.

AK is filmed largely as an observational documentary. Yet the voice-over commentary breaks with the strictly observational mode, as do those moments when members of the crew or cast of *Ran* acknowledge the camera's presence. They do this either by looking directly

[4] 'I always say to my crew: to create is to remember. Memory is the basis of everything.' (Translations come from the English-language version.)

into the lens, as happens on a couple of occasions, or by ignoring the camera while discussing the fact that they are being filmed for the documentary. For the most part, however, *AK*'s cinematography instils distance between its main subject, *Ran*, and itself, even at moments of filming at great proximity. This preservation of distance is also a matter of respect, rather than a mere mark of conformity to a particular filmmaking style. *AK* is respectful of the aura which we are told surrounds Kurosawa, and of the scenes from his film to which this documentary is also privy. The commentary remarks on the inappropriateness and the inherent risks of filming scenes that it is not their place to record: 'de nous parer d'une beauté qui n'est pas à nous [...] Mais nous essaierons de montrer ce que nous voyons comme nous le voyons – à notre hauteur.'[5] This is spoken over a low-angle shot of a warrior with his horse, as *AK*'s camera establishes a deferential relation to what consequently appears as its towering subjects. However, *AK* will capture things in a manner that is its own.

The production of *Ran* is presented as a collective endeavour in which nobody's rank is too high to get involved in menial tasks. There are echoes of this collaborative work in *AK*. Rather than say 'je' (I), the commentary refers always to 'nous' (we), which suggests the teamwork of the documentary project. *AK* shows what lies necessarily beyond the frames of *Ran*, shot from angles that are not already covered by Kurosawa's three-camera system (we are informed that since *The Seven Samurai* (1954), he always uses three for important scenes), and in ways that not only include the director and film-crew but also make-up artists, vehicles and machinery. In some respects, this makes *AK*'s relation to the film on which it is based no different from other documentaries about the making of another film. But *AK* is more than this. Having introduced seven of the people who have worked with Kurosawa for longest, and dedicated the images of the sound man, Fumio Yanoguchi, to his memory (he died while they were editing *AK*), the documentary commentary describes these people and others as parts of the small solar system that gravitates around the man that everyone calls master, 'senseï'. The documentary crew also adopt this as their term of address, as does the commentary. While remaining reverential to Kurosawa's vision, *AK* chooses to gravitate around a different centre from the master himself, as it

5 'appropriating a beauty that does not belong to us [...] but we shall try to show what we see, the way we see it, from our eye level.'

performs a reading of Kurosawa's work authorised by, but separate from, the Japanese director.

Nineteen minutes into *AK*, the remainder of the film is divided into a series of ten sections of uneven length, each of which has a subtitle, which is given in Japanese characters as well as in translation. These are: 'Bataille' (Battle), 'Patience' (Patience), 'Fidélité' (Faithfulness), 'Vitesse' (Speed), 'Chevaux' (Horses), 'Pluie' (Rain), 'Laque et Or' (Gold and Lacquer), 'Feu' (Fire), 'Brouillard' (Fog), and 'Chaos' (Chaos). Within this list of categories, 'Horses' are central, and they become the alternative sun around which *AK* gravitates. As the commentary describes the extended solar system around Kurosawa, the last figure that it lists and that we see partially in the frame is the horse. The voice-over remarks that horses – although the *AK* film crew did not realise it at the time – were to play a symbolic role in what it terms '*notre* histoire' (*our* story) (my emphasis).

Kurosawa refers to horses on more than one occasion and also notes his sympathy with these animals. In one of his recorded conversations, he remarks that the shots that they never film are often the most beautiful. He talks about the early morning starts and the darkness on the road to Mount Fuji. He notes how the horses are led out in the dull light and the peasants are there in their armour. He describes how the braziers are lit when they get to their location, and the men warm themselves. He says that this combination of men and horses is very beautiful but that nobody captures it. While Kurosawa's remarks are spoken in voice-over, the images show us precisely what he talks about. Accompanied by Kurosawa's description but seen through *AK*'s lens, the product is a collaborative, rather than stolen, beauty, which owes its existence to both films. *AK* also traces the symbolic place that horses occupy in other films that are played on the video recorder. We are shown a black and white photograph of Kurosawa as a baby sitting on a rocking horse, and then told that there have been many horses in his life as we view images of horses in extracts from his films and from *Uma* (1941) by Kurosawa's own 'master', director Kajiro Yamamoto. In the final section of *AK*, the commentary describes Kurosawa's daily task in Sisyphean terms, and states that he is painting with horses the inner turmoil that wrecks the soul of these ancient Japanese warriors. Kurosawa's last words of the film ask after the fate of one of the horses: he questions whether one fell in the preceding take. *AK* closes with a solitary warrior on a horse bearing a red banner, winding their way down Mount Fuji's dusty black slopes.

Filmed from different angles and capturing what it sees the way it sees it, *AK* brings out what usually remains hidden. This pertains not only to scenes that are cut or the manual labour that went into the making of *Ran* but also to a beast whose prominence in the documentary permits a reading of Kurosawa's work that does not merely double his own. *AK* begins by recalling how *Ran* remembers *King Lear* but differently, refracted through space and time. By the time the documentary is over, it has also shown how *Ran* remembers its relation to other horses in other films. *Ran* engages consciously with *King Lear* and *AK* engages consciously with these symbolic beasts, even though this was not its original intention. Extra-personal memory serves the creative purposes of both films, yet Marker not only looks back, he also looks out beyond human life to account for how Kurosawa fleshes out his tragic vision. *AK* succeeds in finding its own place on Kurosawa's mountainous battleground, which is demarcated by the elegance, strength and beauty of the horse.

Marker's next film will return him to France, and the death of a friend will prompt a different series of reflections on the memory of a life.

Mémoires pour Simone

Commissioned for the Cannes Film Festival in 1986, *Mémoires pour Simone* is a tribute to Marker's friend from childhood, the French actress Simone Signoret, who died in September 1985. The commentary, provided by actor François Périer, is explicit about the film's focus from the outset and modest about its origins. It will not present us with her life or her career but, rather, the contents of a cupboard from her house in Auteuil, which contains 'des petits bouts de mémoire en vrac' (higgledy-piggledy bits of memory). Memories and memoirs are referred to in the dual sense of the French plural 'mémoires', which, as Jacques Derrida points out in his *Mémoires pour Paul de Man*, is barely translatable (Derrida 1988: 26). The film is also sometimes titled *Mémoire de Simone*, which preserves ambiguity differently by referring to a memory that belongs to Simone as well as someone else. Tenderly, but without becoming overly sentimental and lost in melancholia or grief, these memoirs construct a vision of memory that Signoret herself longed for in her own reflections on the past.

Mémoires consists mainly of extracts from over twenty-five films in which Signoret featured (this is the main reason why it never went on general release: it was impossible to gain permission from all the rights holders). The commentary that weaves the excerpts together is interlaced with citations from her autobiography, *La Nostalgie n'est plus ce qu'elle était* (1976). The film includes excerpts from television interviews, along with photographs, and film and home video footage from Auteuil. *Mémoires* moves seamlessly across the decades, and works associatively rather than chronologically, while beginning and ending with references to Neuilly, the place of her (and Marker's) childhood. It also features 16mm family footage of her daughter Catherine Allégret, shot by Yves Montand. We hear of Signoret's long love affair with Russia, shared by Montand. Her public left-wing support of various people and causes is touched on by the commentary and through footage of a television appearance on Antenne 2, forerunner to France 2 (Pierre Goldman being the most famous of cases). There is a self-reflexive moment for Périer, the commentator, who is able to comment on his own appearance in extracts from *Police Python 357* (Alain Corneau, 1976) and *Thérèse Humbert* (Marcel Bluwal, 1984) in which he co-starred with Signoret. Signoret's cat, César, features several times and is positioned, in true Marker fashion, as the guardian of memories. Some of the film extracts fill the entire screen; others have a black border, as does the television material, which is shown from an oblique angle and reminds us that we are looking at Signoret on screen, the place in which she will live on through images long after her physical death. It is, however, through a refusal to trace the passage of time from life to death, beginning to end, that *Mémoires* fixes an image of the late actress that keeps her forever closer to the cradle than the grave.

At a late point in the film, Périer cites passages from *Nostalgie* over photographic images of her house, shot first from the outside, then from room to room inside, before they focus on Signoret herself. The transition between these still images is made through a series of dissolves; the gentle progression maps the soft photographic treatment of its subject. Signoret discusses growing old, as she terms her wrinkles scars, but says that these markers of the passage of time and of living have been her allies. Photographs of her succeed one another during this meditation on age, each separated from the next with a fade to a white screen, as her face, viewed finally in close-up, generates and reflects this luminescence. The loss that we know has already happened, and as Barthes tells us is the foreknowledge of every photograph, is not merely delayed here, however. Indeed, the camera highlights the radiant beauty of her later years and pays this moment in her life more sustained attention that it did to her youthful good looks, apparent in the early film clips. In a reversal that works in keeping with Marker's fascination elsewhere with the possibilities of diverging from the onward march of time, it is the start, rather than the end, of her life that haunts the photographic images at this point. In her own words in a television interview, she describes actors as eternal children, and her childhood is what the film restores to her in conclusion. While the inevitable passage of time is visible on her face in this sequence, the photographs emanate a relation to her past that the film constructs from the outset. The possibility of seeing childhood rather than only death in the photographic image is as dependent on Marker's memory as it is on Signoret's.

As the commentary recalls, in *Nostalgie* Signoret writes that she has no nostalgia, but then corrects herself: 'j'ai peut-être la nostalgie de la mémoire non partagée' (I may have a nostalgia for the unshared memory (Signoret 1976, trans: 434)). Her regret is that she has shared moments with people who have not seen things in the same way that she has, and her utopia would be a world in which everyone would have the same memory. The commentary remarks on the potentially monstrous consequences of this desire, but affords it the status of a much longed-for childhood treasure. In a subsequent extract from *Rude journée pour la Reine* (René Allio, 1973), we see slow-motion footage of Signoret carrying a child in her arms as she joins in with a game of hopscotch. *Mémoires* thereby introduces child's play before it returns to the place of her own childhood, the memory of Neuilly, with which the film began.

The opening commentary spoke of humour and courage as two of the qualities evident in Simone in 1936 – the courage, it continues, possibly discernible in the way that she used to throw her brown beret up in the air as if defying it to come down. This game is not mentioned in the early years of her autobiography, suggestive of the fact that this may be Marker's memory of her. The camera moves in imitation of the beret being thrown in the air and coming back down to earth, between sky and pavement. In the final image of the film, the camera traces the upward trajectory of this throw, but then remains fixed on a frozen image of tree branches silhouetted against the light of the sky. The commentary refers to a child's wish for the ultimate gift: 'la mémoire partagée d'un moment, fût-il le plus ancien et le plus banal, celui par exemple d'une petite fille [...] en train de lancer très haut, le plus haut possible, un béret marron qui cette fois ne retombera plus.'[6] The film ends by freezing this memory image of play. While he denies neither life's transience nor the very real loss of his friend, Marker leaves her having achieved what she was always trying to do, from his perspective: to throw the beret higher and higher until it fails to come back down. We see from the point of view of the beret being thrown before being sent into oblivion, as we partake in Marker's memory of Simone as a child. Without seeing through her eyes, we share in her utopian vision that is created affectionately through Marker's posthumous gift.

Marker's final project of the 1980s is a television series, whose vast memorial scope looks back to the Ancient Greek world and takes the filmmaker's concern with death and the ontology of the image into new territory.

L'Héritage de la chouette

With a total running time of approximately six hours, the thirteen 26-minute episodes that comprise *L'Héritage de la chouette* (1989) make this an immense documentary undertaking and also Marker's longest to date. The series was a Franco-Greek co-production, funded by the Alexander S. Onassis Foundation, and was first broadcast in 1989 on La Sept (the forerunner to Arte). Its aim, as explained in the first episode and conveyed in the ensuing programmes, is to trace the links that exist between Ancient and Modern Greece and to offer a different view from the many idealised images and the clichés that circulate in the modern world about Ancient Greek civilisation. The voice-over announces in the first episode that everything began on 25 June 1987 when the project to make the series came together.

6 'the shared memory of a moment, be it the oldest and the most banal, that, for example, of a little girl [...] throwing a brown beret as high as possible into the air which this time will never come back down.'

The commentary continues to explain that they had before them the spectre that haunts all cultural documentaries, and that Chekhov is said to have summed up for eternity: 'dire les choses que les gens intelligents savent déjà et que les imbéciles ne sauront jamais' (to say things that intelligent people already know and that idiots never will). On the face of it, this is hardly a welcoming statement to television viewers who are being informed that if they do not already know the information that follows, they never will. François Niney suggests that in stating this Marker indicates a predilection for provocation over pedagogy (Niney 1989: xi). Rather than switch off, then, the viewer is goaded into seeing what he or she does and does not know, and an awareness of one's own ignorance is, as Socrates held, the province of those who are truly wise. The owl symbolises such wisdom and her legacy lives on here through a rich and tightly orchestrated polylogue for television, the many voices and images of which serve alternately to reinforce and contest one another. We are taken back to Ancient Greece by a range of interlocutors, the better to envisage how we might re-emerge from this past along alternative routes.

The structure of each episode varies according to the subject treated.[7] However, the foundation of each is interviews with individual artists and thinkers from the Humanities and Sciences, some self-taught and passionate about the Greek heritage, others widely acclaimed academic scholars. Each interviewee also has his or her own accompanying owl, which features in the background of shots in various guises: as a two- or three-dimensional model, as a virtual image, or even as a mobile suspended from the ceiling. In addition to the interviews, the episodes cut between discussions that

7 The thirteen parts of the series are: 1. 'Symposium, ou les idées reçues' (Symposium, or Received Ideas); 2. 'Olympisme, ou la Grèce Imaginaire' (Olympianism, or Imaginary Greece); 3. 'Démocratie, ou la cité des songes' (Democracy, or the City of Dreams); 4. 'Nostalgie, ou le retour impossible' (Nostalgia, or the Impossible Return); 5. 'Amnésie ou le sens de l'histoire' (Amnesia, or the Sense of History); 6. 'Mathématique, ou l'empire des signes' (Mathematics, or the Empire of Signs); 7. 'Logomachie, ou les mots de la tribu' (Logomachy, or the Words of the Tribe); 8. 'Musique, ou l'espace du dedans' (Music, or the Inner Space); 9. 'Cosmogonie, ou l'usage du monde' (Cosmogony, or the Ways of the World); 10. 'Mythologie, ou la vérité du mensonge' (Mythology, or the Truth of Lies); 11. 'Misogynie, ou les pièges du désir' (Misogyny, or the Traps of Desire); 12. 'Tragédie, ou l'illusion de la mort' (Tragedy, or the Illusion of Death); 13. 'Philosophie, ou le triomphe de la chouette' (Philosophy, or the Owl's Triumph).

take place at various symposia or banquets that have been set up in Paris, Athens, Tbilisi, and Berkeley, California. Scholars who do not feature in the interviews are filmed at these dining tables talking to one another about key concepts while eating and drinking. Their debates range more widely than the philosophy of love, however, the subject of Plato's *Symposium*. The montage of discussions and interviews is organised, as the voice-over specifies in the first episode, to generate 'une conversation sans frontières' (a conversation without borders). Some episodes feature footage from television archives, extracts from a diverse range of films, recordings of plays and guided museum visits. The episodes are also interspersed with images of statues, which represent the Ancient Greeks, their gods, their burial rituals and, most importantly, their continuing presence today in the form of friable stone copies. The Greek etymology of 'television' is vision at a distance. This medium permits distant contact across time and space in order to re-view and resuscitate links to a rich heritage through a form of montage that values the spoken word as much as it does the visual image, the material world as well as the conceptual.

The presence of different points of view is as powerful when driven by the juxtaposition of words as it is by images. In episode 4, for example, the academic George Steiner contends that there is no human connection remaining between the inhabitants of Greece today and those of the Ancient world. The interviews and discussions that surround his statement challenge this. Greek philologist Kostas Georgousopoulos, at the banquet table in Athens, explains that the Greeks of today keep this connection to their past alive when they give their children names from the Ancient world. The weight of the past is carried thus through the names of subsequent generations. Interviews with filmmaker Theo Angelopoulos and ex-patriot Greek singer-composer Angélique Ionatos corroborate this. A statement also appears at the end of the film, the first sentence of which is: 'La Fondation Alexandre S. Onassis tient à faire remarquer à M. George Steiner que si la Grèce moderne existait aussi peu qu'il le dit, ce film, lui, n'existerait pas du tout'.[8] Images have the power to challenge views in a similar manner. We encounter the playwright Alexis Minotis first in episode 11, in a BBC broadcast of 1961, in which he declares that the

---

8 'The Alexander S. Onassis Foundation would like to inform Mr George Steiner that if modern Greece were as non-existent as he says, *this* film would not exist at all.'

reason why his wife never took to directing was that women prefer to be directed. His misogyny speaks for itself here, but we encounter him again in episode 12 in which he explains that the Greeks are the only people who can adequately understand and represent the early tragedies. The interview in which he says this is juxtaposed with extracts from Greek performances of the tragedies, but also with excerpts from a Japanese production of *Medea*, directed by Yukio Ninagawa. The captivating and moving power of the latter performance patently undercuts Minotis's earlier remarks without any commentary being necessary. The dialogue between past and present is as conceptually linked to the spoken word as it is to the image and its material aspects. The television screen seems to serve Marker well in his shift between cinema and the computer.

The variability and invariability of concepts through space and time underpins the entire run of the series. Democracy, in the Ancient Greek and modern world, is set off against slavery in Ancient Greek society and dictatorships closer to the present (episode 3). The most aberrant readings of Ancient Greece feature (for example, through the idealisations of Nazism, explored in episode 2), as do fascinating links between Japan and Greece through culture, particularly tragedy and theatre (in episodes 9 and 12). Nostalgia, memory, history and amnesia are treated in detail (a condensation of concerns that are dear to Marker). Modern Greeks are understood to be nostalgic for a place to which they can never return (exiled Greek writer and diplomat Vassilis Vassilikos says this in episode 4), and politician Michel Jobert says (in episode 5) that a good memory aids the contestation of inaccurate history. In contrast, there is an abiding interest in meanings that are not confined to a particular time and space. Through mathematics, intellectual Michel Serres points out (in episode 6) that some meanings have endured regardless of the passage of time. Serres cites the example of the parallelogram, which we understand in the same way today as someone in Ancient Greece. He expresses his desire to go back to the harmonious combination of mathematics and the verb in the pre-Socratic use of 'logos' rather than the modern-day division of the study of these elements that Ancient Greece combined. Myths are understood to offer such an economy of expression, a silent grammar, which still permits through a kind of shorthand, a designation that connects back to their original usage (Steiner cites several examples in episode 10). Myths are also seen to continue to offer the attractive possibility of dreaming against death. The hierarchies of sexual difference in the Ancient World are explored in episode 11, which privilege male over female sexuality. Ionatos notes some continuity of such asymmetries through to the present day. But the sexism inherent in the secondary positioning of the female sex is then contrasted with the roles of women in tragedy in episode 12. A voyage into the depths and complexities of anything we contemplate (noted by Michel Serres) and a continuous return to the question of what we should think (noted by philosopher and political thinker Cornelius Castoriadis) are what characterise a philosophical approach, as outlined in episode 13, along with a Platonic acceptance of death with dignity, all of which would mark continuities with practices and beliefs from the Ancient world.

The material aspects of the image are apparent throughout, from grainy black and white archive footage to video, and from film to computerised multimedia technology. Some episodes are playful with regard to the use of film and computerised images: episode 6 is emblematic in this respect. Extracts from Norman Maclaren's *Rythmetic* (1956) and *Lignes Horizontales* (1962) are set alongside interviews with mathematical experts. An image of an owl emerges in computerised form here and enters into an interrogative relation to mathematician Daniel Andler's interview. Marker's cat, Guillaume-en-Égypte, also appears in this episode, as does actress Catherine Belkhodja (who has a place in several episodes: at the Paris banquet and elsewhere in images, sometimes as a reflection and sometimes in voice-over). In episode 8, we see Greek composer Iannis Xenakis's machine that enables drawing to be converted into sound, and one of his compositions, *Mycènes Alpha* (1978) plays on a computer screen. Other episodes, for example number 11, restrict themselves, in contrast, to interspersing images of statues and illustrations on pottery to tell the narrative of sexual desire, rather than take this into the multimedia environment. This return to stone is as important to the fashioning of the image in *L'Héritage* as the more technologically sophisticated forays within this series. The television image is as concerned with the imitative aspects of statuary as it is with multimedia creation through pixels.

In episode 11 and its focus on representation of lovers or sex acts, flesh becomes stone as love is pictured in material relics and desire is frozen in statuesque cameos. The turn to stone speaks more broadly for a movement that runs throughout the series. In its negative incarnation, it is associated with the Gorgon's gaze (as French historian Jean-Pierre Vernant explains to schoolchildren in episode 9): the Gorgon is a reflection of what her victims will become as her murderous glance petrifies them. (The Gorgon emerges more positively elsewhere, as we are told that music was born of her cry, which Athena mistook for that of an owl.) The series offers another view of the passage from flesh to stone, however, through the attention it pays to statuary throughout. The images of statues of the Ancient Greeks interspersed throughout *L'Héritage* not only symbolise a return to the past and a reminder of the very links between Ancient and Modern Greece that the series set out to study. They also bring the dead back to us, as copies, rather than the real thing. Yet there is an act of resurrection that passes here through the television image, which causes us to think differently about the ontology of the photographic and cinematic image. In interweaving shots of statues in the series, Marker hereby also resuscitates the link to the ontology of the photographic image, since the statues, whenever they appear, are filmed mainly with a static camera (with the exception of a blue-tinted tracking shot of a row of statues in episode 5). The statues are filmed in the first episode in the basement of the École des Beaux-Arts in Paris, in their various haphazard positions, and also as a stony row of faces in profile, waiting, as if in an air-raid shelter, 'que sonne la fin de l'alerte' (for the all clear). This television series is to unleash them into the present through its manifold reflections on relations to the past.

The Japanese bar in Shinjuku called 'La Jetée' features in episodes 9 and 12, both of which are concerned with death. The fleeting invocation of the bar and, through its name, Marker's 1962 film, also suggests a connection to stillness and the association with preserving the dead or mummifying change that Bazin saw as a defining feature of the ontology of photography and its legacy to film. In part 9, Michel Serres refers to the statues which one cut into pieces and put into the graves of those one was burying. We see a lengthy sequence of shots of these statues filmed from static camera positions in the Goulandris Museum in Athens. They are only partially lit and shot against a black background, suggestive of their having been scattered in a tomb. The episode cuts back to Serres who says that he wants Marker to show the various pieces in the tomb and then, at a particular moment, to lift the bodies up from the place in which they were laid to rest, to show television viewers how statuary puts dead people back on their feet. The voice-over then comments on images filmed by French archaeologists in Denos who filmed exactly how statues buried for two thousand years could be set back on their feet. The commentary terms this a surgical operation, and the stone pieces are re-assembled to the accompaniment of a soundtrack from an operating table: a machine beeps in keeping with a heartbeat. It was through statuary that someone could be made immortal and live through eternity. Through the television image, we return to the capacity for preservation of the photographic image, and we also turn to cinema, yet to reflect on it from the point of view of this different medium.

Episode 9 draws to a close with a shot of a row of faces in the darkness of a cinema auditorium. They are viewed in a line (as the statues were in the first episode of the series), accompanied by the first words of the Japanese man of Alain Resnais's *Hiroshima mon amour*: 'tu n'as rien vu à Hiroshima' (you saw nothing in Hiroshima). The auditorium space is compared to Plato's cave. This comment is attributed by the commentary to Simone Weil in 1940. But, as was pointed out in this study in relation to *La Jetée*, this comparison has been made again more recently in the psychoanalytic film theory of Jean-Louis Baudry. The commentary asks whether Weil knew that the cinema had the means of denying the cave, of disarming the Gorgon and of being able to create its own myths. The opening images of *Hiroshima mon amour* screened earlier in this episode were intercut with Jean-Pierre Vernant's recounting the narrative of the Gorgon to a group of French schoolchildren. The confusion between the lover's limbs and disembodied limbs in *Hiroshima mon amour* returns us to the confusion between life and death, the original and the copy, of the statuary with which we began. Instead of seeing only the mummification of change here, however, there is an attempt to breathe life into its copy through more transitory means, as past and present come together to fashion the afterlife of the cinematic image through the medium of television.

Like myths, which retain the power to see beyond death, television here stages an encounter with what lies beyond the grave. Through televised images of statuary, we connect with the Greek heritage. The television image is, in Marker's hands, a hybrid form that does not permit us to distinguish it neatly from fictional or documentary cinema, computerised images or film. This smaller screen which cuts images to the size of life, rather than allowing them the towering presence of cinema, suggests integration in the space of those who watch it, with a form of contact as transient as life itself. In episode 12, classicist Oswyn Murray likens the ephemeral qualities of the first performances of Athenian tragedy to the brief relation that we have with television programmes, which enter our lives, may stay with us for a day or two, but are soon to be forgotten. The life that is re-injected into the statuary, and what it symbolises throughout this series, is part of the broader reflection on how the past lives on. This is established through dialogue with the erudite interlocutors, and the myriad kinds of other images, that Marker and his production team have sourced and put together. Fleetingly, and in episodic manner, past and present animate one another, as television permits reflection on a legacy that will never die, while also marking out its own role in contributing to how the owl's heritage may live on into the future.

References

Anzieu, Didier (1995), *Le Moi-Peau*, Paris, Dunod; orig. publ. 1985. Trans (1989), *The Skin Ego*, New Haven, Yale University Press.

Anzieu, Didier (1999), *L'Épiderme Nomade et la peau psychique*, Paris, Les Éditions du Collège de psychanalyse groupale et familiale; orig. publ. Éditions Aspygée, 1990.

Bruzzi, Stella (2000), *New Documentary: A Critical Introduction*, London, Routledge.

Derrida, Jacques (1988), *Mémoires pour Paul de Man*, Paris, Galilée.

Lhomme, Pierre (1964), 'Interview', in *Image et son*, 173 (May), pp. 38–43.

Niney, François (1989), 'Label Helène de Chris Marker', in *Cahiers du cinéma*, 422 (July–August), p. xi.

Russell, Catherine (1999), *Experimental Ethnography: The Work of Film in the Age of Video*, Durham, Duke University Press.

Signoret, Simone (1976), *La Nostalgie n'est plus ce qu'elle était*, Paris, Seuil. Trans (1986), *Nostalgia isn't what it used to be*, London, Grafton Books.

Silverman, Kaja (1996), *The Threshold of the Visible World*, New York, Routledge.

5

To *Level 5* and beyond: 1990 onwards

From 1990 onwards, Marker has not ceased to impress. He has been as productive in his later years as he was in his early days. The 1990s begin with a video film made for television, which continues the form and output of his documentary work at the close of the 1980s. This year, and those that follow, see gallery work and video filmmaking emerge side by side, along with the release of the CD-ROM *Immemory* (1998), based on the installation *Immemory One* at the Centre Georges Pompidou in 1997. The installations *Zapping Zone: Proposals for an Imaginary Television* (1990), *Silent Movie* (1995) and *Owls at Noon: Prelude: The Hollow Men* (2005) pursue his commitment to electronic media (see Lupton 2005 and Alter 2006 for discussion of Marker's installation work up to and including *Immemory*). The films of this decade continue to engage the newest technologies, and when Marker reaches *Level 5* (1996), the Internet enters his film space in a transformative manner. He makes film tributes during these years to the late Russian directors Alexander Medvedkin and Andrei Tarkovsky, and to photographer Denise Bellon, in a co-directed work with her filmmaker daughter, Yannick, which returns him to photography. Several short video projects take him to the former Yugoslavia to film the aftermath of the interethnic conflicts of the 1990s and their effects on the people. One of these portraits, *Avril inquiet* (2001), remains unfinished. *Avril inquiet* thus joins an earlier incomplete film, *Le Facteur sonne toujours cheval* (1994: different sources list different dates), on Facteur Cheval and his Palais Idéal. (The film title plays on the name of this man and the title of the book *The Postman Always Rings Twice*). Marker's most recent film to date, *Chats perchés* (2004) takes a politically engaged look at the current state of the world through the geographically specific lens of Paris at the beginning of the millennium, and combines different technologies to conjure a collective vision of change. The cats of the final film look onwards towards better times and furnish a fittingly open-ended, yet hopeful, conclusion to Marker's filmmaking, for the time being.

Berliner Ballade

Broadcast by Antenne 2 (now France 2) on 29 March 1990, *Berliner Ballade* (1990) was made as part of the current affairs programme *Envoyé Spécial*. In this special edition, Marker's contribution is the first of three documentary reports that explore the reunification of Germany after the fall of the Berlin Wall. It focuses on the first elections in the former German Democratic Republic. In its letter-based style and its journey through Berlin, *Berliner Ballade* recalls *Lettre de Sibérie* and *Sans Soleil*. It also includes direct interview footage and thereby attempts to bring together two different strands of Marker's work. Marker declared himself unhappy with the film's blend of subjective impressions and interviews (cited in Kämper and Tode 1997: 306–07). He re-edited the video footage to produce a personal montage of his impressions of Berlin at this time, the result of which is *Berlin '90* in *Zapping Zone*. Fortunately, however, *Berliner Ballade* is still consultable. The title designates a ballad but plays on its homophone in French (balade) to refer to a stroll. This ambulatory portrait of a city in transition is also a study of a changing political climate. The crumbling edifice of the wall – as both political symbol and material entity – is as important to *Berliner Ballade* as the people interviewed in pointing towards a future that might be constructed differently from the past.

The first film image is of a mural painted on the side of a building, which depicts a troop of grey elephants. *Berliner Ballade* is dedicated to Juju, the same dedication that features in the video short *Slon Tango* (added to *Zapping Zone* in 1993), which focuses on an elephant in Ljubljana zoo. Immediately after this mural, it cuts to an elephant in a zoo in Berlin. The musical soundtrack of this opening sequence is the same as that used in *Mémoires pour Simone* over still images taken on the film set of Wolfgang Staudte's unfinished *Mother Courage and her children* (1955). This music establishes an aural link to this earlier

East German shooting location. The voice-over, provided by Catherine Belkhodja, declares: 'Cette fois tu m'écris de Berlin, et ta première visite est bien sûr pour le zoo' (This time you write to me from Berlin, and your first visit is, of course, to the zoo). René Prédal argues that by beginning with his celebrated friendship with animals, Marker 'veut installer une connivence entre le réalisateur et "son" public familier' (wishes to establish complicity between the director and 'his' familiar audience) (Prédal 1995: 23). The familiar elements stretch beyond these animals. *Berliner Ballade*'s images progress from the zoo through shots of statues to a book with its pages being flicked through, and the voice-over reports that he flicks through this city in a search for traces of what Giraudoux wrote about it in 1930. Associatively, the mention of Giraudoux is used to introduce the French writer's love of German poets. Kleist's grave is followed ominously by a shot of trees disguising a villa where we are told the Final Solution for the extermination of Jews was signed in 1942. German history, the voice-over declares, runs between these two places. The associative visual and aural connections made in this first sequence – between other films by Marker, his love of Giraudoux's work, his fascination for filming animals and the specificity of this context – are set off by the opening mural. Wall art (Mauerkunst), along with graffiti, is an important thread in this documentary's record of material signs of change.

Berliner Ballade attends to how the Berlin Wall itself goes into circulation after 1989. The static political boundary that it rendered in imposing material form is now broken up, subject to displacement and to varied uses. Reminders of the human tragedies of the past are there in the form of a series of white crosses where the wall used to be, which commemorate the individuals who died as they tried to get across it. The voice-over informs us that the fall of the wall has generated its own industry. People are filmed chipping away at its remains to sell or keep as a souvenir. In two striking montages, filmed from static camera positions, we see how large sections of the wall have become the canvas for street art. Blocks of the wall are also lined up neatly, like dismantled sections of stage scenery, carefully preserved in East Berlin: 'en attendant quel musée?' (awaiting which museum?) the commentary asks. All of this demonstrates how the wall's mutability has become the occasion for artistic creation and introduces the open-air museum of the street, to which Marker will return in a different city, Paris, in *Chats perchés*. Although this latter film is made in a different political climate, *Berliner Ballade* shares with it a reflection on the state of left-wing politics.

The interviews in *Berliner Ballade* are with cultural figures and politicians from the left and far left. The Communist Party is said still to have its followers, yet people's fading belief in the left more generally is something that the film marks, particularly in Jutta Braband's interview (Secretary for the United Left), and in the election results (the right-wing Christian Democratic Union won). The communist writer Stephen Hermlin, the most pessimistic of the interviewees, states that he is on the losing side once again. The film closes with a defiant ballad, however, performed by singer-poet Wolf Biermann, which notes how a future for the people in the east had been forgotten about, but that things have changed. All they ask is to be left to decide their own way forwards. During the song, images of people at his performance are intercut with shots of the former site of the wall. The different facets of this documentary are brought together thus through montage to commemorate a troubled past and look forward to an uncertain future.

Marker follows up this short documentary for a television series with a feature-length film, also made for television, which commemorates his friendship with Russian director Alexander Medvedkin.

Le Tombeau d'Alexandre

Marker's earlier work, *Le Train en marche*, had already registered his admiration for Medvedkin. Yet it was not until 1993 and the release of *Le Tombeau d'Alexandre* that the emotional and intellectual profundity of their special bond was brought to light. Emma Widdis notes the effusiveness of Medvedkin's writing to Marker (see Widdis 2005). This is evident through until the last letter, of 19 January 1989, when Medvedkin was already very ill. Medvedkin writes: 'I embrace you and want to see you more often. OUR FRIENDSHIP MUST HAVE NO END' (cited in Widdis 2005: 124). Medvedkin died later that year in Moscow. *Le Tombeau d'Alexandre*, released four years later, and whose credits list Medvedkin as a 'fantôme' (phantom), is a filmic extension of their epistolary relationship beyond the grave. This documentary permits Marker, through an interceding commentator, to perpetuate contact with the dead.

The French film was made first of all as a two-part television programme shown on La Sept/Arte in France. It has since been released in its French- and English-language forms on DVD under the Arte label (the English title is *The Last Bolshevik*), accompanied by Medvedkin's *Happiness*. *Le Tombeau* comprises six long posthumous letters from Marker to Medvedkin. The written letters form the text of the voice-over commentary, read by Jean-Claude Dauphin in French and by Michael Pennington in English. The tone of the letters is rather more direct and questioning than is suggested by the uncritical warmth of Medvedkin's above remark about endless friendship. But Marker's candour is coupled with his creation of a positive vision of his friend's life, work and ideology, in spite of some ambiguities that the film can never quite lay to rest. The two parts of the film, 'Le Royaume des Ombres' (The Kingdom of the Shadows) and 'Les Ombres du Royaume' (The Shadows of the Kingdom) are separated by a brief entr'acte, 'Chat écoutant la musique' (Cat listening to music). The mode of address moves between talking about Medvedkin in the third person to speaking to him directly. The intermittent voice-over returns in each letter, and each also features interviews on screen – with Medvedkin's daughter Chongara, friends, scholars, young and old, all of whom are avid Medvedkin enthusiasts – alongside extracts of his films, and excerpts from films by his contemporaries.

The first letter in 'Le Royaume des Ombres' begins with colour images of Medvedkin in one of his last interviews, apparently berating Marker for not writing more often. The voice-over gives a brief chronology of Medvedkin's life, from 1900 to 1989, in relation to key events in Russian history, which the entire film will then elaborate on in detail. It moves from the early years to October 1917, through the civil war of the 1920s and his service in Budenny's 'Red Cavalry', to the Stalin trials of the 1930s, followed by the death of Stalin, and finally his own death in the midst of perestroika. The historical events are related to Medvedkin's filmmaking, much of which was censored, and much of which has now been lost. The trajectory of *Le Tombeau* begins broadly chronologically and then doubles back in temporal terms, both within each individual instalment and from one letter to another. François Niney terms this Marker's 'montage à échos' (montage of echoes). Niney describes this formal structure as the most adequate to the idea of working on the period that is longer than a lifetime and that opens out to refer back to past and forwards to future generations (Niney 1996: 15). The opening out of Medvedkin's life to a broader history and time in this film, however, complicates Marker's interest in the word–image relationship and their conjunction through montage.

The film's epigraph, by George Steiner, focuses attention on images from the outset: 'It is not the literal past that rules us: it is images of the past.' In keeping with this statement, the film places images under scrutiny through a frequent use of stills, photographs and motion footage, which then have a bright rectangle or circle placed over them in order to focalise our attention, and encourage us to think or to remember. Elsewhere, motion footage is paused to the same end. The film also mixes archive footage with handheld video footage, along with special effects and animation to emphasise its concern with the different phases in the technology and history of the image, from photography through to the era of television and video. The letters, along with the specifically poetic associations of the 'tombeau' of the French title – the name given to a homage paid by one poet to another (and French for 'tomb') – reinforce the importance of the written word, both to the filmmakers' relationship and to this particular tribute.

Jacques Rancière argues that Marker is giving a lesson on memory in this film, which involves the hierarchical organisation of word over image (Rancière 2006: 168–69). While we might agree with Rancière when he says that Marker uses words to explain images, we are in fact being taught to question the filmic construction of that very lesson through word and image. The homage designated by the term 'tombeau' can also be musical. The documentary thereby places itself, through its French title, within a tradition of poetic and musical homage, and this suggests an amplification of reading it solely in terms of an essayistic use of language. The images of *Le Tombeau* bear a crucial relation to words, but the poetic–musical connotation of the title suggests that this film will point up the limits of documentary as a language of information and explanation. The challenge of this film lies in its questioning of how we glean historical knowledge and information through film, even as these things are precisely what the documentary still seeks to impart.

While *Le Tombeau* does not include extracts from the works of poets, it does feature many citations from the works of composers, Russian and other. Several of Alfred Schnittke's works are credited individually (*In Memoriam, Quintette, Trio, Concerto de violon*), as are extracts from the work of Mussorgsky, Sergei Rachmaninov, D. Pokrass, Arthur Honegger, Antonio Vivaldi, Moondog and additional music by Michel Krasna. The musical resonance of the film's title is apparent in the first letter. Midway through it, we are introduced to an old man sitting in a church listening to the liturgy. He is presented as one of Medvedkin's contemporaries, Ivan Kozlovsky, who was a famous singer and performer in his younger years. The voice-over commentary asks what Kozlovsky is hearing in his head. At the end of the first letter, the montage returns to Kozlovsky in the church and repeats the question that the voice-over raised earlier, asking what music the man was hearing. The film furnishes a response to the commentary's question by showing a scene from *Boris Godunov*, the opera by Mussorgsky, based on the work of the poet Alexander Pushkin. In the opera, Kozlovsky played a simpleton who sang of the pain and suffering that awaits the Russian people. The poetic and the musical come together here as Marker inserts an image from Kozlovsky's younger years into his present in the church. Marker creates a mental and aural image for Kozlovsky's thoughts based purely on his own supposition and the logic of associations within this particular letter, which closes on a melancholy musical note as a result. Commentary, image and music combine in this sequence, yet the poetic–musical element is inserted where there is no knowledge on the part of the filmmaker of the thoughts of his subject. In supplying information about the anonymous churchgoer, Marker's use of word and image covers over a gap in what can be known about Kozlovsky. The conjunction of poetry and music at this point in the first letter suggests that *Le Tombeau* will be fissured in terms of the knowledge that commentary and image can supply. In accordance with this, *Le Tombeau* turns on questions of trust and mistrust of the image through the complex system of montage on which it depends. Ultimately it is montage itself that is deconstructed by the film's scrutiny of images and its attention to what lies beyond the language of information.

The relation between cinematic image, fiction and reality and the subsequent way in which images are manipulated to inspire trust or mistrust is a constant preoccupation of the film. The two parts of *Le Tombeau* take their name from a famous statement by Maxim Gorky about cinema, which is then inverted, mirroring the very mirror effects that Marker's film plays with throughout when speaking of the 'Kingdom of the Shadows'. Gorky coins the phrase 'kingdom of the shadows' in an article of 4 July 1896, having been to a projection of the films of the Lumière brothers and then attempted to describe what he had seen. Marker's film shows how the shadows of the cinematic realm step into the real. We are told that many viewers of the era would mistake the actor who played Stalin for the real-life politician, and that the Stalin show trials used the same lights in the court room that Vertov used to film Lenin's funeral. The first mention of Gorky's phrase in the film refers to the confusion between fiction and reality in the service of propaganda. We are shown images of the Odessa steps filmed in colour by a handheld camera and told that it takes ninety seconds to descend the steps that Eisenstein's *Battleship Potemkin* takes seven minutes to show. Intercut with images from the Odessa steps sequence of *Potemkin* are present-day images of people descending the steps. A statue at the top of the steps, which appears in a montage of stilled images, commemorates the heroes of Potemkin, but these figures, along with the legend itself, come solely from Eisenstein's film, not from historical reality. Yet what the commentary terms one of the greatest lies in the history of images is the acceptance of an image from a theatrical reconstruction of the storming of the Winter Palace in 1917 as if it were archive footage of the actual event (the images were filmed in 1920 on the third anniversary of the event). And it is this act of reading the fictional reconstruction as archive footage of historical fact that *Le Tombeau* exposes.

In contrast to an erroneous trust of the image, and faith in its provenance, the film brings out Medvedkin's sincerity. Medvedkin's *Happiness* takes its reference points from reality. *Le Tombeau* shows a still image of the Kolkhoz's landscape taken from Medvedkin's film-train, followed by the corresponding scene from *Happiness*. Both sources are film but fiction this time bases itself on real life and historical fact. Prior to the entr'acte, the commentator declares that his job is to question images, which is precisely what he has been engaged in doing throughout. Montage has served to expose lies and, through examples from Medvedkin's films, to approach truth. Yet in an extension of the poetic–musical resonance at the end of the first letter, the entr'acte suggests that this editing technique does not serve to tell the whole story.

The brief film placed in the interval has been read elegantly by Jean-

André Fieschi to distil the very essence of *Le Tombeau*. The interval picks up on animal references within the film (Medvedkin's love of cats and other animals features in archive footage and a brightly coloured pie-bald horse spins round occasionally in Marker's film). It features Marker's cat, Guillaume-en-Égypte, who is lying across an electronic keyboard ostensibly listening to the music of Federico Mompou. We see shots of varying distance of the cat and its surroundings, put together seamlessly in relation to Mompou's music. Fieschi writes that this is 'un chat de montage' (a montage cat) (Fieschi 1996: 20). He continues: 'Ce chat ment. Mais en vérité, il ne ment pas. Il est l'hôte vaguement indifférent d'un mensonge (d'une manipulation) qui vient servir la vérité, d'une pause où se dé-monte et se démontre, en entr'acte, la rhétorique du cinéma (et celle de la terreur)'[1] (*ibid.*: 20). The rhetoric of cinema as montage is indeed on display here but, rather than being accompanied by words which speak for the image, images speak for themselves in tune with the music. The film reflects us back on its own processes in this interval. *Le Tombeau*'s return to music as it draws to a close contrasts revealingly with the earlier Kozlovsky scenes.

The figure of Kozlovsky in the first letter is, as Rancière notes, distinct to the point of being opposed to Medvedkin in terms of the difference between the lives they led (Rancière 2006: 162–63). In the final letter, however, the vision of an old man listening to music could not be closer to Medvedkin. Yakov Tolchan is first introduced in the second letter, and the commentator states that he would listen to this man, after Medvedkin's death, as if he were the late director. Tolchan was Medvedkin's camera operator, and his testimony in relation to the life and times of the director returns throughout the film. In the final letter, he is filmed from an angle where he seems no longer to be aware of the camera or anyone in the room, and he stares ahead of himself into space. It becomes apparent that he is listening to music, and the commentator explains that, after they had finished talking, Tolchan invited him to stay and listen to his favourite piece. Music, we are told, is the only thing that Tolchan believes in now. This time, there is no commentary to suggest what he is thinking or seeing (as with Kozlovsky), we just see him lost in his appreciation. With regard

---

[1] 'This cat lies. But, in truth, it does not lie. It is the vaguely indifferent host of a lie (of a manipulation), which works in service of the truth, of a pause in which the rhetoric of cinema (and that of terror) is dismantled and revealed, in entr'acte.'

to Tolchan, the film allows the music to have the last word as we watch him listen.

The montage of *Le Tombeau* juxtaposes images of fiction and the real to show how each is read in terms of the other and makes sense according to a logic of signification that is neither strictly documentary nor strictly fictional. Sometimes the montage is spatial. A split-screen effect occurs occasionally, as two still images are placed alongside one another in the service of scrutinising possible relations between Medvedkin and different historical figures. This film which gives us information about the life of a Russian filmmaker, relatively unknown outside of specialist circles, is deliberately open-ended as a documentary, hence the letter-based structure which renders this personal rather than objective in terms of the information it seeks to impart. Julian Graffy notes that Marker's 'hero remains something of an enigma' (Graffy 1993: 57). Rather than see this as a failing on the part of the documentary filmmaker, we might read this as being one of his aims. *Le Tombeau* provides an incomplete portrait of Medvedkin, which tacitly acknowledges the limits of documentary's power to furnish complete knowledge of one slice of history, and of an historical subject, who was also Marker's friend. Bound to incompletion, this film grants Medvedkin's final letter-based request and confirms that his friendship with Marker will indeed have no end.

Le 20 heures dans les camps

Marker's next film is the first of several video shorts on the aftermath of the interethnic conflicts of the 1990s, which take him to different areas of the former Yugoslavia. *Le 20 heures dans les camps* (1993) focuses principally on a group of young Bosnian refugees who make televised news programmes that are broadcast to the Roska refugee camp, housed in a derelict army barracks in Ljubljana, Slovenia. These fledgling producers and presenters receive their information from radio and satellite television stations (Radio Sarajevo, Sky and CNN are mentioned explicitly). They create their own programmes on the basis of pirating the contradictory reports gleaned from their different sources. Their equipment was provided by the Belgian organisation Causes Communes. In addition to this aspect of their television production, another group of refugees also films the testimonies of those living in the camp as part of a memory project aimed at bearing witness to experiences that would otherwise vanish without a trace. François Périer provides the general voice-over for the film. Mathieu Kassovitz lends his voice to the French translation of interviews with the Bosnian men and Catherine Belkhodja does likewise for the women. Interspersed throughout are interviews with Théo Robichet (credited frequently as part of the earlier SLON team) who comments analytically on why the television and memory projects are so necessary for these people. Filmed on Hi 8 video, *Le 20 heures* gets as close as it can to the refugees and listens to their stories.

The start of the film is alluring in its fast-paced combination of music with a strong beat and swift montage of images. Périer's voice-over states that such an opening will be familiar to viewers of satellite television but warns that this one carries clandestine passengers. The sequence is paused three times to reveal distorted images of people, one of whom is recognisable as one of the Roska television presenters we see in the ensuing film. Robichet explains that the first time he met these people he felt that they were all shut away inside themselves, and that the need to open out, both beyond the walls that confine them, as well as beyond themselves, is what generated the idea for these projects. In place of an opening establishing shot of their location – the most habitable section of the former Yugoslav army barracks – there is a montage of still images of broken windowpanes and derelict rooms in a dilapidated building, which is accompanied by percussive sound effects. Périer's voice-over explains that the army wrecked everything when they left but a symbol remained: a map with a hole cut out of it where Bosnia Herzegovina used to be, which is spread out on the floor of one of the rooms. This fragmented view of the refugees' broken environment, accompanied by the absent homeland symbolised through the ruined map, gives a material sense of the devastation, disorientation and loss that informs the personal accounts from individuals throughout the film. When we do see a shot of the exterior of the barracks, along with a sign that names the place, the external view of this paradoxical safe haven for shattered lives serves only to reinforce the sense of isolation to which Robichet refers. A later sequence adds to this. Leonard Cohen's song, 'Everybody Knows', plays over a travelling shot of the outside of a low-level building – viewed from the exterior of a wire fence – which comes to rest on a close-up of a tearful white-haired old lady with her head in her hands. We see this place from the outside, and the fence is a further barrier, which also suggests the physical enclosure of the people. The lyrics to Cohen's song encapsulate the pessimism of a worldview in which injustice prevails. Yet the aim of the film is to see through the facades of the buildings and the people in order to unlock and record memories that are still raw.

Once a week the television crew go into one of the rooms of the camp to interview people. One of the participants in the memory project explains the need to preserve these moments for the future. *Le 20 heures* shows the beginning of one of their films: a montage of close-ups on sad or tearful faces and then expressive shots of hands gives way to a focus on objects. We see a close-up of cutlery and a white plastic cup on some dishes, a photograph, a collection of teddy bears. The objects are signs of life that trigger a memory of happier times and serve as a material connection to a now inaccessible past. The presence of the television crew's video camera serves as a catalyst for talking through some of the refugees' painful experiences of losing loved ones in the conflict. We get only the briefest of snapshots of information, which matches the restricted view that we see of their quarters inside the camp. But these encounters provide valuable testimony in the drive towards a previously inaccessible truth, which an overly manipulative approach to existing images in the world media – or indeed a failure to record anything at all – would never reveal. As if also affected by the stripping away of media lies, Périer's voice-over confesses to the only lie contained in the film we are watching, which is in its title. He explains that the evening news programme is broadcast to the camp at seven o'clock and not eight o'clock in the evening. The appropriateness of a French television convention to signal the time of the news is thereby questioned.

Le 20 heures closes with a series of messages addressed by members of the television team to the world media and to other refugees. They ask for increased objectivity on the part of journalists' coverage of news, express utopian desires for only love and not war and wish that all refugees will be able to return to their homeland one day. This video message in a bottle reaches out to a broader audience on a note of hope and encouragement rather than despair and accusation. Through communication and the preservation of memory, the film shows how the refugees have created their own means of access to the slow, painstaking, and uncertain road forwards. In an earlier part of the film, one of the female interviewees explains that she cannot see a future for herself as things stand. The significance of the closing gesture of the film is that it focuses on how things need to change in order to envisage a different future for others, as well as the possibility of creating one for themselves, that does not repeat the past. In spite of their plight, they see ultimately beyond the confines of their own walls and their own experiences, and this is arguably the most poignant aspect of the film. Their visions of change reach outwards to others and forwards in time as they hope for a better future for everyone.

Casque Bleu

This 26-minute documentary is based on the testimony of François Crémieux who served in Bihac, Bosnia for six months in 1994 as part of the UN peacekeeping force during the conflict. *Casque Bleu* was released in the same year that Marker's multimedia installation, *Silent Movie*, was first exhibited and was broadcast on Arte in October 1995. On the face of it the two works could not be more different. Marker's tribute to one hundred years of cinematography in the installation returns to the early years of the twentieth century to commemorate what he calls an *Ur-Kino*, or cinema of origins: a pre-historic state of film memory which coincides with a state of perception anterior to consciousness. Marker points out what would have been obvious to spectators of cinema at its origins: that silent cinema was never silent. Rather than the absence of sound, he speaks of its defining feature as follows: 'that other kind of mutism, the muffling of another kind of signal, much more meaningful than the words: the erasing of colors, the Black-and-White' (Horrigan 1995: 17). He talks of the collective unconscious of the film industry holding its breath in order to enjoy 'a privileged stage of perception' (*ibid.*: 17), as if trying to prolong its childhood through this black and white period, before joining the colour of realistic representation. Marker's career bears witness to a sustained love affair with black and white images, especially, although not exclusively, in his works based around photographs. *Casque Bleu* is marked by its historical context in terms of the fluent narrative Crémieux provides. But in its form the documentary privileges the muted phase of black and white (in spite of being shot using colour video), along with stillness, in order to frame the testimony of a witness who is anything but silent.

Almost exclusively, we watch a fixed frame close-up of the loquacious and candid Crémieux, who reflects on his experiences and on the United Nations' place in Bosnia, along with the specific role played there by the French. Apart from the opening image, which is a vibrantly coloured map of ex-Yugoslavia and the surrounding area, the rest of *Casque Bleu* does not exploit the colour video on which it was filmed. Crémieux's face is pale and partially in the shadow, and he sits in front of a black background. His fluent speech is interspersed with nineteen white intertitles on black backgrounds that segment his narration. Additionally, black and white photographs are placed in front of the camera periodically: some look like pages of a book turned before the lens, others as though they are loose-leaf images.

Crémieux, a volunteer, spent six months in preparation for his service in Bihac and then six months there. He speaks about the various motivations soldiers may have for joining the force – principally financial – and also about the missions set for them, along with the briefing sessions that they received. Their lesson on the history of Yugoslavia lasted only fifteen minutes and their briefings were deeply racist. These sessions encouraged the soldiers to be wary of anyone they met, while registering an institutionalised fascination for the Serbs, which dates back to an historical Franco-Serb alliance. As he sums up his experience at the end of the film, he notes a sense of pointlessness when, on returning home, he heard that the Serbs had bombed Bihac, the very place that the UN had spent two years protecting. This negative reflection does not colour the entire film, however. He notes how the army was respectful of political power, even though it could have been very critical; and his own relationship to authority was dutiful and obedient, even though he thought prior to departing that he may refuse to carry out some orders.

He explains that his most emotive moments during his service were associated with meeting the children around their base. His testimony is interspersed with several photographs of children at this point, either on their own or in groups. He says that he came closer to the war through narratives of their experience than when he went on military activities. It was through the living that the effects of war registered themselves on him most profoundly. He recalls how he participated in missions to collect dead bodies from the frontline but notes that the bodies were so dehumanised that this had virtually no effect on him. Significantly, we do not see photographs of dead bodies when he talks about the mission he goes on. And when we hear a tale about orders to shoot dogs at the base – first given on health grounds, then pursued as a grim form of sport – we see an image of men sweeping the ground and do not glimpse the hapless dogs.

With the final sheet of photographs, which appears as Crémieux reflects back on his experiences, he declares that people like Marker who are willing to listen to him for almost an hour are rare. His address to Marker uses the plural 'vous' and thereby opens out to include the broader audience of which we are part, even though the interview has been edited to just under half of its original length. Like *Le 20 heures dans les camps*, *Casque Bleu* testifies to things that usually remain hidden from view. What we hear in this film seems more remarkable than what meets the eye. The very basis of the film's effect lies in its ability to focalise our vision on the verbal testimony of its witness, which enlivens and exceeds the photographs and the fixed frame. Just as Marker's reference to muteness in early cinema moves away from absence of sound to absence of colour, from silence to black and white, Crémieux's voice provides a form of vision that gestures beyond what the photographs document. Such 'vision' works in conjunction with the muting of colour that characterises what we see, but it is dependent on the sonority of the human voice.

Marker will collaborate with Crémieux again in 2000 on a visit to Kosovo. In the meantime, his subsequent two films engage with death and time in divergent but equally arresting ways.

Level 5

Level 5 (1996) is the culmination of the explorations of time, memory and history inaugurated by *La Jetée* and *Sans Soleil*. Raymond Bellour notes that the film received a good critical reception (Bellour 1999: 227), and it was certainly reviewed widely upon its release. It features Catherine Belkhodja, the muse of Marker's later years, in the role of the female protagonist Laura (named after the title character of Otto Preminger's *film noir* of 1944). Belkhodja had already provided voice-overs within several of Marker's films – *Le 20 heures dans les camps*, *Berliner Ballade*, *Le Tombeau d'Alexandre* and *L'Héritage de la chouette*

– and had also featured as a mute image in the latter. Additionally, she figured in *Owl gets in your eyes* (grouped with *Tchaika* and *Petite Ceinture* to constitute the very brief *Three Video Haikus* of 1994) and in stills and imaginary silent film footage within the installation *Silent Movie* (1995). In *Level 5*, she is a fleshed-out, speaking being. Indeed, once released, Belkhodja became spokesperson for and promoter of the film. She appeared in an episode of *Le Cercle de Minuit* television series, devoted to war and cinema on 4 February 1997, and was also interviewed by the French press (see Belkhodja 1997). The film focuses on a particular episode at the end of the Second World War – the Battle of Okinawa – and gives a more detailed elaboration of this atrocity than that provided in *Sans Soleil*. *Level 5* also develops Marker's obsession with Hitchcock's *Vertigo*, already apparent in the two previous films. In an article, published first in the journal *Positif*, and which features subsequently in the cinema section of the CD-ROM *Immemory*, Marker writes about the logic of the second chance, which underpins *Vertigo*, but he displaces this into the realm of video games, which is directly relevant to *Level 5*. He asks: 'Qu'est-ce que nous proposent les jeux vidéo, qui en disent plus sur nos inconscients que les œuvres complètes de Lacan? Pas l'argent ni la gloire: une nouvelle partie. La possibilité de recommencer à jouer. "Une seconde chance." *A free replay*'[2] (Marker 1994: 84). The unconscious delights in repetition rather than change, and it is the possibility of replaying the past that both Marker and Laura experiment with here by means of video and a computer. As with *La Jetée* and *Sans Soleil*, *Level 5* confronts the impossibility of escaping time. Laura has her own means of dealing with the historical and personal tragedies that this film lays bare, however, in which she re-maps both temporal and spatial connections to her own past and that of Okinawa through a mesmerising range of images.

Level 5 is essentially Laura's video diary, punctuated by log-ins dated from September 7 to November 29 in an unspecified year, with separate entries marked out by a white date on a black screen. She directs the diary explicitly to her dead male lover who passed away under mysterious circumstances after he returned from a trip to Okinawa. Her address to camera broadens out to implicate all specta-

2 'What do video games offer us, which say so much more about our unconscious than the complete works of Lacan? Neither money nor glory: a new game. The possibility of playing again. "A second chance." *A free replay.*'

tors, but perhaps especially Chris, 'l'as du montage' (the montage ace), to whom she says she will give all of these images one day to see what he can do with them. In the film we watch, this passing over of a diverse stock of images from Laura to Chris has already happened. Marker plays the role of Chris, whom we hear in voice-over at intervals throughout. He says that he took up Laura's challenge at a time when other people's images interested him more than his own, and he used the subject of war as a key to re-enter Japan's history. In addition to her diary entries, which are shot statically, we also see Laura working on the video strategy game devoted to the Battle of Okinawa, left incomplete by her lover, the details of which tragedy allow her to reflect on her own more personal loss. Intercut with Laura's diary entries are interviews with commentators and witnesses of Okinawa: Nagisa Oshima, Kenji Tokitsu, Ju'nishi Ushiyama and Shigeaki Kinjo. *Level 5* also features extracts from films by Nagisa Oshima and John Huston, footage shot by Gérard de Battista and Yves Angelo, along with the computer images of the game itself and those from the film's equivalent of cyberspace, the Optional World Link, whose acronym returns us once again to one of Marker's favourite creatures, the O.W.L. Synthesised voices and associated computer sounds are interspersed with Laura's and Chris's human voices, and music – choral, instrumental or synthesised – lends the entire film an eerie, melancholic feel.

Part of what gives this extraordinary film its power is the sheer horror of the documentary facts that are presented. Okinawa's history is less well known in the West than is that of the atomic attacks on Hiroshima and Nagasaki, but its pivotal place within the Second World War served to give rise to these subsequent cataclysmic events. One of the aims of *Level 5* is to show the role that the Battle of Okinawa played in determining the course of history. Rather than be captured by the Americans, the Japanese persuaded the people of Okinawa that death was preferable by their own hands. This led to one of the biggest massacres of all time, in which members of families killed their loved ones in order to spare them from what the propaganda was telling them would be an even worse fate. Chris's commentary and the testimony of the interviewees concur that Okinawa was quite literally sacrificed by Japan in order to block the progression of the Americans to the other islands. An analogy is made with the Japanese game of Go, in which one sacrifices one piece in order to save the rest. In interview, Marker comments on the need to present the eyewitness account of the Okinawa atrocities in a way that would make these documentary elements stand out from the myriad other tragedies that the television viewer may watch in a day (cited in Walfisch 1996: 31). The form of *Level 5* is thus crucial to the possibility of viewers experiencing the specificity of the events recounted and being affected by them, as Marker desired. Its most striking effects come from the mixed media involved in its making. Yvonne Spielmann defines Marker as an intermedia artist on the basis of the similarities and continuities established between the analogue and the digital in this film, which also crosses into the space of hypermedia through the use of the computer (Spielmann 2000: 24). Filmed on analogue video and then blown up to 35mm, engaging the logic of the video game but featuring computer imagery created on an Apple Power Macintosh 8100, this is a hybrid film in its material aspect. Placed alongside the multi-coloured deviations into the world of the video game and cyberspace, the drained colour of the individual testimonies emerges all the more prominently, and the combination becomes an attempt to jolt the viewer out of indifference to the barrage of images of suffering he or she sees on a daily basis.

Laura comments early on in the film on the inconceivable task faced by a young boy, Kinjo, who had to kill members of his own family. At a later stage, she comes across his testimony in the database: he is now an old man and has converted to Catholicism. He tells of how he killed his mother with his elder brother's help, how his father went away to kill himself and how he and the elder brother killed their younger siblings. The filming of the eyewitness account begins by focusing on him as he talks, but then places his testimony as a voice-over as we see an aerial image of Okinawa's terrain and the tranquillity of what Laura terms the Yves Klein blue of its sea and skies. There is a jarring contrast between the serenity of the images and the barbarity of the acts Kinjo recounts. The sequence also cuts twice to Laura and her stupefied absorption in his testimony, which concludes with her putting her head in her hands. Laura embodies the position from which a viewer might begin to relate to others' pain in Marker's film, in which her suffering is no less palpable than that of the people of Okinawa but is a conduit to this pain rather than its equivalent. Belkhodja remarks in interview that she did not feel that she was up to the task of playing her character: 'J'avais l'impression que je ne pouvais pas porter toute cette douleur du monde sur mes frêles épaules' (I had the impression that I could not carry all the pain of the world on my fragile shoulders) (Belkhodja 1997: 21). Yet she bears this weight, and it is her character Laura's unique function in the film that enables her to occupy this difficult position.

Level 5 begins by cutting between different shots of two people's hands operating a computer mouse. One is older than the other and male, perhaps corresponding to Chris and Laura. We then hear a woman's voice and see a series of disparate images. The location from which the disembodied voice emanates has the same kind of ambiguity and oscillation that Michel Chion associates with the phantom vision of the 'acousmêtre', the kind of narrator who is not easily located either inside or outside the image. Indeed, Chion states that the beginning of Preminger's *Laura* has precisely these qualities (Chion 1994: 129): the voice subsequently identified as that of Waldo Lydecker explains where he was the night that Laura died, but the film reveals ultimately that it is a dead man who speaks these words about a woman who is alive. In Marker's film, in contrast, it is the voice of a woman that we hear and that we subsequently identify as that of Laura. She reads out a passage from her dead lover's work, over images of lights in motion projected onto a statuesque mould of a face, which serves as their screen. The final image in this opening sequence is of a complex lattice pattern, which then remains faintly on screen – a ghost of an image – as Laura appears in the flesh. Throughout his filmmaking, as we have seen, Marker troubles any straightforward documentary relationship between a voice-over and images on screen. In *Level 5* he takes this one step further. For Jacques Rancière, *Level 5* is an attempt to break with a tension between images that speak for themselves and words that make them speak, thereby engaging the relationship that he saw in *Le Tombeau d'Alexandre* in more critical terms (Rancière 2006: 169–70). One of the ways in which it does this, in his view, is through Laura's embodiment of the fictionalisation of the poetic function of the commentator's voice. One important facet of the film's commentary, Laura's voice, steps into the visual frame as a fictional rather than a documentary commentator, and occupies physical space. Chris is in the more conventional position of being heard and not seen. It is Laura's occupation of a space between fictional character and documentary voice-over that permits her to work through her own traumas while remembering suffering that is not her own.

Level 5 negotiates the fine line between memory and forgetting that *Sans Soleil* also explores, but it refuses the amnesiac relation to Okinawa that Japanese and world history had previously sanctioned. By moving between Laura's life and that of the people of Okinawa, the insistent question that the film enables us to ask is how one might use electronic memory to relate to the suffering of others. The role that film played in the process of remembering was central to *Sans Soleil*. Film is also important in fashioning the protagonist in *Level 5* (especially Laura's relation to classics by Preminger (*Laura*), Resnais (*Hiroshima mon amour* and *L'Année dernière à Marienbad*) and Hitchcock (*Vertigo*)). However, it adds computer technology and the virtual reality of cyberspace to this. Laura states that the ethnologist of the future should be told that it was customary in our era to confide in 'un esprit familier et protecteur' (a familiar and protective spirit), and that it was usual to store our memories in its databases. She then corrects this in a slight modification of what Krasna writes in *Sans Soleil*: 'en fait on n'avait plus de mémoire, il était notre mémoire' (in fact, we no longer had a memory, it was our memory). Electronic texture is, as with *Sans Soleil*, the only eternity we have left, but the means of accessing this are broadened out beyond celluloid and its synthesised variations here to the difference that multimedia makes. This fits with Marker's broader interests in installation work beyond this film. The conceptually driven concern with multimedia and its relation to survival, through the re-contextualisation of different kinds of document (archive footage, photographs, interviews), extend this film into a different relation to space, time and the documentary, all of which relations centre on Laura.

Laura's connection with Okinawa's painful history is figured first of all in terms of a relation to Resnais's *Hiroshima mon amour*. She states: 'Je peux me reconnaître dans cette petite île, parce que ma souffrance la plus unique, la plus intime est aussi la plus banale, la plus facile à baptiser, alors autant lui donner un nom qui sonne comme une chanson, comme un film, Okinawa mon amour.'[3] She hereby likens herself to the female protagonist of Resnais's film (played by Emmanuelle Riva who relives the personal trauma of lost

---

3 'I can recognise myself in this little island, because my most unique and intimate form of suffering is also the most banal, the easiest to baptise, so one might as well give it a name that sounds like a song, like a film, Okinawa mon amour.'

love through an adulterous encounter in Hiroshima, several years after the end of the Second World War). When Laura utters these words, she speaks directly to her diary camera, but this declaration of recognition is matched by the similarity between the filming of the witness accounts and her diary. Although they are filmed from different angles, and Laura's address to camera is more direct, the parity of attention treats Laura – in formal terms of the camera's approach to her – as another witness rather than a mere spectator, neither undermining her personal experience, nor presenting it as the same as what the Okinawa people have been through. Laura wishes to rewrite the past, to alter it. She sits at her computer and attempts to redraw the battle lines to defend Okinawa, and to change the historical outcome of the Battle in her video game to give it a happier ending, but the machine always prevents this. Although the rewriting of history by means of the video game replay proves to be impossible, the film in which she features uses video to bring to light this neglected aspect of the official history, to open up the archives and to permit them to tell a different story.

The 'free replay' to which Marker referred in his reading of *Vertigo* offers a way of re-visiting the past. The film engages with the Platonic logic of anamnesis (which Laura actually mentions in a latter part of the film and attributes to a legend of Jewish tradition) in which life becomes a process of rediscovering what one once knew. The trope of the video game that mimics an unconscious love of repetition reinforces this. But in allowing a different story to emerge from the official historical amnesia, this replay also gives rise to something new. For Laurent Roth, Marker's films embalm time (recalling Bazin's description of the ontology of the photographic image and the subsequent cinematic mummification of change), but only so that such embalmed time can 'traverse a future which it already contains' (Roth 1997: 45). When he writes more specifically about *Level 5*, he states that the film's communication with the beyond is not with a new space or time: 'this beyond has always been there before: Chris Marker is not an author of science fiction. Anticipation only serves him to explore those zones of virtual memory which a new game's roll of the dice will actualize' (Roth 1997: 60). The embalmment that guards against the passage of time prevents a relation to the future. Even by mummifying duration, there is something static about a looped temporal structure that never gives rise to something that is not already there, that can never create the possibility for evolution, development and change. Marker's work takes the 'virtual' further into the technological dimension of cyberspace than Roth's use of the term allows for, however. It thereby opens up to a different temporal and spatial logic crucial to the relation to memory and history that *Level 5* will create, one that is not so rooted in the tragic ontology of the image and its link to death.

The actual–virtual tension, to continue with Roth's terminology, pertains to Laura's location in the present of her office and the porous membrane through which she gains access to the virtual reality of cyberspace, the Optional World Link. Laura enters a gallery of masks through the O.W.L., which permits her to adopt various guises and to communicate with people through them. The montage of masks and the accompanying range of sonic and visual distortion show her as part of this virtual space and its infinite variations, which expands the more constrained location of the actual space that she occupies – her office of ten by six foot. Although flattened out as a function of this electronic texture and given depth only through the perspective generated by special effects, the virtual image and Laura's place in it questions the location of her reality. For Bouchra Khalili, during the multiplication of the masks, the play of the varied images opens a temporal abyss: 'L'espace se dissout dans cet excès de mise en abîme, faisant sombrer Laura avec lui dans une autre dimension qui n'est que du temps, sans repère, sans passé ni avenir, une mémoire à nu'[4] (Khalili 2002: 155). Although this suggests rightly that Marker's engagement with cyberspace is inseparable from his ongoing explorations of time, his film renders more emphatic a concern with the virtual and the actual in spatial terms too.

Laura does make one move into another actual space beyond her office in the course of *Level 5*. The interlude features an open space of greenery, populated by emus, kangaroos and parrots, which is difficult to locate geographically. Laura walks freely among the animals and birds, accompanied by music and her voice-over. She complains of a headache that is caused by temporal flux. She wants to live in the present and dispense with other aspects of time, but these return constantly to trouble her. This move beyond her office brings her

4 'Space dissolves in this excess "mise-en-abime", making Laura sink with it into another dimension, which is only time, with no reference point, no past or future, a memory stripped bare.'

into contact with animals rather than the human world, as if there were no possibility for commerce with people anymore, other than through the virtual reality of the O.W.L. The acronym suggests that human dialogue and contact has to pass through the figure of this symbolic bird, which is also a creation of cyberspace, in order to exist. Consequently, this exit to the physical world outside her office is fleeting.

Laura's relation to the immateriality of virtual space is a constant in *Level 5*. She literally materialises in front of the camera at one point, and this suggests possible ways of transportation, being and appearance that do not belong to our world. Laura logs on to O.W.L. in order to research into information about Okinawa and has conversations with people in this virtual space. Chris mentions in voice-over that the network is reputed to permit people to log in to the nervous systems of their correspondents, which gives it the feel of the matrix to which William Gibson refers in *Neuromancer* (his name and the book are referred to by Laura at the beginning of the film), and which the Wackowski brothers turned into their blockbuster trilogy. The virtual life for Laura, in contrast, is not fleshed out through physical encounters. Prior to and after her entry into the gallery of the masks, when she logs on, her image and those of the O.W.L. become part of the same space, either through her reflection on the screen of her computer, where she seems to have crossed over to the other side of the screen, or through the computer being reflected on the special plastic face mask that she wears in order to log in. The layers of electronic texture clothe her and fashion her visibly at these moments, and this recalls the palimpsests of *2084*. In a reversal of the move made by her counterpart in Preminger's *Laura*, who goes from being an image to a woman of flesh and blood, she steps into the computer image of cyberspace throughout the film. Pierre Eisenreich recognises that Marker is engaging with and expanding space here: 'Chris. Marker semble avoir dépassé aussi bien la fiction que le documentaire en laissant augurer un espace fractal, certes infini, mais vide de tout repère'[5] (Eisenreich 1998: 89). Neither space is located definitively in relation to either documentary or fiction. An ability to access the facts of Okinawa's past is dependent on the power of fiction and on the resources located in the virtual realm.

5 'Chris. Marker seems to have gone beyond fiction as well as documentary by inaugurating a fractal space, certainly infinite, but void of any reference point.'

Like *Le Tombeau d'Alexandre* before it, *Level 5* is appropriately incomplete, selective in the elements it seeks to elaborate upon and aware of the fact that there is no such thing as full knowledge or closure in the way that memory and history are continually rewritten, remembered or forgotten. The random access memory of the computer database, in which each fact stored is equidistant from any other, is a more appropriate spatial metaphor than the linear, temporal structure of a strip of celluloid to account for the way in which Laura accesses the history of Okinawa, along with the haphazard resurgence of things from her own memory, sometimes triggered by the mere mention of a word. She scrolls down lists of names pre-entered into the computer database and clicks on the names of those whose tale she wishes to hear; she narrates encounters she has on O.W.L., which connect her back to her memories, her present life or to her lover's incomplete game. All this is shared with the lover whose death she simultaneously admits and denies.

'Level 5' named the final level in a game that she and her lover used to play, when they attributed points to others' discourse: she states that they never awarded anyone a '5' and questions whether one needs to die to reach this level. Laura's acceptance–denial of her lover's death is announced explicitly after one of her conversations with a man, Michel, on the O.W.L. who informs her that he is going to kill himself and that his fame will make her famous too as the last person who spoke to him before dying. She challenges him and says that she thinks he is bluffing. She adds: 'même si tu me disais que tu étais mort, je pourrais parler avec toi, parce que l'homme que j'aimais est mort et je lui parle tous les soirs.'[6] Her acceptance–denial of her lover's death could be read purely on a thematic level, but her dual place as poetic function and fictional character places her within the image with an enhanced status. Her unwillingness to accept the physical fact of death (even though she also admits it) means that this serves on both a structural and thematic level to defy associations with death and embalmment that underpin the ontological connection between the photographic and cinematic image. In part, this is a function of the shift into the terrain of multimedia technology, but *Level 5* never abandons the more conventionally indexical image and its link back to photography.

6 'even if you told me that you were dead, I could still talk to you, because the man that I loved is dead and I talk to him every evening.'

The relation between death and the image is brought out literally and questioned in ethical terms through her viewing of footage from Okinawa. Laura's trawl through these and other archives isolates instances in which the presence of a camera, and the operator, are taken to be responsible for driving people to death. She questions whether one woman from Okinawa would have jumped to her death had she not turned to see a camera pointed at her. We are shown the grainy black and white footage of this woman and the film is frozen as she turns to see the camera, prior to leaping into the abyss. The camera here performs more than the 'sublimated murder' of which Susan Sontag speaks in relation to the photograph's capacity to violate someone (Sontag 1979: 14–15): it is actually taken to be responsible for the woman's death. Laura highlights the wrongs of this and seeks to question such a drive to death on the part of the person filming. This works in line with her own contesting relation to death and the filmic image.

Through the displacement of documentary commentary and its embodiment in the fictional character of Laura, she signifies her lover's absence by fleshing it out, and gives her body instead of his image as a marker of her death-defying behaviour. It is through aural, rather than physical or visual, contact that the link to her lost loved one is preserved, through the spoken word that is addressed to him, rather than his image that might preserve him forever in the Bazinian account. Her melancholic failure to accept the loss of her loved one preserves him here technologically in a modification of the mummifying properties of the image: as an invisible but implied, even though impossible, presence, *he* is embalmed by *her* image and commentary. If she were to stop talking to her loved one, this would end both the fiction and the documentary. Her central position in this respect also offers a different way of seeing temporality and death, at great personal cost, which allows her to connect with the time of others, and their suffering. Connecting with others and with the past through the technology that she has at her disposal permits communication across spatial and temporal distance, even the distance between life and death. The position defined for the viewer in the fiction is identified with a space beyond the present. We, along with Chris, are direct recipients of the address to camera that permits communication with her dead lover, and we are therefore in the very impossible position that she believes exists. It is precisely because this space opens out to other viewing positions that the film is able to replay its relation to memory and history differently. It does not rewrite history as a fiction but opens out one person's memory, one people's history, to the memories and histories of others, to introduce us to what we do not already know and cannot know in the same way as anybody else.

As with *Sans Soleil*, there is no closure in *Level 5*, yet the process of relating to others through the multimedia layers of this film is altogether more devastating in Laura's case than it was for Krasna. Laura spirals downwards, unable to draw her personal process of mourning to a close and visibly affected by the Okinawan tragedies that she studies on a daily basis. Chris tells us that he had hoped that the war had ended for her but that this was not to be (this reference harks back to the first Okinawa interviewee who talks of Okinawans who still have a tremendous sense of injustice with regard to what happened: for them the war is not yet over). Laura's final unkempt appearance in the film is in a series of shots that she controls, which move increasingly closer to her until we lose sight of her in extreme, blurred close-up. The film ends with Chris's entry into her diary room space. In an inversion of her namesake's reappearance in Preminger's film, the lady has vanished, and Chris, pseudo-detective, arrives on the scene with his handheld camera. The computer states that it does not know 'how to Laura', and the closing theme music sings of a future encounter in an unspecified place and time. Laura communes with extreme suffering and death throughout this film, and there is a suggestion, in her final farewell and disappearance, that she has crossed over to the other side, rather than remaining in the liminal space between life and what lies beyond. By leaving the issue of her fate open, however, the end of the film perpetuates her questioning of the boundary that death represents. This final part of Marker's loosely connected trilogy re-engages issues of stasis, time and mobility present in the previous films, then, by entering the most difficult territory of all – that of personal and historical trauma. *Level 5* undoes the work of death inherent in an overly static vision of the past, and testifies to the necessary yet risk-ridden journey of giving time and life to the pain of memories that need to be remembered, stories that need to be told.

Une Journée d'Andrei Arsenevitch

Marker's next film is a tribute to Russian director Andrei Tarkovsky, who passed away in December 1986. Made in 1999, *Une Journée d'Andrei Arsenevitch* forms part of the 'Cinéma, de notre temps' (Cinema, of our time) collection run by Janine Bazin and André S. Labarthe. It was first broadcast on Arte on 17 May 2000. It has since been released on DVD under the Argos label as one of the accompaniments to Andrei Tarkovsky's *The Sacrifice* (1986), his final film, which was produced by Argos Films. Marker's *Journée* centres on a particular day in the life of the Russian filmmaker, and on a moment that Tarkovsky describes in the posthumously published French version of his diary in 1993 as 'peut-être le plus important de ma vie' (perhaps the most important of my life) (Tarkovsky 1993: 400). The event to which Tarkovsky refers here is his being reunited with his son, Andrioushka, and his mother-in-law, Anna Semionova, after six years of exile. Up until this moment, the Russian authorities had refused travel visas to Tarkovsky's family. It was only upon hearing that the filmmaker was terminally ill that they arranged for his relatives to visit him in Paris, where he and his wife Larissa had been staying. The day in the life of Tarkovsky is also, as Bernard Eisenschitz states, a life contained in a day (Eisenschitz 2005: 19), but this life is constructed through an erudite reading of his work. The moment of emotional re-encounter extends outwards beyond the frame of the images that form the record of the day, to recall other days, other Tarkovsky films. *Journée* comprises 16mm footage of the day filmed by Marc-André Batigne and Pierre Camus, numerous extracts from Tarkovsky's films, photographs by Pierre Fourmentraux, and video footage by Marker, who also wrote the commentary and did the editing. It includes further footage of Tarkovsky, bed-ridden but continuing to work on his final film, along with testimony from Alexander Medvedkin who expresses his deep regret after his fellow filmmaker's death (from *Medvedkine 88*, by Françoise Widhoff). In keeping with the eclectic and associative aspects of Marker's editing, *Journée* brings many segments of film and video together. However, his recognisable style respects the specificity of the Russian director's filmmaking, and pays homage to Tarkovsky's desire to use cinema to 'sculpt in time'.

Marina Vlady – actress, writer and partner of Léon Schwartzenberg, the cancer specialist who cared for Tarkovsky throughout his illness – is the narrator. (Marker will offer a touching commemoration of Schwartzenberg's own death in *Chats perchés*.) Alexandra Stewart provided the voice-over for the English-language version. Unlike some of Marker's films in which a more oblique relation exists between image and commentary, here the relationship is more direct. This permits us to focus less distractedly on what goes on within a shot, on time within the images, and the transitions between them. We hereby approach time through the image, and this brings the film close to Tarkovsky's vision as outlined famously in his text *Sculpting in Time*. For the Russian director, and in contrast to Kuleshov's and Eisenstein's theories of the 1920s, it is rhythm and not montage that is the main formative element of a film. Rhythm, for him, is pre-eminent within the cinematic image, rather than deriving solely from the way in which images are assembled together (Tarkovsky 1986: 119). Marker's *Journée* brings different times together through the varied films that he juxtaposes.

Journée begins with the first shot of the mother from Tarkovsky's *Mirror* (1975), who is seated on a fence and filmed from behind as she smokes and looks out across a field. We hear the sound of a train on the soundtrack, before the voice-over commentary of Marker's film announces that Larissa was watching out for the arrival of the plane from Moscow. *Journée* cuts to an image of Larissa at this point, whom we view from behind standing in front of a window. As the voice-over remarks, with her blond hair in a bun, she resembles the mother of *Mirror*. An analogy between the two women's hairstyles and the position from which we view them then serves to bind together film and life: 'un chignon russe, vu de dos, c'est le signe de l'attente' (a Russian chignon, viewed from behind, is the sign of waiting). The film cuts back to *Mirror* as it makes this comparison, and Tarkovsky's camera moves slowly around the mother's plaited hair, before Marker's film returns us to the airport and to the emotional reunion of Larissa, her son and her own mother.

It is appropriate that *Mirror* is the film with which Marker's *Journée* begins, since not only is this the most autobiographical of Tarkovsky's films, it also combines newsreel footage and acted sequences. This resonates with the shift between documentary images (16mm and video) and extracts from Tarkovsky's work, which structures *Journée*. In *Sculpting in Time* Tarkovsky expresses his anxiety about films that combine subjective time and authentic documentary time, which contain different 'time-pressures' (Tarkovsky 1986: 130). Yet his work in *Mirror* showed how documentary could become an organic part of the film, and he was able to draw the material together in what he terms 'a single time-sense' (Tarkovsky 1986: 130). In Marker's film, the voice-over commentary assures progression and flow between images. One image summons many more, and his editing is characteristically non-linear, but the smooth integration of documentary and acted scenes creates a harmonious continuity rather than the disjunctive cuts of montage cinema. The opening shot from *Mirror* has further resonance, since mention of the woman's chignon echoes Marker's fascination with the spiral of Kim Novak's and Hélène Chatelain's hair in *Vertigo* and *La Jetée* respectively, in which he sees the spiral of time, explicitly in the Hitchcock film, and by reference back to this film in his photo-roman of 1962. There is an element of implicit self-recognition here, then, facilitated by the felicitously titled *Mirror*, that refers us simultaneously to Tarkovsky's film and a moment from his life, and to Marker's filmmaking beyond this. The image of waiting tacitly recalls the vertiginous temporal spiral that haunts Marker elsewhere, through the image of a woman. Yet here its perilous connotations seem tamed, calmer and more resigned, in keeping with the patient interest in time on the part of the other filmmaker rather than with the restlessness of montage. Indeed, the spiral stabilises as a circle in *Journée* as Marker works in tune with Tarkovsky.

Partway through the film, Marker inserts video footage shot by him seven months earlier while on location in Gotland, Sweden with Tarkovsky's film crew for *The Sacrifice*. We see Tarkovsky, his crew and actors running through the final scene. The commentary describes this as one of the most complex scenes in the history of cinema, which could not be shot again. It was dependent on a single take, which lasts approximately six minutes and in which all the action was to be captured by a tracking shot of the camera. Alexander, the main protagonist, has just set light to his house, which burns in the background as the action between characters takes place in the foreground of the shot: the house had already been reconstructed once after the first attempt at filming this scene failed, and could not be rebuilt a second time. As Tarkovsky films and directs, *Journée* cuts to the final version of *The Sacrifice*, full screen, yet this runs only for a few seconds before the image is partially masked by a black circular border and we hear Tarkovsky's instructions in voice-over, translated by an interpreter. *Journée* cuts back to Tarkovsky on set, before it shows another image from the final version of *The Sacrifice*, full-screen. We then see Tarkovsky run actors through their roles. *Journée* accompanies these documentary images of Tarkovsky and his actors, with circular inserts from *The Sacrifice*, which show how Tarkovsky's instructions were followed perfectly in the second take. The commentary outlines how Tarkovsky envelops the four elements of air, water, fire and earth (a characteristic of his work described at some length earlier in Marker's film). It also explains how the travelling shot – breaking with Godard's famous association of it with morality – becomes a matter of metaphysics: the image opens out to the infinite through the matter that is filmed. Tarkovsky wanted to place cinema on the same level as the other arts, while recognising this art form as a living being. This suggests that he takes the time-pressure within a film frame as a physician might take the body's blood pressure; but the physician also speaks as a metaphysician. For Tarkovsky: 'the image stretches out into infinity, and leads to the absolute' (Tarkovsky 1986: 104). While Marker views Tarkovsky's interest in the tracking shot as a mode of access to the metaphysical dimension, his own film provides this access through editing.

Marker builds out from the Russian director's tracking shot to create something new, which works in accordance with his own style. The circular inserts of *Journée* create a spatial montage, in which we view the making of scenes from Tarkovsky's film at the same time as the final product. Marker's documentary video footage is juxtaposed simultaneously with a selection of the acted scenes: the single time-sense, which brings together two different times, is achieved here by Marker who hollows out a space in his own footage, through which we see *The Sacrifice*. This montage condenses time differently from the cuts elsewhere in *Journée* between the 16mm footage of the reunion day and Tarkovsky's films; instead, it allows two separate times (the present shooting of *The Sacrifice*, the future of the finished version) to co-exist within the same image. We glimpse Tarkovsky's metaphysics through the circular window opened in Marker's images. The form of the circle features elsewhere in *Journée*. Boris Pasternak's prophecy that Tarkovsky would make seven films is recounted over an image of a séance table created through iris masking. A later sequence concerning the bold pianist Maria Yudina, who reportedly told Stalin what she thought of his regime and lived to see another day, concludes with the spinning shape of the centre of a record, again produced through masking. Marker's film continues the circular trajectory as it draws to a close.

Over shots of the exterior of the Hartmann Clinic in Neuilly-sur-Seine, we are told that Tarkovsky died here during the night of 28–29 December 1986. The commentary remarks that the Russian Orthodox Cathedral, where his funeral took place, bears the name of a film: Saint Alexander Nevsky. It is Eisenstein to whom we are referred here indirectly through an allusion to the title of one of his films. Marker's passion for montage, coupled with the critique of this very kind of cinema through Tarkovsky's writings, means that Eisenstein remains a reference point, but one that has to stay in the background in the context of *Journée*. We hear French newscasters announce Tarkovsky's death, along with a cello suite by Bach, played by Mstislav Rostropovitch. Black and white photographs of some of those who attended the funeral are laid down to the music, one upon another, like cut flowers on a grave. *Journée* ends as it began, with images from Tarkovsky's films: the opening shot of *Ivan's Childhood* (1962) and the final shot of *The Sacrifice* are juxtaposed, each of which features a child and a tree. Marker's film suggests the closure of a circle in conclusion, 'une boucle bouclée' (a closed circle), yet this reading is proffered tentatively since the last film was made before Tarkovsky knew that he was ill, furnishing another enigma for people to ponder. The commentary suggests openly that viewers must find their own key to Tarkovsky's films.

By way of a coda to Marker's film, it is worth noting a posthumous twist that has arisen since its release. In 2004, the French translation of Tarkovsky's diary was re-published in revised form. His son, Andrioushka, provides a preface, which is entirely new, and in which he confirms that this edition: 'peut donc être considérée, par ses ajouts et ses corrections, comme sa version définitive' (may be considered, through its additions and corrections, as the definitive version) (Tarkovsky 2004: 6). Although many entries have been altered substantially, it is the entry of 7 February 1986 that is relevant here, since, with regard to Marker, it restricts itself to reporting that he brought the 16mm footage to Tarkovsky the day beforehand and then includes only the most cursory remarks about the day itself as seen through the film. It erases the subsequent material present in the 1993 edition, in which Tarkovsky expresses gratitude to Chris for arranging filming of perhaps the most important moment of his life, along with the exact words cited in *Journée* that relate to his saying silly things and to Larissa's words and emotions. It also omits an ensuing compliment, which is paid to Marker in the 1993 version, in which Tarkovsky writes that he found some of the passages of the 16mm film excellent and that he hopes to use them in an autobiographical film that he planned to make with Franco Terilli (see Tarkovsky 1993 and 2004: 400 and 534 respectively). Marker, who is so attentive to exposing in whose name and at whose expense the rewritings of history and memory occur, is now subject to a similar degree of creative editing. Rather than see the 2004 diary as definitive, it seems preferable to add this to the enigmas that Marker's reading of Tarkovsky's work leaves open to be visited by future reader-viewers. The 1993 and 2004 diaries will then stand as competing narratives, which alternately reveal and conceal what the filming of that day really meant to the late great Russian director.

Un Maire au Kosovo

In 2000, Marker returned to the former Yugoslavia with François Crémieux. The resultant 28-minute film, *Un Maire au Kosovo*, focuses principally on the testimony of Bajram Rexhepi, mayor of Kosovo. (The incomplete film, *Avril inquiet* (2001), is based on interviews with Kosovans.) Having trained as a surgeon and exercised his profession in Kosovo during the conflicts of the late 1980s and early 1990s, he earned the respect of soldiers and lay people alike, and the temporary government of Kosovo asked him whether he would become mayor. The film begins with images of the town of Mitrovica in North Kosovo, famous, we are told by the voice-over (provided by Frederico Sanchez), because of the bridge that divides it, which separates Albanians from Serbs. For the few Albanians who still live on the other side, a footbridge was constructed: we see people cross the bridge and come up the hill on the other side towards the camera. They are captured in slow motion, along with a soldier who tells the camera operator not to shoot. A subsequent image of burning vehicles harks back to more violent times in this area. The commentary informs us that the moment the Kosovans ceased to be pictured as refugees on the roadside, they disappeared from the media eye, and Kosovo became an abstraction. The people and conflicts of this region have been the subject of much discussion and, as the commentary reports, we rarely hear from the people themselves. This film aims to change this.

Rexhepi is interviewed indoors, in fixed frame close-up, and also while driving, in a profile shot (which only the bumpy road disturbs), with the passing landscape and townscape just visible beyond him. Marker's voice is audible at times. The interviews with Rexhepi are interspersed with filming of an anniversary ceremony of the UÇK, the Kosovo liberation army, at which soldiers are gathered together in festivities and awarded medals, and people in folk costumes dance and sing. Occasionally, we are shown images of dilapidated interiors and exteriors of buildings, vehicles and debris, some of which are shot from static camera positions and resemble photographs. Parts of the UÇK ceremony are shown in slow motion, most strikingly the dancing. Rexhepi's testimony is balanced. He is adamant that everyone has had enough of war in this area now and that they need to find another way of dealing with their differences. When asked about the future, he says that he is not entirely optimistic but neither is he pessimistic. The impression with which we are left after Rexhepi's testimony is one of a level-headed, fair-minded man, which makes the final intertitle concerning the media assessment of the subsequent elections all the more jarring: 'Aux élections d'octobre 2000, Bajram Rexhepi a été battu par la LDK d'I. Rugova. Verdict de la presse: "les modérés l'ont emporté sur les ultras..."'.[7] The voice-over states at the outset that the use Rexhepi makes of his authority risks shaking some received ideas. Although the press verdict indicates how entrenched these ideas are, Rexhepi's preceding words question both their accuracy and fixity.

Le Souvenir d'un avenir

Marker's next film returns him to the photographic image. Co-directed with Yannick Bellon, *Le Souvenir d'un avenir* (2001) is his third photofilm, made up almost entirely from black and white photographs taken by Denise Bellon, Yannick's mother. It pays tribute to the work of Denise Bellon by focusing on the period in her career from the 1930s to the 1950s. The title is a citation from a poem by Claude Roy, quoted in full at the end of the film, but the voice-over declares early

7 'In the elections of October 2000, Bajram Rexhepi was beaten by I Rugova's LDK. Press verdict: "the moderates beat the extremists".'

on that each of these photographs 'montre un passé mais déchiffre l'avenir'(shows a past but deciphers the future). (Roy was Yannick's brother-in-law; and to continue the embedding of the film in the Bellon family, it is dedicated to Claude and Loleh, her sister.) The 'memory of a future' refers to how the photo-film will look back and look again at its images with knowledge of what the future holds. The fluent voice-over commentary, provided by Pierre Arditi, furnishes the narrative that links together the otherwise disparate images. The voice-over also inspired a special issue of *Images documentaries*, but the editor remarked on a sense of discomfort at hearing Arditi's, rather than Marker's, voice. Catherine Blangonnet-Auer expresses frustration and regret at the disjunction between Marker's text and the voice that speaks it. She says that she could hear Marker's detached, slightly ironic tone echoing in Arditi's voice, and that François Périer is better at approximating this (Blangonnet-Auer 2006: 11). It is interesting that Blangonnet-Auer does not expect to hear Yannick Bellon's voice and is only surprised that the commentator is not Marker. To forge a relation to the mother through photography is to recall Barthes's *La Chambre Claire*, which is written in the light of his own mother's death, yet no mention is made in this photo-film of Denise Bellon's death in 1999. Marker and Bellon do not set this up as a work of mourning. Temporal progression still leads to death here, though, echoing the trajectory of a lifetime, while broadening it to include historical devastation as the photo-film shows a future that is now past.

Like *La Jetée* and *Si j'avais quatre dromadaires* before it, the camera eye of *Le Souvenir* provides movement where there is none in the original images themselves, using pans and zooms. Stasis is injected with life through this second retrospective look of a different camera eye at what Denise Bellon's camera first recorded. This photo-film is very distant from the utopia that *Dromadaires* envisaged in conclusion and is closer to the dystopian projections of *La Jetée*. Michael Almereyda comments indeed on Marker's ability to look at Bellon's photographs and see 'impending doom in nearly every image' (Almereyda 2003: 36). Unlike both previous works, however, *Le Souvenir* makes use of film footage in addition to the photographs we see, without ever supplanting photography with film. (The photographic image also gives way temporarily to other documents: magazines are opened up (*Marie Claire, Paris Match*), as is a signed copy of Breton's *Les Vases Communicants*.) The future presaged by the photographic images is designated by means of the commentary and through recourse to the archive footage.

Le Souvenir charts signal aspects of Denise Bellon's career, which include six years with the Alliance Photo agency, her proximity to the Surrealists (especially André Breton) and her travels to Africa. We also see images of the World Exhibition in Paris in 1937, the French cinema of the period – referred to as its Golden Age – and French cities (Lyon, Marseille, Paris) of the inter-war and immediate post-Second World War period. The specificity of her gaze as female photographer is registered as the images show the various cultural figures, along with ordinary people, mutilated war heroes and legionnaires that she was able to approach and capture on film, while also recording family images of her two daughters. The commentary describes how she turns ordinary things into works of art. Her gaze is referred to as prophetic in what the photo-film picks up on as an uncanny ability to capture images that tell of the future. The power of the commentary to bridge past and future is apparent throughout.

After a succession of film posters of the pre-war period, we are told that later on Henri Langlois will see in one of the stars, Jean Gabin, the prefiguration of a resistance fighter. This prompts the question of who Henri Langlois was. Two of Bellon's photographs show reels of film in a bathtub, followed by the image of a sturdy black pram. Langlois, founder of the Cinémathèque française, was responsible for preserving many of the films from the period by reportedly storing them in his bathtub and transporting them through the streets of Paris in the pram. The voice-over muses on the thought that *Battleship Potemkin* may have been transported thus, a tacit allusion to the Odessa steps sequence in which a pram containing a baby tumbles down the staircase. From Gabin, through Langlois, to Eisenstein, we move from the pre-Second World War period to the post-war period, and then back to the 1920s. Changes in terminology and names are also registered by the commentary in ways that establish links between the past and the future. As it comments on the names of bridges in Paris, the voice-over notes that there is a Pont Neuf, a Pont Bercy, but that there is yet to be a Pont Bir Hakeim. 'Bir Hakeim' is looked up in a dictionary: the definition states that it is near to Auschwitz, and this gives a premonition of the horrors to come, along with a sense of why that particular bridge had yet to assume this name. Recourse to film footage continues this future connection to death.

In viewing some of Bellon's photographs, *Le Souvenir* actualises its knowledge of the future. At these moments, the photographic image is overlaid in superimposition by a filmic image. It is film, rather than photography, that obtains a spectral presence here. The celebration of the body that the commentary sees in Bellon's photographs of the 1930s is associated with freedom, but a filmic image of mass open-air exercise routines, which appears faintly over the image of the photographed body, suggests its future appropriation by totalitarian regimes. Similarly, a still image of a parachute in peacetime is combined with filmic images of parachutists during the war, as the commentary notes the changing association of the term 'parachutist'. We see a photograph of a body lying by a river, and the commentary connects this to the future dead of the coming years, as a superimposed filmic image shows a German bomber plane. The frozen moments in time that are now past are ghosted by moving images of the future that the photographs evoke. The superimpositions are initially suggestive of dissolves, yet the hinted transition does not take place: we always return to the photographs, as the commentary continues its trajectory. The animated, sinister future is recognised although not allowed to replace the photograph. Its time will come. This work locks both stasis and movement into a forbidding image of history – one with which we are all too familiar. *Le Souvenir* animates stasis by inserting the photograph into the mobility of historical time, and it registers that its catastrophes are not open to change in the vision of this particular photo-film.

The double vision of this overlap of photographic and filmic images records the temporal quicksand through which the future becomes the past. The future that this film sketches out, through commentary and image, is bleak and is already known, rather than to be created. Marker's next film, *Chats perchés*, will use similar techniques to concern itself contrastingly with what is yet to come. It is time for the return of the cat.

Chats perchés

In 1977, Marker observed that cats are never on the side of power, and associated revolution with the grin of Lewis Carroll's infamous feline. In 2001, the appearance of grinning yellow cat graffiti all over Paris was to become the subject of his *Chats perchés* (2004). The film bears the

English title of *The Case of the Grinning Cat*, which suggests a detective mystery to be solved, but with the same sense of tracking innocence rather than criminality to which Marker referred when speaking of his approach in *Le Fond de l'air est rouge* (Marker 1978: 6). *Chats perchés* was screened on Arte in December 2004, and was released on DVD by Arte-Les Films du Jeudi in the same year with an accompanying short story by François Maspero, *Les Chats de la liberté*. In Maspero's tale, as in Marker's film, the yellow cats symbolise peace and freedom. In the run-up to the year 2000, fin-de-siècle angst generated many scare stories about how the human race would come to an end. Marker's post-millennial film, which focuses on events from 2001 to 2003 both in Paris and on the world stage, shows various pathways towards such annihilation. However, *Chats perchés* is dedicated to all those who, like M. Chat, are trying to construct a new culture. The film crosses Paris from the Left to the Right Bank in search of the cats. It also scales the city from the subterranean tunnels of the metro, its waterways (canal and river) to its rooftops. The treatment of the cats is variously ironic and tender. Their genealogy is traced from the Cheshire cat, through Miyazaki, Japanese advertisements and Manga, as well as western art history. The film paints a somewhat bleak picture of the times it traverses. Yet through a combination of mixed media, *Chats perchés* hints at how the human race might create the necessary conditions for the survival of the planet and all of its inhabitants.

The film exists in the shadow of the 9/11 terror attack on the Twin Towers, and reflects back on this momentarily from its starting point in November 2001 as it records public events, news stories and the mysterious feline graffiti in Paris over the next two years. Reminders of the heightened state of security are present in the 2001 footage: announcements on the French metro caution people to be vigilant at all times, and the transparent green bin liners which replaced the solid green bins are seen on the streets. *Chats perchés* tracks the graffiti cats, along with other representations and living incarnations: we meet Boléro, the black and white cat of the Strasbourg–Saint-Denis metro station, and Caroline, a cat stranded up a tree. The misfortunes that beset the cats are placed on a level with those that affect the human population. Although the juxtaposition of the fate of a cat alongside political occurrences is sometimes amusing, the relation between the human and feline world is one that Marker takes seriously. When Boléro gets his paw caught in an escalator, the film announces this on an intertitle as a catastrophe alongside that of the first round of French presidential election results on 21 April 2002, in which far-right-wing Jean-Marie Le Pen and right-wing Jacques Chirac were left as the only candidates. The film takes a critical look at broader political events relating to the US invasion of Iraq and re-exposes the fiction of the existence of weapons of mass destruction. Anti-war demonstrations are shown in Paris, which unite protesters of all nationalities. Mass protest itself is a recurrent feature of the film, among which feature demonstrations against the far-right wing in France; trade union demonstrations; protests by contract workers in the entertainment business and from young women regarding the wearing of the veil in French schools; a die-in for AIDS; and a placid Tibetan protest. The other gatherings of the masses that the film shows are funerals: tributes are paid to cancer specialist Léon Schwartzenberg and actress Marie Trintignant who died within the period of filming. The cats disappear for a substantial part of the second half of the film, and the intertitles (there is no commentary) remark that this is not surprising, given the events that have occurred. The insistent search for the cats – who do eventually return – is linked to the possibility of a better future.

The production of temporal meaning is bound, as in many of Marker's previous works, to the juxtapositions of editing. His associative montage drives the film forwards, while visual flashbacks and aural echoes give reminders of other times and places, through the resurgence of memory. The chronology has its 'haltes de mémoire' (memory stops): for example, journeys along the canal Saint-Martin recall early French cinema as images of a boat called the 'Marcel Carné' bring forth echoes of Arletty's voice from *Hôtel du Nord* (1938). The montage remains non-linear. Montage images still succeed one another regardless of the temporal direction in which they lead, but alongside the succession of images are those that exist simultaneously. Marker makes use of techniques that involve simultaneity, as well as temporal reversibility and displacement. The cats, graffiti and living, are thus perched between the different times of film and new media, looking forwards and backwards, and they watch over us from the height of their frequently precarious positions. The creation of a culture of freedom and peace is indebted to the positioning of cats and people between different technologies of the image, the streets and the Internet, collective and solitary pursuits.

A new media element is present from the first image onwards. *Chats perchés* begins with a flashing message on a computer screen, accompanied by an owl, which announces the arrival of new mail in the recipient's inbox. A computerised voice reads out the page of a website, which gives instructions to people to meet in front of the Centre Georges Pompidou. They are told to walk around the golden urn on the forecourt, while opening and closing their umbrellas. Through a slow dissolve, the urn then replaces the images of the people. All of this, we are informed by an intertitle, happens under the gaze of a cat. The film zooms in on, and then freezes the image of, the graffiti creature that will preoccupy the perambulating filmmaker. Dissolves involve temporal transition, albeit at the conventionally slower pace than a straight cut. The passage of time with which this technique is usually associated does not always materialise, however (as in *Le Souvenir d'un avenir*). The movement of the world is slowed down occasionally at these moments to permit contemplation of a different relation to time, which is disturbing at first but which gradually opens out to more enabling possibilities.

An example of this occurs early on. Bagpipes play on the soundtrack, as 'Flashback' appears on an intertitle. This aural link to a commemoration of the victims of 9/11 accompanies the superimposition of the very faint image of the Twin Towers under attack, over images of the Paris skyline. The traumatic, iconic memory image ghosts the present time of November in Paris 2001, and produces layers within the same frame. The Paris image then loses that of New York's tragedy, as we move forwards with a spectral memory rather than remain in the past. The association with catastrophe apparent through flashback at this point recurs throughout the film as glances back in time are linked with trauma. Music furnishes the link to the past in a later sequence, as the opening soundtrack to Resnais's *Hiroshima mon amour* plays over images of people at a die-in on the Champ-de-Mars to raise consciousness for AIDS. The start of Resnais's film is not shown but the Champ-de-Mars images recall it. The entwined bodies of the die-in participants combine an associated sense of love and death, and one image dissolves into another, as colour turns to black and white and movement to a succession of stilled images. The connection to death in this combination of movement and stasis recurs differently in relation to news of actress Marie Trintignant's death.

This news registers as if a bad dream. The film images of her funeral procession are superimposed on a static shot of a sunflower at her graveside. There are flashbacks to news headlines relating to Trintignant and her partner, singer Bertrand Cantat (later convicted of her death by manslaughter), and to extreme close-ups of Trintignant's eyes, which are superimposed over the disturbed sleep of an anonymous traveller on the metro. Successive flashbacks to headlines continue to appear over images of travellers reflected in the glass windows of the metro train. Trintignant and Cantat are re-united, albeit fleetingly, as images of them both appear on screen simultaneously. New York, Hiroshima and Vilnius – Trintignant's place of death – are sites of different losses, which through the connection to the present and the AIDS epidemic also stretch out globally. The places appear literally or associatively through flashes and dissolves, as time slows and dilates to register tragedy without creating a hierarchy between one loss of life and another. These associations link to the non-hierarchical temporality created by means of the technique of morphing elsewhere in the film.

Chats perchés employs morphing through sequences designated by the gaze of a 'morpheye'. Morphing allows for a transition between images that would usually only be permitted by a dissolve or a cut. Vivian Sobchack explains that the morph is associated with non-hierarchical temporality since it is bound up with the reversibility of time. Sobchack suggests that it is no accident that this form coincides with our era of cosmetic surgery and body sculpting: 'Faced with the visible representation and operations of an impossible meta-physical object, we fool ourselves into thinking we can conquer both our human flesh and temporality to get out of this world alive' (Sobchack 2000: 153). Marker's film is not interested in physical rejuvenation and does not suggest a return to halcyon days: as we have seen, the flashbacks to past times are to sites of trauma rather than peace. Correspondingly, morphing is not used in this film to reverse things that have already happened. Furthermore, it is associated with deception or mendaciousness rather than truth. The 'morpheye' in *Chats perchés* focuses on politicians. It emerges for the first time in the run-up to the first round of the French Presidential elections. Rival candidates are subject to its slow transforming gaze, while their words are heard in voice-over. It also operates in relation to George W. Bush's pronouncements. In Marker's hands morphing is a lot less smooth or spectacular than in some films: it involves a change in a static image, which is slow and slight, and lends the politicians a mechanical air. Morphing becomes a visible and sluggish distorted form of movement here. By associating the capacity of morphing with politicians, the film suggests that political change in fact needs to emerge from somewhere other than their discourse. It will come, rather, from the demonstrations and protest that feature throughout, which connect with the revolutionary strand of Marker's earlier work in their continuing commitment to change. The graffiti image of the smiling cat, captured in different poses and guises, is an unchanging symbol of faith in peace, and all those who strive towards this are allied with this creature.

Rather than be associated with the narcissism of remaining forever young, an interest in reversible temporality through technologies of the image in this particular film has a broader humanitarian thrust. Flashbacks return to trauma and the 'morpheye' to political posturing, yet both are mobilised in order to recognise a need for change. *Chats perchés* suggests that the world and the survival of the human race depend on an ability to conquer the destruction of flesh (and fur), not so that individuals delude themselves into beating time and being able 'to get out of this world alive' but so that ensuing generations have a world in which to go on living. The move into the future on the part of the human race is said to depend on it being accompanied by the cats. This is a film about survival and, through its localised temporal and spatial focus (Paris at the start of the new millennium), exploring what is necessary to achieve this. The connection to an invisible, unknowable time turns away from the self-centred interest in the preservation of the individual to look onwards and outwards to others. Collective acts of protest against injustice unite people in the interests of questioning the status quo. There are touches of irony and humour throughout, as the film avoids moralising while suggesting an ethical responsibility on the part of the living to those – human and animal – that are yet to be born. In place of a god lies a cat: a faint black and white cat's head is superimposed on a cloud at one point in the film. *Chats perchés* allows us to glimpse a new time and culture through the contemplation of cats, whose association with the film's modified ways of seeing and being envisages an inhabitable planet for us all.

References

Almereyda, Michael (2003), 'Deciphering the Future', in *Film Comment* (May–June), pp. 36–37.

Alter, Nora M. (2006), *Chris Marker*, Urbana and Chicago, University of Illinois Press.

Belkhodja, Catherine (1997), 'Chris Marker ne laisse pas souffler la vérité', in *L'Humanité* (19 February), p. 21.

Bellour, Raymond (1999), 'Level Five', in *L'Entre-Images 2: mots, images*, Paris, POL, pp. 227–33.

Blangonnet-Auer, Catherine (2006), 'Introduction', in *Images documentaries*, 55/56, pp. 9–11.

Chion, Michel (1994), *Audio-Vision: Sound on Screen*, Columbia, Columbia University Press. Trans. Claudia Gorbman.

Eisenreich, Pierre (1998), 'Les Petites Fictions du documentaire', in *Positif*, 446 (April), pp. 87–89.

Eisenschitz, Bernard (2005), 'Une Journée d'Andrei Arsenevitch', in *Le Sacrifice: textes et documents réunis par Bernard Eisenschitz*, Paris, Argos Films, pp. 19–20.

Fieschi, Jean-André (1996), 'Poulpe au regard de soie!', in Jean-André Fieschi, Patrick Lacoste and Patrick Tort (eds), *L'Animal-Écran*, Paris, Centre Georges Pompidou, pp. 13–30.

Graffy, Julian (1993), 'Review of *The Last Bolshevik*', in *Sight and Sound*, 9 (September), p. 57.

Horrigan, Bill (1995), *Silent Movie*, Ohio, Wexner Centre for the Arts.

Kämper, Birgit and Thomas Tode (1997) (eds), *Chris Marker: Filmessayist*, Munich, Institut Français de Munich.

Khalili, Bouchra (2002), '*Level 5* ou le reposoir', in Philippe Dubois (ed.), *Théorème 6: recherches sur Chris Marker*, Paris, Presses Sorbonne Nouvelle, pp. 141–57.

Lupton, Catherine (2005), *Chris Marker: Memories of the Future*, London, Reaktion.

Marker, Chris (1978), *Le Fond de l'air est rouge: scènes de la troisième guerre mondiale 1967–1977*, Paris, François Maspero.

Marker, Chris (1994), 'A free replay (notes sur *Vertigo*)', in *Positif*, 400 (June), pp. 79–84.

Niney, François (1996), 'Remarques sur *Sans Soleil* de Chris Marker', in *Documentaires*, 12 (Summer–Autumn), pp. 5–15.

Prédal, René (1995), 'Un cinéma direct à la première personne: Chris Marker', in Christophe Avrot, Anthony Fiant, Stéphanie Papin, René Prédal (eds), *CinémAction*, 76, pp. 18–24.

Rancière, Jacques (2006), 'Documentary Fiction: Marker and the Fiction of Memory', in *Film Fables*, Oxford, Berg. Trans. Emiliano Battista.

Roth, Laurent (1997), 'A Yakut Afflicted with Strabismus', in *Qu'est-ce qu'une madeleine?*, Paris, Yves Gevaert, pp. 37–63.

Sobchack, Vivian (2000), 'Meta-Morphing "At the Still Point of the Turning World" and Meta-Stasis', in Vivian Sobchack (ed.), *Meta-morphing: Visual*

Transformation and the Culture of Quick-Change, Minneapolis, University of Minnesota Press, pp. 131–58.

Sontag, Susan (1979), *On Photography*, London, Penguin; orig. publ. 1971.

Spielmann, Yvonne (2000), 'Visual Forms of Representation and Simulation: A Study of Chris Marker's *Level 5*', in *Convergence: The Journal of Research into New Media Technologies*, 6: 2 (Summer), pp. 18–40.

Tarkovsky, Andrei (1986), *Sculpting in Time: Reflections on the Cinema*, Austin, University of Texas Press.

Tarkovsky, Andrei (1993), *Journal 1970–1986*, Paris, Cahiers du cinéma.

Tarkovsky, Andrei (2004), *Journal 1970–1986*, Édition définitive, Paris, Cahiers du cinéma.

Walfisch, Dolores (1996), 'Interview with Chris Marker', in *Vertigo*, 7 (Autumn), p. 38.

Widdis, Emma (2005), *Alexander Medvedkin*, London, I. B. Tauris.

Conclusion

My own love affair with Chris Marker's films began in the unlikeliest of settings and on the most inappropriate of screens. I watched *La Jetée* on a computer terminal at the Bibliothèque nationale de France and was transfixed. I had already seen *Sans Soleil*, but was unable to respond to its complexity on a first viewing. *La Jetée* subsequently gave me a point of access to the later film, which then led me through all of the others in turn, the culmination of which series of encounters is the writing of this book. Roland Barthes, a recurrent voice throughout, says that one always risks failure when one talks about what one loves, and this may be true (Barthes 1984). It certainly enables us better to understand the absence of the Winter Garden photograph from *La Chambre Claire*, mentioned briefly in the introduction to this study. Barthes chooses not to show this early image of his mother because he knows that nobody else would be affected by it in the same way that he is. The unshared image thus becomes synonymous with an unshared love, which Barthes, like Marker, refuses to lament.

Separate from the unrequited kind, which involves a lack of reciprocity, this love that is not shared recognises inevitable and valuable differences between people's experiences. The monstrousness of a collapse into sameness, where everyone would experience things and remember them in exactly the same way, was touched on in Marker's *Mémoires pour Simone*. It is by acknowledging, rather than denying, these necessary distinctions and specificities that the drive towards connectedness is established. Fur and scales come to matter as much as human flesh in Marker's various visions of solidarity or collective struggle through the years, the militant spark of which has never been extinguished. The rethinking of filmic time and alternative lives in his many and varied works is enabled, rather than blocked, by an engagement with death and stasis. The time of others that has been traced throughout this study may appear to jar occasionally with an ethical vision, since its production or recollection sometimes involves negotiating violence on fiercely contested political terrain. Yet Marker's films move unceasingly beyond such conflict as they track new, more peaceable modes of existence.

In *Sans Soleil*, the filmmaker takes us to the end of memory's path and invites us to look back with him. If all that lies at the journey's end is a series of regrets, then the film of life culminates in melancholia for what has been lost, as well as what was desired but never possessed. There is certainly something of this in Marker's oeuvre, which aches at times for what was and what could have been. If, however, we join with him in confronting the pathos of personal and historical tragedy, human limitations and finitude, while also looking out from this vantage point, a different way of seeing and being materialises that gestures forwards, even as we glance back. This book began with an epigraph from Marker's novel *Le Cœur net*, which stated that death is not the opposite of life, and that the antonym of living is still to be discovered. In his hands and through his eyes, film becomes the search for this other to life – an indelible marker of hope and generosity to something that lies somewhere beyond our reach, and which as yet has no name, but which some may call the future.

References

Barthes, Roland (1984), 'On échoue toujours à parler de ce qu'on aime', in *Le Bruissement de la langue*, Paris, Seuil; article orig. publ. in *Tel Quel* (1980).

Filmography

Comprehensive lists of Chris Marker's broader film collaborations and installation work appear in: Birgit Kämper and Thomas Tode (eds) (1997), *Chris Marker: Filmessayist*, Munich, Institut Français de Munich; Philippe Dubois (ed.) (2002), *Théorème 6: recherches sur Chris Marker*, Paris, Presses Sorbonne Nouvelle; Catherine Lupton (2005), *Chris Marker: Memories of the Future*, London, Reaktion; and Nora Alter (2006), *Chris Marker*, Urbana and Chicago, University of Illinois Press.

Les Statues meurent aussi (1950) 30 min., b/w, 35 mm

Co-directed with Alain Resnais
Camera: Ghislain Cloquet
Sound: René Louge
Music: Guy Bernard
Voice-over: Jean Négroni
Editing: Alain Resnais
Commentary: Chris Marker
Production: Tadié-Cinéma Production
Distribution: Présence Africaine

Olympia 52 (1952) 82 min., b/w, 16 mm blown up to 35 mm

Camera: Chris Marker, Robert Cartier, Charles Sabatier, Joffre Dumazadier
Voice-over: Joffre Dumazedier
Editing: Suzy Benguigui
Production: Peuple et Culture
Distribution: Peuple et Culture

Dimanche à Pékin (1956) 22 min., col., 16 mm blown up to 35 mm

Camera: Chris Marker
Music: Pierre Barbaud
Voice-over: Gilles Quéant
Editing: Francine Grubert
Production: Argos Films, Pavox Films
Distribution: Argos Films

Lettre de Sibérie (1958) 62 min., col., 16 mm blown up to 35 mm

Camera: Sacha Vierny
Sound: René Louge, René Renault, Robert Hamard
Music: Pierre Barbaud
Voice-over: Georges Rouquier
Editing: Anne Sarraute
Production: Argos Films, Procinex
Distribution: Argos Films

Description d'un combat (1960) 60 min., col., 35 mm

Camera: Ghislain Cloquet
Sound: Pierre Fatosme
Music: Lalan
Voice-over: Jean Vilar
Editing: Eva Zora
Production: Wim van Leer
Distribution: Israel Film Archive

Cuba Si! (1961) 52 min., b/w, 16 mm blown up to 35 mm

Camera: Chris Marker
Sound: Jean Neny
Music: E G Mantici, J Calzada
Voice-over: Nicolas Yumatov
Editing: Eva Zora
Production: Pierre Braunberger
Distribution: Les Films de la Pléiade

Le Joli Mai (1962) 165 min., b/w, 16 mm blown up to 35 mm

Camera: Pierre Lhomme, Etienne Becker, Denys Clerval, Pierre Villemain
Sound: Antoine Bonfanti, René Levert

Music: Michel Legrand, Boris Mokroussow
Voice-over: Yves Montand
Editing: Eva Zora, Annie Meunier, Madeleine Lecompère
Production: Sofracima
Distribution: Sofracima

La Jetée (1962) 29 min., b/w, 35 mm

Editing: Jean Ravel
Music: Trevor Duncan, Choirs of the Russian Cathedral in Paris
Principal Actors: Hélène Chatelain, Davos Hanich, Jacques Ledoux
Voice-over: Jean Négroni
Sound: SIMO
Mixing: Antoine Bonfanti
Production: Argos Films
Distribution: Argos Films

Le Mystère Koumiko (1965) 54 min., b/w and col., 16 mm blown up to 35 mm

Camera: Chris Marker
Sound: Jean Neny
Music: Toru Takemitsu
Production: Apec, Sofracima; Service de la Recherche ORTF
Distribution: Sofracima

Si j'avais quatre dromadaires (1966) 49 min., b/w, 35 mm

Camera: Chris Marker
Sound: Antoine Bonfanti
Music: Lalan, Trio Barney Wilen
Voices: Pierre Vaneck, Catherine Le Couey, Nicolas Yumatov
Editing: Chris Marker
Production: Norddeutscher Rundfunk, Apec
Distribution: ISKRA

Loin du Viêt-Nam (1967) 115 min., b/w and col., 35 mm and 16 mm blown up to 35 mm

Co-directed with Alain Resnais, William Klein, Joris Ivens, Claude Lelouch, Jean-Luc Godard, [Agnès Varda]
Voice-over: Maurice Garrel
Editing: Chris Marker
Commentary: Chris Marker

Sound: Antoine Bonfanti, Harrick Maury, René Levert
Production: SLON
Distribution: Sofracima

La Sixième Face du Pentagone (1968) 28 min., col., 16 mm

Co-directed with François Reichenbach
Camera: Chris Marker, François Reichenbach, Christian Odasso, Tony Daval
Commentary: Chris Marker
Sound: Antoine Bonfanti, Harald Maury
Editing: Carlos De Los Llanos
Production: Les Films de la Pléiade, Pierre Braunberger
Distribution: Les Films de la Pléiade, Les Films du Jeudi

À bientôt j'espère (1968) 55 min., b/w, 16 mm

Co-directed with Mario Marret
Camera: Pierre Lhomme
Sound: Michel Desrois
Voice-over: Chris Marker
Montage: Carlos De Los Llanos
Production: SLON
Distribution: ISKRA

Ciné-Tracts (1968) b/w, 16 mm

Anonymous, silent films.
Marker inaugurated the project and is said to have contributed some films to the series.

On vous parle du Brésil: Tortures (1969) 20 min., b/w, 16 mm

Editing: Chris Marker
Production: SLON
Distribution: ISKRA

Jour de tournage (1969) 11 min., b/w, 16 mm

Camera: Pierre Duponey
Production: SLON
Distribution: KG Films

On vous parle du Brésil: Carlos Marighela (1970) 17 min., b/w, 16 mm

Camera: Chris Marker
Production: SLON
Distribution: ISKRA

On vous parle de Paris: Maspero, les mots ont un sens (1970) 20 min., b/w, 16 mm

Camera: Chris Marker
Voice-over: Chris Marker
Production: SLON
Distribution: ISKRA

La Bataille des dix millions (1970) 58 min., b/w, 16 mm

Camera: Santiago Alvarez, Noticierios ICAIC
Music: Léo Brouwer
Voices: Georges Kiejman, Edouard Luntz
Editing: Valérie Mayoux, Chris Marker
Production: KG Production, SLON, RTB, ICAIC
Distribution: ISKRA

On vous parle de Prague: le deuxième procès d'Artur London (1971) 28 min., b/w, 16 mm

Camera: Pierre Duponey
Editing: Chris Marker
Voice-over: Chris Marker
Production: SLON
Distribution: ISKRA

Le Train en marche (1971) 32 min., b/w, 16 mm

Camera: Jacques Loiseleux
Voice-over: François Périer
Production: SLON
Distribution: ISKRA

Vive la baleine (1972) 30 min., col., 35 mm

Co-directed with Mario Ruspoli
Camera: Mario Ruspoli
Sound: Chris Marker

Commentary: Chris Marker
Music: Lalan
Voice-over: Louis Casamayor, Valérie Mayoux
Editing: Chris Marker
Production: Prodix
Distribution: Argos Films

On vous parle du Chili: ce que disait Allende (1973) 16 min., b/w, 16 mm

Camera: Miguel Littin
Voice-over: Régis Debray
Editing: Chris Marker
Production: SLON
Distribution: ISKRA

La Solitude du chanteur de fond (1974) 60 min., col., 16 mm blown up to 35 mm

Camera: Pierre Lhomme, Yann le Masson, Jacques Renard
Sound: Antoine Bonfanti, Michel Desrois
Production: Seuil Audio-visuel
Distribution: NEF-Diffusion

L'Ambassade (1973) 20 min., col., Super 8

Production: EKF
Distribution: ISKRA

Le Fond de l'air est rouge (1977) 240 min., b/w and col., 16 mm blown up to 35 mm

Sound: Chris Marker
Voices: Simone Signoret, Jorge Semprun, Davos Hanich, Sandra Scarnati, François Maspero, Laurence Cuvillier, François Périer, Yves Montand
Montage: Chris Marker
Production: ISKRA, INA, Dovidis
Distribution: ISKRA

Junkopia (1981) 6 min., col., 16 mm blown up to 35 mm

Camera: Chris Marker, Frank Simeone, John Chapman
Special effects: Manuela Adelman, Tom Luddy, Sara Ström
Music: Michel Krasna

Production: Argos Films
Distribution: Argos Films

Sans Soleil (1982) 110 min., col., 16 mm blown up to 35 mm

Camera: Sandor Krasna/Chris Marker
Sound: Michel Krasna
Voice: Florence Delay (French), Alexandra Stewart (English)
Editing: Chris Marker, Anne-Marie L'Hote, Catherine Adda
Production: Argos Films
Distribution: Argos Films

2084 (1984) 10 min., col., 16 mm blown up to 35 mm

Co-directors: CFDT audiovisual group
Camera: Robert Millie, Christian Bordes, Pascal Le Moal
Voice-over: François Périer
Production: La Lanterne, CFDT audiovisual group
Distribution: ISKRA

AK (1985) 71 min., col., 35 mm

Camera: Frans-Yves Marescot
Sound: Catherine Adda
Music: Toru Takemitsu
Voice-over: François Maspero
Editing: Chris Marker
Production: Serge Silberman/Greenwich Film S. A. (Paris), Herald Nippon Inc. (Tokyo), Herald Ace (Tokyo)
Distribution: AAA

Mémoires pour Simone (1986) 61 min., col., 35 mm

Extracts from numerous films featuring Simone Signoret
Voice-over: François Périer
Production: Festival de Cannes

L'Héritage de la chouette (1989) 13 episodes of 26 min., col., video

Voice-over: André Dussollier
Production: Attica Art Productions, La Sept, FIT Productions
Distribution: La Sept

Berliner Ballade (1990) 29 min., col., video Hi 8

Camera: Chris Marker

Voice-over: Catherine Belkhodja
Editing: Chris Marker
Production: Antenne 2, Envoyé Spécial
Distribution: Antenne 2

Le Tombeau d'Alexandre (1993) 118 min., col. and b/w, video

Voice-over: Jean-Claude Dauphin (French), Michael Pennington (English)
Editing: Chris Marker
Production: Films de l'Astrophore, Michel Kustow, EPIDEM OY, La Sept, Arte, Channel 4, CNC
Distribution: Balfour Films

Le 20 heures dans les camps (1993), 28 min., col., video Hi 8

Directed in collaboration with the Roska television producers
Voice-over: François Périer
Voices: Catherine Belkhodja, Mathieu Kassovitz
Editor: Chris Marker

Le Facteur sonne toujours cheval (1994?) 52 min., col., video: unfinished film

Three Video Haikus (1994) 'Petite Ceinture', 1 min., 'Chaika', 1 min 29 sec., 'Owl Gets in Your Eyes', 1 min 10 sec.

Casque Bleu (1995) 27 min., col., Betacam video

Interview with François Crémieux
Production: Chris Marker, Films de l'Astrophore
Distribution: Films de l'Astrophore

Level 5 (1996) 106 min., col., Betacam video blown up to 35 mm

Camera: Chris Marker, Yves Angelo, Gérard de Battista
Sound: Michel Krasna
Editing: Chris Marker
Actor: Catherine Belkhodja
Production: Films de l'Astrophore, Argos Films
Distribution: Connaissance du cinéma, Argos Films, Maxfilm

Une Journée d'Andrei Arsenevitch (2000) 56 min., b/w and col., video and 16 mm

Camera: Chris Marker, Marc-André Batigne, Pierre Camus
Voice-over: Marina Vlady
Editing: Chris Marker
Production: AMIP, La Sept/Arte, INA, Arkeion Films for the series 'Cinéma, de notre temps', run by Janine Bazin and André S. Labarthe

Un Maire au Kosovo (2000) 27 min., col., video

Co-directed with François Crémieux
Voice-over: Frederico Sanchez

Avril inquiet (2001) 52 min, col., video: unfinished film

Le Souvenir d'un avenir (2001) 42 min., b/w, 35 mm

Co-directed with Yannick Bellon
Photographs: Denise Bellon
Sound: Michel Krasna
Theme music: Federico Mompou
Voice-over: Pierre Arditi
Production: Les Films de l'équinoxe, Arte France
Distribution: Les Films de l'équinoxe, Arte France

Chats perchés (2004) 59 min., col., video

Video: Chris Marker
Sound: Michel Krasna
Editing: Chris Marker
Production: Les Films du Jeudi, Laurence Braunberger and Arte France
Distribution: Les Films du Jeudi

Select bibliography

Books and articles

Alter, Nora M. (2006), *Chris Marker*, Urbana and Chicago, University of Illinois Press.
A lively, engaging and comprehensive study, which includes a selection of interviews with Marker, translated into English.

Bazin, André (1998), 'Chris Marker: Lettre de Sibérie', in *Le Cinéma français de la Libération à la Nouvelle Vague (1945–1958)*, Paris, Cahiers du cinéma, pp. 257–60; orig. publ. in 1983.
A landmark early essay focused on Marker's *Lettre de Sibérie*, which is more broadly relevant to his essayist style.

Bellour, Raymond and Laurent Roth (1997), *Qu'est-ce qu'une madeleine? À propos du CD-ROM Immemory de Chris Marker*, Paris, Yves Gevaert.
Stimulating essays on Marker, which range more widely than his CD-ROM *Immemory*.

Dubois, Philippe (ed.) (2002), *Théorème 6: recherches sur Chris Marker*, Paris, Presses Sorbonne Nouvelle.
A diverse and useful series of articles on Marker's work.

Gauthier, Guy (2001), *Chris Marker: écrivain multimédia, ou voyage à travers les médias*, Paris, L'Harmattan.
The first single-authored book-length study on Marker's output: a richly informative overview.

Kämper, Birgit and Thomas Tode (eds) (1997), *Chris Marker: Filmessayist*, Munich, Institut Français de Munich.
A very helpful guide to Marker's work up to the date of publication. The book contains a detailed bibliography and filmography along

with some interesting articles.

Kear, Jon (1999), *Sunless: Time and History in the Work of Chris Marker*, London, Flicks Books.

An illuminating study.

Lupton, Catherine (2005), *Chris Marker: Memories of the Future*, London, Reaktion.

An excellent, comprehensive book on all facets of Marker's career, which illuminates his work with reference to key cultural contexts and political events.

Pourvali, Bamchade (2003), *Chris Marker*, Paris, Cahiers du cinéma.

A succinct and suggestive introduction.

Special issues

Image et son, 161–62 (1963) (April–May), 'Chris Marker'.

A good selection of articles on Marker's early years.

Positif, 433 (1997) (March), 'Dossier Chris Marker'.

A rich series of articles across the range of Marker's work. It also contains testimony from Pierre Lhomme, Antoine Bonfanti and Valérie Mayoux on their experience of working on his films.

Film Comment, XXXIX:3 (May–June) and XXXIX:4 (July–August) (2003), 'Around the World with Chris Marker': Part I, 'Lost Horizons'; Part II, 'Time Regained'.

The first English-language dossier on Marker, which features essays from some key scholars in the field along with a very helpful filmography.

Index

20 heures dans les camps, Le 151–54, 156
2084 112, 125–27, 164

À bientôt j'espère 73, 76–79
AK 57, 112, 127–31
Alleg, Henri 83
Allégret, Catherine 132
Allende, Beatriz 110
Allende, Salvador 82, 95–97, 110
Almeida, Juan 33
Almereyda, Michael 175, 183
Alter, Nora 4, 10, 11, 30, 37, 142, 183
Alvarez, Santiago 84
L'Ambassade 3, 97–100
L'Amérique rêve 11
Amphitryon 38 15–16, 37
Andler, Daniel 138
Angelo, Yves 158
Angelopoulos, Theo 136
L'Année dernière à Marienbad 47, 58, 60, 161
Anzieu, Didier 121–25
Apollinaire, Guillaume 60
Arcady team, the 20, 24, 33
Arditi, Pierre 175
L'Aveu 87–89
Avril inquiet 162, 173

Barthes, Roland 7, 10, 50, 61, 65, 82, 94, 133, 175, 185, 186

Bataille des dix millions, La 84–87
Batigne, Marc-André 168
Battista, Gérard de 158
Battleship Potemkin 51, 104, 110, 149, 176
Baudry, Jean-Louis 52, 140
Bazin, André 6, 7, 10, 21–22, 24, 26, 37, 46, 48, 54, 61, 65, 139, 162, 166
Bazin, Janine 168
Belkhodja, Catherine 138, 144, 152, 156–67
Bellon, Denise 142, 174–77
Bellon, Yannick 142, 174–77
Bellour, Raymond 5, 6, 10, 48, 65, 156, 183
Bensmaïa, Réda 51, 65
Berenizi, Jacopo 1, 93
Berio, Luciano 104
Berliner Ballade 143–45, 156
Bhégin, Cyril 99, 111
Blangonnet-Auer, Catherine 175, 183
Bonfanti, Antoine 40, 61, 77, 102
Boris Godunov 148
Braunberger, Pierre 11, 32
Breton, André 175, 176
Bruzzi, Stella 115, 141
Bullfight/Okinawa 2

Cacérès, Bénigno 15–16, 37

Cahiers du cinéma group 4
Camus, Pierre 168
Cantat, Bertrand 181
Capa, Robert 51
Carroll, Lewis 104, 111, 177
Casamayor, Louis 93
Casque Bleu 154–56
Castella, Bob 101
Castoriadis, Cornelius 138
Castro, Fidel 32–37, 62, 68, 84–87, 107
Cèbe, Pol 78, 91
Chambre Claire, La 7, 10, 50, 65, 175, 185
Chat écoutant la musique 2, 146, 183
Chatelain, Hélène 47, 170
Chats perchés 2, 9, 72, 94, 142, 144, 169, 177–82
Chion, Michel 160, 183
Chronique d'un été 40–41
Ciné-Tract 79, 108
Clarke, Shirley 76
Classe de Lutte 78
Cloquet, Ghislain 12, 31
Coates, Paul 49, 65
Cœur net, Le 1, 186
Cohen, Leonard 70, 152, 153
Compañero Presidente 96
Coréennes 2, 6, 63
Costa-Gavras, Constantin 87, 88
Coubertin, Baron Pierre de 17
Couey, Catherine le 60
Crémieux, François 154–56, 173
Cuba Si! 11, 32–37, 38, 63, 65, 68, 84, 101, 105, 109
Cuvillier, Laurence 107

Darke, Chris 11, 37
Dauman, Anatole 11, 21, 22, 37
Dauphin, Jean-Claude 146
Debray, Régis 96–97
Delahaye, Michel 40, 65
Delay, Florence 115
Deleuze, Gilles 5, 6, 10

Demy, Jacques 33, 37, 57
Dépays, Le 2, 6, 100, 111
Derrida, Jacques 131, 141
Description d'un combat 11, 27–32, 33, 67
Deux ans après 4
Dieu, la mort et le temps 8, 10
DiIorio, Sam 39, 41, 65
Dimanche à Pékin 4, 11, 18–21, 46
DOC 2
Dubois, Philippe 11, 37, 48, 65
Dumazedier, Joffre 16, 17

Eisenreich, Pierre 164, 183
Eisenschitz, Bernard 168
Eisenstein, Sergei 51, 89, 90, 104, 149, 169, 172, 176
Eisler, Hanns 74
Esprit 1

Facteur sonne toujours cheval, Le 142
Fargier, Jean-Paul 107, 111
Feuillade, Louis 42
ffrench, Patrick 51, 65
Fieschi, Jean-André 150, 183
Fond de l'air est rouge, Le 74, 86, 87, 96, 101, 104–11, 177–78
Fourmentraux, Pierre 168
Frampton, Daniel 49, 65
Francovich, Alain 45, 65

Gabin, Jean 176
Gatti, Armand 21
Gauthier, Guy 4, 10, 31, 37, 40, 65
Georgousopoulos, Kostas 136
Gibson, William 164
Gilliam, Terry 45
Giraudoux, Jean 2, 15, 16, 37, 38, 41, 57, 83, 144
Giraudoux par lui-même 2, 15, 37
Glaneurs et la glaneuse, Les 4
Godard, Jean-Luc 5, 41, 74, 171
Goldman, Pierre 132
Gorky, Maxim 148–49

Graffy, Julian 151
Grimault, Paul 24, 34, 37
'Groupe des Trente' 18
Guéry, William 24, 34, 37
Guevara, Che 33, 75, 81, 82, 83, 96, 105, 106

Hanich, Davos 47, 107
Happiness 89, 90, 92, 146, 149
Harispe, Antonio 20
Hennebelle, Guy 77, 78, 111
L'Héritage de la chouette 52, 112, 126, 134–41, 156
Hesse, Bertrand 28
Hikmet, Nazim 102
Hiroshima mon amour 12, 140, 161, 180
Hitchcock, Alfred 51, 115, 123, 157, 170
L'Homme et sa liberté 2
Hommes de la baleine, Les 93
Horak, Jan-Christopher 6, 10
Huston, John 158

Illégaux, Les 28
Immemory 6, 49, 142, 157
Ionatos, Angélique 136, 138
Irigaray, Luce 52, 65
ISKRA *see* SLON
Ivan's Childhood 172
Ivens, Joris 74

Jara, Victor 103
Jetée, La 2, 19, 38, 45–56, 63, 64, 65, 69, 70, 100, 114, 115, 120, 123, 124, 139, 140, 156, 157, 170, 175, 185
Jobert, Michel 137
Joli Mai, Le 3, 38–45, 50, 102, 116
Jour de tournage 88
Journée d'Andrei Arsenevitch, Une 71, 168–73
Junkopia 112–14

Kafka, Franz 27

Kämper, Birgit 11, 37, 143, 183
Kassovitz, Mathieu 152
Kaufman, Mikhail 90
Kawin, Bruce 54, 66
Kear, Jon 197
Khalili, Bouchra 163, 183
King Lear 128, 131
Klein, William 74
Kozlovsky, Ivan 148, 150
Kristeva, Julia 122
Kuleshov, Lev 169
Kurosawa, Akira 127–31

Labarthe, André S. 168
Langlois, Henri 50, 176
Laura 160, 161, 164
Ledoux, Jacques 49
Lelouch, Claude 74
Lee, Min 73, 111
Lee, Sander 52, 66
Leer, Wim van 27
'Left Bank' group 4
Legrand, Michel 57
Lenin, Vladimir 73, 86, 90, 92, 149
Lettre de Sibérie 3, 11, 21–27, 33, 48, 67, 143
Level 5 2, 3, 45, 69, 117, 127, 142, 156–67
Levin, Meyer 28
Levinas, Emmanuel 7, 8, 9, 10, 12, 13, 37
Lhomme, Pierre 39, 40, 41, 66, 102, 116, 141
Littin, Miguel 96
Loin du Viêt-Nam 73–78
Lointain Intérieur 22
London, Artur 87–89
Lupton, Catherine 4, 10, 31, 37, 58, 66, 93, 101, 111, 142, 183

Mailer, Norman 76
Maire au Kosovo, Un 173–74
Marcorelles, Louis 40, 66
Mardore, Michel 36, 37
Marret, Mario 76–78

Maspero, François 82–84, 107, 128, 178
Mayoux, Valérie 84, 93–95, 111
Medvedkin, Alexander 78, 89–93, 142, 145–51, 168
Medvedkin groups, the 39, 73, 77, 78, 92
Melville, Hermann 94
Mémoires pour Simone 112, 131–34, 143, 185
Mendoza, César 109
Michaux, Henri 22, 26, 83
Minotis, Alexis 136–37
Mirror 169–80
Möller, Olaf 56, 66
Mompou, Federico 150
Montand, Yves 41, 87–88, 100–04, 107, 132
Morin, Edgar 40–41
Mulvey, Laura 5, 10
Murray, Oswyn 141
Mussorgsky, Modest 122, 148
Mystère Koumiko, Le 38, 56–60, 65

Naficy, Hamid 26, 37
Négroni, Jean 12, 46
Nerval, Gérard de 122
Ninagawa, Yukio 137
Niney, François 8, 10, 135, 141, 146, 147, 183
Nouvelle Vague 4, 58
Nuit et brouillard 74–75

Olympia 52 11, 15–18, 34, 109
Olympiad 17
On vous parle de Paris 82–84
On vous parle de Prague 87–89
On vous parle du Brésil: Carlos Marighela 80–82
On vous parle du Brésil: Tortures 79–80, 81–82
On vous parle du Chili 82, 95–97
On vous parle series 33, 74, 110
Oshima, Nagisa 158
Owls at Noon 142

Palach, Jan 109
Parapluies de Cherbourg, Les 57
Pasternak, Boris 171
Penley, Constance 49, 66
Pennington, Michael 146
Périer, François 107, 125, 131, 132, 152, 153, 175
Petit bestiaire 2
Petite Planète 2
Peuple et Culture 2, 15, 16
Pierrard, André 21
Pinochet, Augusto 97, 109
Pourvali, Bamchade 51, 66
Prédal, René 144, 183
Preminger, Otto 156, 160, 161, 164, 167
Pushkin, Alexander 148

Quand le siècle a pris forme 112
Quéant, Gilles 18

Ran 127–31
Rancière, Jacques 147, 150, 160, 183
Ravel, Jean 50
Renfermée: La Corse, La 6
Resnais, Alain 4, 11, 12, 13, 15, 41, 47, 51, 53, 58, 74, 140, 161, 180
Rexhepi, Bajram 173–74
Riboud, Marc 76
Richardson, Tony 101
Riefenstahl, Leni 17
Riva, Emmanuelle 161
Rivette, Jacques 41
Robbe-Grillet, Alain 58, 60
Robichet, Théo 152
Rodowick, David 5, 10
Rostropovitch, Mstislav 172
Roth, Laurent 109, 111, 162, 163
Rouch, Jean 40–41
Roud, Richard 4, 10, 89, 111
Rouquier, Georges 22, 24
Roy, Claude 174–75
Ruspoli, Mario 93
Russell, Catherine 117, 141

Sacrifice, The 168, 170–72
Salut les Cubains 33
Sanchez, Frederico 173
Sans Soleil 3, 45, 49, 62, 68, 111, 112, 114–25, 126, 127, 143, 156, 157, 161, 167, 185, 186
Scarnati, Sandra 107
Schwartzenberg, Léon 168–69, 179
Scott Fitzgerald, Frances 103
Sculpting in Time 169–73
Semprun, Jorge 87, 88, 107
Serres, Michel 137, 138, 139
Seven Samurai, The 129
Signoret, Simone 87, 88, 102, 104, 107, 108, 131–34, 141
Si j'avais quatre dromadaires 9, 34, 38, 48, 60–65, 79, 90, 100, 101, 115, 175
Silberman, Serge 127
Silent Movie 142, 154, 157
Sillitoe, Alan 101
Silverman, Kaja 118, 120, 141
Simeone, Frank 112
Sixième Face du Pentagone, La 70, 74, 75–76, 78, 106
Slansky, Rudolf 87, 88
SLON 73–111, 152
Sobchack, Vivian 181, 183
Soderbergh, Steven 119
Solaris (1972) 119
Solaris (2002) 119
Solitude du chanteur de fond, La 97, 100–04
Sontag, Susan 6, 10, 61, 66, 166, 184
Souvenir d'un avenir, Le 48, 174–77, 180
Soy Mexico 9, 38
Spielmann, Yvonne 159, 184
Stalin, Joseph 87, 88, 146, 149, 171
Stalker 121
Staring Back 2, 6
Statues meurent aussi, Les 11, 12–15, 18, 31, 32, 46, 51, 53, 62
Staudte, Wolfgang 143

Steiner, George 136, 137, 147
Stewart, Alexandra 115, 169
Susini, Marie 6

Takemitsu, Toru 57, 128
Tarkovsky, Andrei 119, 121, 125, 142, 168–73, 184
Tautin, Gilles 108
Tazieff, Haroun 115
Terilli, Franco 173
Terrenoire, Louis 32
Tessier, Danièle 115, 123
Three Video Haikus 157
Tode, Thomas 11, 37, 143, 183
Tokyo Ga 120, 121
Tolchan, Yakov 150–51
Tombeau d'Alexandre, Le 2, 70, 89, 145–51, 156, 160, 164
Toute la mémoire du monde 51
Train en marche, Le 79, 89–93, 145
Travail et Culture 2
Trintignant, Marie 179, 180–81
Tryon, Chuck 5, 10
Twelve Monkeys 45

Uma 130

Van Cauwenberge, Geneviève 40, 66
Vaneck, Pierre 60
Varda, Agnès 4, 18, 27, 33, 37, 74
Vassilikos, Vassilis 137
Vergès, Paul 106
Vernant, Jean-Pierre 139, 140
Vertigo 51, 120, 123, 157, 161, 162, 170
Vertov, Dziga 90, 149
Vierny, Sacha 21
Vilar, Jean 28, 108
Vive la baleine 9, 93–95
Vlady, Marina 168

Weil, Simone 140
Wenders, Wim 120, 121
Widdis, Emma 145, 184
Widhoff, Françoise 168

Wilson, Emma 47, 66
Winter Garden photograph 7, 185
Wollen, Peter 46, 66

Xenakis, Iannis 138

Yamamoto, Kajiro 130

Yanoguchi, Fumio 129
Yudina, Maria 171
Yumatov, Nicolas 34, 60

Zapping Zone 2, 6, 81, 142, 143
Zátopek, Emil 17, 109
Zora, Eva 29, 33

Lightning Source UK Ltd.
Milton Keynes UK
17 August 2010

158518UK00001B/3/P